Virtual Reality with VRTK4

Create Immersive VR Experiences Leveraging Unity3D and Virtual Reality Toolkit

Rakesh Baruah

Apress®

Virtual Reality with VRTK4

Rakesh Baruah
Brookfield, WI, USA

ISBN-13 (pbk): 978-1-4842-5487-5 ISBN-13 (electronic): 978-1-4842-5488-2
https://doi.org/10.1007/978-1-4842-5488-2

Managing Director, Apress Media LLC: Welmoed Spahr
Acquisitions Editor: Spandana Chatterjee
Development Editor: Siddhi Chavan
Coordinating Editor: Divya Modi

Cover designed by eStudioCalamar

Cover image designed by Pixabay

Distributed to the book trade worldwide by Springer Science+Business Media New York, 233 Spring Street, 6th Floor, New York, NY 10013. Phone 1-800-SPRINGER, fax (201) 348-4505, e-mail orders-ny@springer-sbm.com, or visit www.springeronline.com. Apress Media, LLC is a California LLC and the sole member (owner) is Springer Science + Business Media Finance Inc (SSBM Finance Inc). SSBM Finance Inc is a **Delaware** corporation.

For information on translations, please e-mail rights@apress.com, or visit http://www.apress.com/rights-permissions.

Apress titles may be purchased in bulk for academic, corporate, or promotional use. eBook versions and licenses are also available for most titles. For more information, reference our Print and eBook Bulk Sales web page at http://www.apress.com/bulk-sales.

Any source code or other supplementary material referenced by the author in this book is available to readers on GitHub via the book's product page, located at www.apress.com/978-1-4842-5487-5. For more detailed information, please visit http://www.apress.com/source-code.

Printed on acid-free paper

*To my mom, dad, and sister, who have given
me more than any one person deserves.*

Table of Contents

TABLE OF CONTENTS

About the Author

Rakesh Baruah is a writer and creator with 15 years of experience in new media, film, and television in New York City. After completing an MFA in screenwriting and directing for film from Columbia University, Rakesh joined the writers' room of a hit primetime network drama as an assistant. The experience opened his eyes to the limits of television and the opportunities promised by immersive 3D content. In 2016 he began a self-guided journey toward virtual reality design that has taken him through startups, bootcamps, the Microsoft offices, and many, many hours in front of a computer. He shares what he's learned with you in a style and format designed specifically for the person who, in high school, preferred English class to trigonometry.

About the Technical Reviewer

**Doug Holland** holds a master's degree in software engineering from Oxford University and is a Senior Software Architect at Microsoft Corporation. He is a former C# MVP and Intel Black Belt Developer and has been working with Microsoft's Mixed Reality partners since the release of HoloLens.

Acknowledgments

This book was a labor of love motivated by a drive to help others through the frustration I have felt learning a new technology mostly on my own. Fortunately, through my journey from writer to coder, I have been able to collect relationships that have made what once was a daunting dream into a reality: a resource for virtual reality design that I wished I had available to me when I was first starting.

This book would not be possible without the unyielding patience, support, and attention from my team of Apress editors: Spandana Chaterjee, Divya Modi, Sidhi Chavvan, and Doug Holland. Also, thank you to the teams at Extended Reality and Unity who have made their transformative technology available to regular people like me. Even though they decided not to grant me a certification of completion, I'd like to thank the team at devCodeCamp in Milwaukee, Wisconsin, without whom I wouldn't have had the discipline to delve into the daunting world of .NET programming. Specifically, I thank Michael Terrill, my instructor at the bootcamp, who did not let me quit when I wanted to most.

I'd also like to thank my mother for letting me live in her house while I worked on this book and my father for always smiling and encouraging me when I woke him up at 6 a.m. to share whatever random harebrained insight I'd had in the middle of the night. Thank you to Sarika for being a true friend; to Jerry for being more than a teacher; and to Matt for always finding time to help me brainstorm. Thank you to Niraj for showing me the way to adapt; to the minds at Oculus for their wonderful tech; and to the VR and GameDev Twitter communities for helping me feel like a part of something larger than myself.

Introduction

There I was, sitting in the writers' offices of a big-time, network TV show, and it dawned on me: This isn't going to last. It turns out I was right; not because the show ended (as of this writing it's still going strong), but because I wouldn't be invited back for the next season. Fortunately, before I found myself unemployed, I'd been given a glimpse into the world of big media at the peak of its success. The cliff was coming, and I needed to pack a parachute fast.

Before I'd gone back to school to get a master's degree in screenwriting and directing, I'd worked in all things screen—television, Internet media, interactive TV, and film. I loved the technology of media, but I knew nothing of its art. Graduate school helped me overcorrect. By the time I received my degree, I'd become an analogue hermit, reading plays and writing exclusively by hand. I'd skipped out on the explosion of apps. I cared about writing, lighting, story, drama, actors—all that quaint detritus of a simpler time. When I finally got the opportunity to work in a real-life, Hollywood environment (even though it was in Queens, New York), I was perfectly anachronistic. I didn't care about mobile technology, yet TV and cable were dying. Fortunately, something new was just beneath the surface.

I came to virtual reality (VR) technically savvy about computer production and classically trained in story. VR seemed like the perfect medium for me. I loved computers, I loved video games, I loved movies, and I was hopelessly deficient in attention. The journey I've been on since 2016 has led me to a space brimming with opportunity and excitement. Hollywood (the real one, in Los Angeles) is making movies using VR tools and techniques. For the idealist in me who feels morally compelled to help people, VR reaches into spaces like education and health. VR has turned out to be a medium of coding, pictures, stories, gaming, service, community, and entertainment. Because I've been a lifelong dilettante too antsy to stop learning just one thing, VR has been a safe haven for me. I can keep exploring and people think it's work.

I designed this book for the version of me who was sitting at a desk in 2016 in a writers' room in Queens looking into an uncertain future that appeared only dark and stormy. It has been my experience that learning the principles of computer programming and VR design is not difficult; it only feels hard because the people who understand it are too busy being brilliant to explain their genius to dummies like me. Fortunately, because of the Internet and software like Unity and the Virtual Reality Toolkit, even humanities majors like me can join the ranks of the technologically savvy. Sure, I might feel like a poseur, but it's hard to doubt even yourself when you make a computer program, put on a headset, and watch what you imagined come to life before your eyes.

In this book I have done my best to speak to the person like me—the worker bee curious to know more and terrified of being left behind. Much to my dismay, I am not good at video games, and much of the literature about learning to use Unity seemed to me to be about making video games. However, the contemporary marketplace appears to support my instinct that VR is much more than just diversion and entertainment. It offers real productivity power. Throughout this book, you will learn the fundamentals of C# coding, Unity, and the Virtual Reality Toolkit (VRTK). I've presented them using simple but extensible exercises that target scenarios the average person might encounter in a classroom or office.

My vision for this book was "Making VR for Creative Professionals." Although it might, at times, be a bit complex for the complete beginner and at others too dumbed-down for the programming pro, I am confident that anyone, regardless of their pedigree, will complete the chapters and exercises in this book with a feeling of time well spent. There's a bit of film-making theory for the computer pros and some computer science for the liberal arts majors. I like to think of myself as someone who straddles the space between art and science. Being on brand, I do both poorly, but this book might just hit the sweet spot of what I know best. If you ever wanted to create your own VR experience, then I sincerely hope you find your imagination stoked and your self-doubt silenced by the time you reach the last page of this book. If that is the case, then the journey I have taken for the past four years will have been worth every step along the way.

OVERVIEW

VRTK and Unity 2019

What Is Virtual Reality?

I like to think the present day of virtual reality (VR) development began in 2010, in Southern California, in the hands of a 17-year-old, in his parents' garage. The boy's name was Palmer Luckey, and four years later he would sell the device he created to Facebook for more than $2 billion.

Of course, Palmer didn't invent VR or the VR headset. In fact, part of the reason Palmer was able to create a novel device like the Oculus Rift was because he had been an avid collector of almost 100 defunct headsets others had made through the decades. We can trace the origins of VR as we know it today to the latter half of the 20th century, when a former head of the U.S. Department of Defense's Information Processing Office took a position as an associate professor of electrical engineering at Harvard. With the help of his inspired students, he created the first VR system and head-mounted display. Forebodingly, they called it the Sword of Damocles. The year was 1968.

For the next 40 years VR loomed as the next *next big* thing, only to be surpassed by computer graphics, 3D movies, the Internet, social media, and smartphones. Coincidentally, it was the technology that passed VR that made VR possible. Faster processors, stronger graphics cards, global positioning, gyroscopes, and accelerometers—all the things that made the iPhone so much more powerful and popular than its predecessors— found their way into Palmer's, and eventually Facebook's, Oculus Rift. The VR system and head-mounted display created by the Harvard professor in the 1960s weighed so much that it would crush its user if it wasn't mounted to the ceiling. Today, we can wear a VR headset like the Oculus Go outside while rolling in the grass (Figure 1).

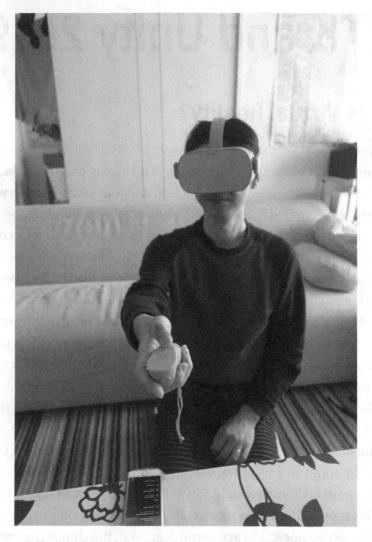

Figure 1. *Released in 2016, the Oculus Go VR headset empowered users to experience simulations free from desktop computers. Source: kobakou via Flickr.com https://www.flickr.com/photos/ kobakou/CC BY 2.0*

We can't let the salad days of VR until 2010 mislead us to believe the medium was on a respirator. VR continued to grow away from the commercial spotlight in musty offices like those at NASA's Jet Propulsion Laboratory and MIT. It made brief appearances through flash-in-the-pan technologies like the Nintendo Power Glove and Sega VR, but its real incubation continued in heavy industry where companies like Autodesk pushed 3D modeling and stereoscopic imaging further through devices for medicine, flight simulation, automobile design, architecture, construction, and military training. By 2010, VR had been maturing in the shadows of the personal computer and information technology revolution. Its promise extended its practice until transformations in affordable equipment closed the distance.

Although the hardware for VR has caught up with the vision of its pioneers, the concept of VR hasn't changed one bit. From the stain of paint on a cave wall to the Renaissance and beyond, humans have tried to transform that which they experience into two-dimensional form. Unfortunately, we haven't really moved much further beyond the discovery of perspective by the Italian masters. Until today. Today, not only does the hardware for VR exist at a scale we mere consumers can afford, but so does the software that empowers artists and developers to create their own virtual experiences from home. 3D modeling software, game engines, visual scripting tools, OpenVR, webVR—every day it seems the list gets longer of what is possible to create with very little overhead. VR, today, is the same concept it was 70 years ago. It's the convincing representation of immersion in a digitally fabricated world. The only thing that's changed is that today it's possible.

How Does VR Work?

The evolution of technology over the past 20 years, particularly in the field of mobile computing, has been the nutrient for VR's bloom. At its essence, VR is a computation process akin to animation. Our computers draw images on a screen, then manipulate those images over time, creating the illusion of movement. Faster, cheaper, more powerful technology has pushed the boundaries of VR beyond what has been known because drawing three-dimensional objects to a screen up to, and in some cases past, 100 times a second is a computationally intensive process. Factor in the calculations a computer must perform to re-create the illusion of natural physics and it becomes apparent how powerful our VR systems have had to become for us to consider them merely proficient.

Computers manage the mathematically and computationally heavy lifting of creating immersive, virtual experiences by organizing their work into a process called the graphics rendering pipeline (Figure 2). The pipeline consists of three stages: the application stage, the geometry stage, and the rasterization stage. The application stage is the part of the pipeline process that most directly includes us, the developers. During the application stage of the pipeline, the developer uses a program, such as Unity, to design the style and execution of a scene. The geometry stage of the pipeline handles the dizzying number of operations required to locate, move, and transform the 3D objects in the scenes we create. Finally, the rasterization stage of the pipeline handles the drawing of each pixel to our screen, paying special attention to the color, texture, and shading properties of each pixel.

Figure 2. *The graphics rendering pipeline moves the geometry of 3D shapes from software, through the graphics hardware, and on to a screen. Source: By PaterMcFly / Vierge Marie, CC0,* `https://commons.wikimedia.org/w/index.php?curid=58106609`

That we can create and consume VR experiences so easily today is a direct result of the affordability and availability of powerful computing components. Most of the tasks performed in the graphics rendering pipeline occur in the hardware of our machines. As they involve matrices of values moving, multiplying, subtracting, and adding in mere milliseconds, the calculations required to faithfully render a three-dimensional scene in an immersive VR experience are impossible for humans to replicate. That is why the most robust VR experiences still require headsets connected to computers. To generate a realistic representation of the moon's reflection in a puddle of water in VR, for example, relies on enormously comprehensive calculations that determine the angle of reflection of each ray of light of each moving point in the scene. The volume of calculations that occur per second, per frame is truly remarkable. It is the machine and its performance of algorithms inspired by human ingenuity that bring virtual experiences as close to reality as they have come.

What Is Unity?

The application stage is the phase of the graphics pipeline that most directly affects us, the developers. Many applications fit into this phase of the graphics pipeline. The one of interest to us, in this book, is Unity. Launched in 2005 as a democratizing tool for video game design on the MacOS platform, Unity has grown into a multiplatform application used by industries ranging from engineering design to artificial intelligence. Its popularity has stoked the growth of a rich online ecosystem comprised of passionate, independent developers and industry professionals. That so many tools, extensions, assets, tutorials, videos, and books exist in service of the Unity developer only reinforces the platform's rate of adoption. The ubiquity of its resources, its ease of use, the breadth of its applications, and its low barrier to entry contribute to the popularity of Unity as the first, and only, choice of hundreds of thousands of developers.

Unity succeeds as an application portal into the overwhelmingly technical realm of the graphics rendering pipeline because of the balance it strikes between performance and usability. Although Unity, no doubt, has within it the capacity to intimidate a user, its elegantly simplified mimicry of more expensive software endears it to novices and experts alike. The way Unity works, although not simple, is straightforward, and intuitive to anyone who has had even minimal exposure to the principles of computer graphics, whether it be through applications like Photoshop, Adobe Premier, or iMovie. Even developers, confident through years of programming but new to graphic design, find Unity approachable. Originally intended for the creation of video games, Unity has evolved into a bridge between computer science and computer art.

As an application, Unity provides us, as designers and developers, with the tools we need to tap into the powerful graphics rendering pipeline inside of our computers. Its buttons, windows, icons, and sliders hide from us the complex math required to generate VR experiences. By developing a familiarity with Unity's appearance and functions, we earn entry into the promises of visual effects amplified by the graphics processing unit (GPU). As a program, Unity abstracts the details of matrix manipulation and repetitive multiplication. Unity allows us to place objects in a scene and trust the pipeline to render what we intend into VR. Unity is both our canvas and our palette for creating immersive reality. By creating and manipulating game objects in Unity, we have ultimate control of the inputs into the graphics rendering pipeline—vertices, meshes, materials, textures, and lights.

The Making of 3D Space

The elemental ingredients the graphics pipeline accepts to create its magic are vertices, meshes, materials, textures, and lights. The pipeline takes objects we place into a Unity scene and animates them to a screen. As the application portal of the pipeline, Unity translates our designs into instructions for the machine's central processing unit (CPU) and GPU. The inputs we provide Unity, and in turn the graphics pipeline, stem from the simplest of shapes, a point.

3D graphics programs locate points in our scene along three axes: x, y, and z. In Unity, the z axis moves in the same direction as the camera's lens, the y axis points directly above it, and the x axis points to its sides. A convenient way to visualize the three-dimensional axes of Unity is to use your left hand as a mock coordinate plane (Figure 3). If you make an L shape with your left hand using your pointer finger and thumb, then the direction your middle finger points when extended mimics the z axis in Unity. Accordingly, your thumb represents the x axis and your pointer finger the y axis.

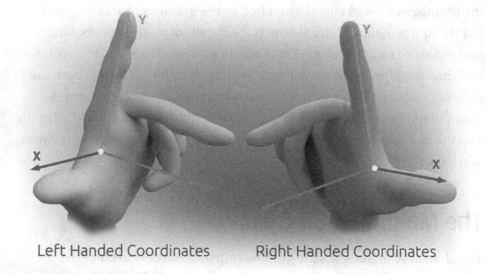

Left Handed Coordinates   Right Handed Coordinates

Figure 3. *Unity uses a left-handed coordinate system as a frame of reference for the developer. Source: By Primalshell - Own work, CC BY-SA 3.0, https://commons.wikimedia.org/w/index.php? curid=27531327*

The fundamentals of creating and manipulating 3D objects in Unity come from the geometry most students cover in high school. The x, y, and z coordinates of a point together form a vertex. If a vertex is a point in space then the distance between two vertices composes a line, called an edge. Three edges form a triangle; two triangles form a square; and six squares form a cube, of which each side is a face. Like corners, vertices are the points in 3D space that together form the shape of an object (Figure 4).

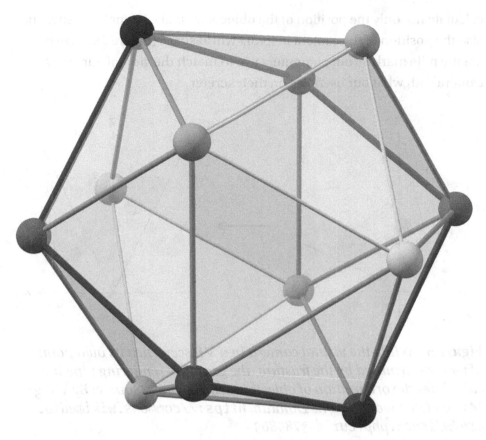

Figure 4. *Vertices are points that join edges to form polygons. They are the markers the graphics rendering pipeline uses to determine the location, rotation, and size of an object in three-dimensional coordinate space. Source: By PaterMcFly/Vierge Marie, CC0,* `https://commons.wikimedia.org/w/index.php?curid=58106609`

Vertices matter to us as VR developers because they are the hooks into which the 3D graphics rendering pipeline connects to our content. Every immersive scene begins with a virtual camera looking through a frustum, its field of view. For an application like Unity to pass information about our scene to the graphics rendering pipeline in our computer it must first calculate not only the position of the objects we place in our 3D scene, but also the position of the camera in its 3D world space (Figure 5). Vertices are the mile markers our computers use to match the view of our virtual camera with what our users see on their screen.

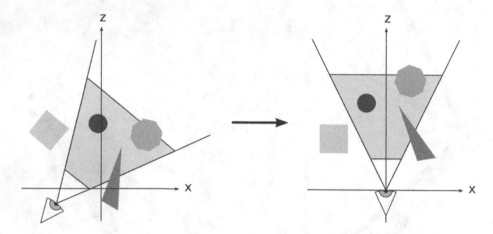

Figure 5. *While the virtual camera in a VR scene has its own point of view determined by the frustum, the graphics rendering pipeline calculates the orientation of objects in world space. Source: By Vierge Marie - Own work, Public Domain,* `https://commons.wikimedia. org/w/index.php?curid=3789863`

Because vertices so heavily inform the orientation between our camera, our computer, and our scene, they go through hundreds of calculations before they become pixels we can see during playback. The number of vertices, therefore, influences not only the visual detail of our scene, but also the speed at which it is processed. Too much detail in a scene, too many vertices, can create a bottleneck in the graphics rendering pipeline, in turn creating a lag for the viewer. Simple shapes with few vertices render quickly. Complex shapes with many vertices do not. Any lag between a user's input into a VR experience and its playback is called latency. High latency in an immersive experience is the difference between success and nauseating failure.

The shapes formed by vertices are polygons, the simplest of which is the triangle. The triangle is fundamental to 3D graphics because its three points are the minimum required to define the orientation of a plane. Once our computers know the mathematical orientation of a plane, they can compute what is called the normal, the perpendicular vector that intersects the surface of a plane (Figure 6). Although this might sound unnecessarily theoretical for our purposes in this book, the normal vector and triangular polygons form the basis (linear algebra pun!) of the magic we've come to call visual effects.

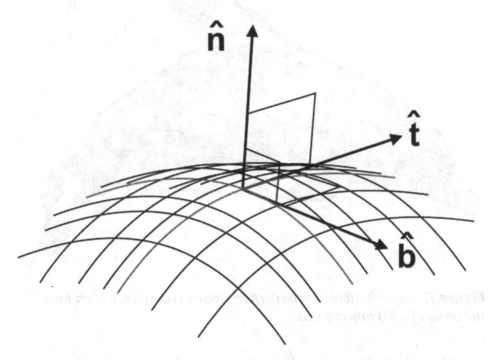

Figure 6. *The normal vector n portrays the perpendicular intersection of vectors t and b. The normal vector of a triangular surface plays a key role in the calculation of 3D computer graphics.*

The triangles formed by vertices, and the polygons formed by triangles, together create the outline of objects in three-dimensional space. By tracking the relative position of the vertices connected by edges to form polygons in a scene, the graphics rendering pipeline repeatedly calculates the location of objects in our scenes, how they are portrayed by the camera, how they respond to physics, and how they react to light. The set, or library, of the vertices and their connecting edges associated with an object in virtual space form the foundation of the object's mesh (Figure 7).

Figure 7. *Edges between three vertices create triangles, which form the basis of a 3D object's mesh*

I like to think of a mesh as the outline created by connecting the nodes in a point cloud of a three-dimensional object. In my mind's eye, a virtual mesh is like the chicken-wire armature of a papier-mâché sculpture I made in elementary school art class. The triangles and polygons created by vertices and their edges form the illusion of a surface our human brains identify as a cohesive shape. By reducing the appearance of an object in three dimensions to a mesh comprised of triangles, the graphics rendering pipeline in our computers can more quickly calculate the appearance of the object under different conditions.

Because a mesh connects the disparate vertices of an object into a discernible whole, a mesh allows us to manipulate the appearance of an object to a user of our immersive experience. By creating the illusion of a planar surface between vertices, a mesh enables us as designers to add materials and textures to an object. Materials in 3D design applications like Unity refer to the optical properties of an object. Textures are the 2D images we can apply to materials to create unique detail (Figure 8). For example, a sphere can take on the likeness of either a basketball or a fortune teller's ball in a Unity scene of our making. The outcome of its appearance emerges from the combination of materials and textures we apply to the sphere's mesh. The material of a basketball will be duller and more diffuse than the material we use for a crystal ball, which will be shinier and more specular. The textures, too, will be unique.

Figure 8. *Textures applied to uniform spheres create the illusion of distinct 3D objects*

The final component of the graphics rendering pipeline with which we concern ourselves is the shader. A shader, in 3D graphics, is a mathematical operation performed by a computer to determine the appearance of an object influenced by the impact of light (Figure 9). As a mathematical function, a shader takes in as inputs an object's mesh, material, and texture to determine the path a light ray, reflected from the object, will travel to reach the virtual camera in our scene.

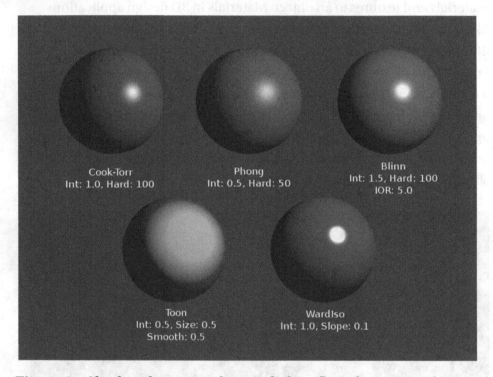

Figure 9. *Shaders determine the way light reflects from a 3D object. The mathematics required to create them is complex and has been conveniently abstracted by 3D modeling and animation software. Source: Di Blender Foundation - Blender Reference Manual, CC BY-SA 4.0, https://commons.wikimedia.org/w/index. php?curid=58923022*

Rasterizing vs. Ray-Tracing Current evolutions of rendering pipelines have moved from rasterizing triangles on a screen to ray-tracing paths of light, which calculates the trajectories of vectors between a virtual camera and an opaque surface. Although unique, the processes share enough high-level detail for the scope of this book to ignore their differences.

Shaders can create the illusion of lapping waves and undulating trees in our virtual experiences. How a material and its texture appear to move beneath light is the question a shader function answers. As shaders calculate the reflection of light off each vertex of an object in our scene, their calculation can become computationally expensive as the number of polygons in our scene increases. The balance between the prudent design of objects, the placement of virtual lights, and the judicious application of shaders comprises a large bit of the artistry involved in crafting immersive experiences.

The presentation of 3D immersive scenes is a computationally expensive task. The fidelity of VR experiences we see today is the result of advancements in the affordability and accessibility of powerful computer processors and GPUs. In concert with the availability of head-mounted displays replete with infrared tracking sensors, gyroscopes, and accelerometers, the accessibility of robust graphic rendering tools in consumer-grade GPUs have put the dreams of 20th-century computer graphics pioneers within reach of more modest developers like you and me.

Of course, VR is not the only evolution in spatial computing. Augmented reality (AR) and mixed reality (sometimes referred to as MR and other times as XR) are also mediums rife with rich promise. Whereas VR defines a wholly immersive experience in which computers fabricate all the pixels in a user's field of view, AR and MR overlay virtual objects onto the real world. Devices such as the Microsoft Hololens offer headsets with nearly transparent lenses that create the illusion for users of objects like menus hovering in their environment. The Microsoft Azure cloud service even offers a tool set called Spatial Anchors, which enables designers to place computer-generated, 3D art in real-world locations visible only to AR-enabled devices. Smartphones from both Apple and Google also include AR features that companies like IKEA have already leveraged for business. AR and MR merge the real and the digital. VR replaces the real with the made. Fortunately for us, as developers, the pipelines for the creation of AR, MR, and VR content share much in common. In fact, Unity has many built-in features and optional add-on libraries that make it a powerful tool for AR and XR creation. A large portion of what this book covers in regard to Unity's workflow is immediately transferable to MR experiences beyond VR.

The ubiquity of the graphics rendering pipeline at the heart of so much new media serves as a testament to its importance. Combined with the facility and ease of use of a 3D game engine like Unity, the powerful tools of the graphics rendering pipeline have become available to most anyone with a laptop. The mathematics involved in the realistic re-creation of reality in a computer is profound enough to drop Isaac Newton's jaw, but an application like Unity, with its intuitive graphical user interface (GUI) and drag-and-drop simplicity, places the power of creating new, original, convincing worlds into the hands of everyday people.

Unity handles the heavy lifting required to render reality in a stereoscopic headset. With the real work outsourced to software and the machine, we, as artists and developers, are free to create almost anything we can imagine. Because the technology of the future exists today, the only limiting factor to the creation and sharing of new, immersive worlds is our own unfamiliarity with the tools we have at our disposal.

Although Unity has a tremendous amount of promise as an engine for creation, its versatility can be more of a burden than a boon to the inexperienced VR developer. Artists and designers use Unity to create an assortment of different experiences ranging from mobile 2D puzzle games to console-ready first-person shooters. Film studios use Unity for animation. Architectural firms use Unity for industrial design. The bounds of Unity's power grow with every new update and release. The cost of this power can be, unfortunately, Unity's ease of use.

Introducing VRTK, the Virtual Reality Toolkit

Many different VR systems from different manufacturers exist today. Unity, conveniently, integrates with most. However, each headset manufacturer has traits unique to its design that might require a download of their proprietary software development kit (SDK). One of the many appealing features of Unity is its promise of cross-platform development, but the requirements of targeting a specific VR system might compromise our vision as designers. Fortunately, the release of the Virtual Reality Toolkit version 4 (VRTK) from the developers at Extended Reality, Ltd., in March 2019 has made creating VR experiences for all platforms more accessible to less experienced developers.

By the admission of its own raison d'être, VRTK is a free, open-source VR development framework to streamline the VR prototyping process for novices and experts alike. Its drag-and-drop features add a layer of distance between the knobs and controls of Unity and an even further abstraction from the nuts and bolts of code. Although Unity is a powerful program to facilitate the creation of 3D experiences, the integration of user input via mounted headsets, infrared sensors, and wireless touch controllers can become a tedious cycle of sweat and obscenity for even a seasoned developer. This isn't through any fault of Unity and its team of developers, of course. It is the state of affairs for a bleeding-edge medium like VR. As the community endeavors to create efficient solutions to complex spatial computing problems, open source frameworks like VRTK emerge to bridge the distances between expectations and reality, virtual or otherwise.

VRTK works by hooking into the input and event management systems of Unity. We'll go into further detail on these topics in sections where we explore the interaction between users and our Unity scenes, but suffice it to say, for now, that VRTK provides a clear, useful interface to more quickly re-create commonly performed actions in a VR scene. The fundamental feature of an immersive experience is the response of the virtual environment to user input. If users move their head, for example, then our virtual environment should update to accommodate the users' new point of view. If a user touches an object in a virtual scene, that object should somehow respond.

Feedback is the fabric of our reality; the senses are our portal to the world. As an interface to facilitate the creation of interactive features in our immersive experiences, VRTK is a powerful tool to help us more quickly and more easily execute our ideas for VR projects. By removing obstacles to creativity imposed by complicated programming and 3D modeling, VRTK through its ready-made scripts and prefabricated materials opens an avenue of opportunity formerly impeded by constraints like time and focus. With the help of the VRTK framework in the Unity ecosystem, you will become more able to rapidly prototype the VR experience you envision in your head. After all, what is VR in its essence but the ability to share exactly what we imagine with others no matter the distance between us in the material world? Consider this book, then, your ticket to a brand new era of creativity and communication that knows few bounds.

CHAPTER 1

Setup

To begin developing immersive experiences with Unity and VRTK, we must first download and install the required tools. These tools include: Unity, an integrated development environment (IDE), and Git for either Windows or Mac.

I'm not going to lie to you: Setting all of this up might not be easy. There are many steps, and many points at which something could go wrong. I will try to be as agnostic in regard to platform as I can, but I am accustomed to developing with Unity on a PC running Windows 10. Unity is cross-platform, though, for both your development environment as well as deployments. Both Windows and MacOS are supported. To be certain that I provide you with the most accurate depiction of what I know and have learned, I will refrain from speculating about what you might encounter in your environment. At the same time, I will do my best to anticipate errors you might receive while downloading, installing, and running your program.

With all that said, the resources available online for the tools we need to run Unity and VRTK on our machines are abundant. All that you require to find the answers you might need is enough information to know the question you want to ask. It is with that axiom in mind, the standard operating procedure of the developer's secret weapon—Google—that I relay to you what I know. VR and the tools for its creation like VRTK are a bleeding-edge medium. As such, unknowns, hiccups, and missteps abound. I will do my best to make the trial by fire as illuminating as it will be hot.

© Rakesh Baruah 2020
R. Baruah, *Virtual Reality with VRTK4*, https://doi.org/10.1007/978-1-4842-5488-2_1

In this chapter you will learn how to do the following:

- Download and install Unity.

- Download and install an IDE.

- Download and install Git.

- Clone the VRTK GitHub repository.

- Set up the Unity Editor for a VR project.

- Run the VRTK sample scene in Unity.

Downloading and Installing Unity

Let us begin. Unity is a robust 3D engine that provides an interface to create many kinds of experiences. Because of its versatility, Unity can demand significant resources from your local machine. Before downloading and trying to install Unity on your computer, confirm that your system meets the minimum standards for Unity development. As of this writing, the most recent version of Unity to have been released is Unity 2019.3 (August 28, 2019). The Unity web site also allows the download of its Unity Hub application, which makes it easier for developers to manage installs, licenses, and projects. I, personally, use Unity Hub, but foregoing the Hub for just a Unity installation will not impair your ability to follow along with the text. Next I provide the system requirements listed by Unity on its web site. Check the most recent requirements to confirm your computer's setup will work with the version of Unity or Unity Hub you download and install.

System Requirements for Unity Development

The following are the system requirements:

- OS: Windows 7 SP1+, 8, or 10, 64-bit versions only; MacOS 10.12+.

- Server versions of Windows and OS X are not tested.

- CPU: SSE2 instruction set support.

- GPU: Graphics card with DX10 (shader model 4.0) capabilities.

The rest depends primarily on the complexity of your projects.

Additional Platform Development Requirements

Additional requirements are as follows:

- iOS: Mac computer running minimum MacOS 10.12.6 and Xcode 9.4 or higher.

- Android: Android SDK and Java Development Kit (JDK); IL2CPP scripting back end requires Android Native Development Kit (NDK).

- Universal Windows Platform: Windows 10 (64-bit), Visual Studio 2015 with C++ Tools component or later and Windows 10 SDK.

From the Unity web site you can download a free version of the application for beginners. To use VRTK with Unity you must run a version of Unity no earlier than version 2018.

The Code Editor, an Integrated Development Environment

Although Unity is an interface that allows easy, direct creation of VR experiences, it still requires the use of a third-party IDE. As you will learn, Unity allows us to write scripts to perform actions in our Unity program. For Unity to read these scripts, we must provide it with an IDE, or code editor. I like to think of an IDE as a word-processing application like Microsoft Word. An IDE simply provides us a place to write and store our code. Because we write Unity code in a programming language called C#, we cannot use a word processor that only understands human language syntax. A key difference between an IDE and a word processor is the IDE's inclusion of a compiler. A compiler translates the C# code we write in our IDE into the machine code computers understand.

If you ask a dozen Unity developers from around the world their preferred IDE to use with Unity, you'll get a dozen answers. The only right answer is the one that is right for you. Unfortunately, finding an IDE that interacts IDE-ally (code editor pun!) with your peccadillos is a product of taste, time, and experience. To jump-start things, however, I offer you two of the most common code editors Unity developers tend to choose for their creative process. If you will use Unity on a Windows machine then I recommend Microsoft Visual Studio Community Edition, which is an optional install within the Unity Installer. As a Windows 10 developer, I personally prefer the Microsoft Visual Studio IDE, which has been updated to a 2019 edition called VS 2019. Visual Studio is a fully loaded code editor that can create enterprise-level applications. However, it is a large install with demands on your computer's hardware. Its power might be excessive for a developer interested only in creating Unity applications. Another popular choice for a code editor to use with Unity is the lightweight Visual Studio Code, commonly called VS Code. It shares many similarities with its older sibling, Visual Studio, yet its smaller footprint and cross-platform compatibility make it popular among Mac developers and creators operating streamlined machines. Both code editors are available for free online. The free version of Visual Studio is its Community Edition.

- Visual Studio Code and Unity (ideal for Mac users):
  `https://code.visualstudio.com/docs/other/unity`

- Visual Studio and Unity:
  `https://visualstudio.microsoft.com/vs/unity-tools/`

The download addresses for Visual Studio and VS Code lead to both detailed requirements for your system and installation instructions for use with Unity. These IDEs are not the only options available to you to create VR experiences in Unity. They are, however, the most popular and therefore most helpfully discussed in online forums.

Downloading and Installing Git

The third application we must download to make full use of Unity and VRTK is called Git. Git is a free and open source distributed version control software. It allows for the sharing of code online. Downloading Git for your operating system allows you to connect to code repositories other developers have set up to share their code. I like to think of Git as a Google Drive or DropBox for code. Software packages are too large and unwieldy to share as attachments to e-mails or as single documents in a shared folder. Git enables us to clone people's projects so that we can manipulate and run their code on our local machine. For the purposes of the exercises in this book, we will use Git and its Git Bash feature to download the VRTK files required for integration into Unity. Information for downloading, installing, and setting up Git for Windows and Mac OS can be found here:

- Git for Windows:
  https://git-scm.com/download/win

- Git for Mac:
  https://git-scm.com/download/mac

Once you've downloaded and set up the necessary applications to begin developing immersive experiences in Unity and VRTK, meet me in the next section where we will test whether or not everything is ready and up to code (get it?).

Setting Up Unity and VRTK

When Unity, an IDE, and Git are set up on our local computers, we are finally able to create a Unity project and install VRTK. Bookmark this section, as it will be a valuable resource during your immersion into Unity and VRTK. You might find yourself referring to it often. To install VRTK into a Unity 3D project, follow these steps:

1. Open Unity and create a new 3D project.

2. Select the default layout of the Unity application by selecting Main Menu ➤ Window ➤ Layout ➤ Default (Figure 1-1).

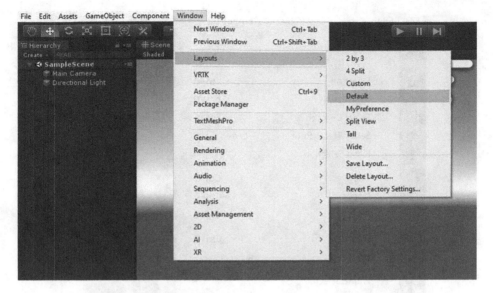

Figure 1-1. *Select the Unity Default layout*

3. In Unity, navigate to Main Menu ➤ Edit ➤ Project
    Settings (Figure 1-2).

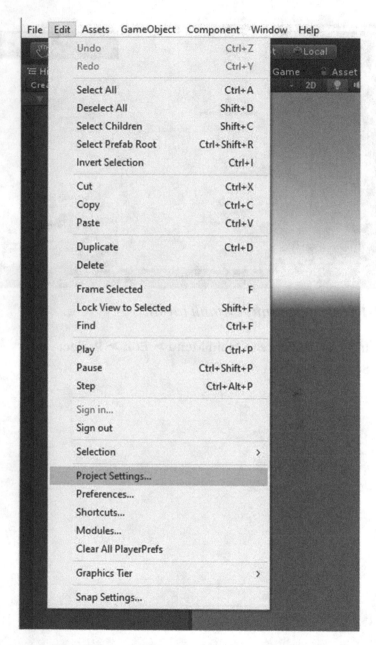

Figure 1-2. *Select the Project Settings for the Unity project*

4. In the Project Settings dialog box, navigate to the left-hand tab titled Player (Figure 1-3).

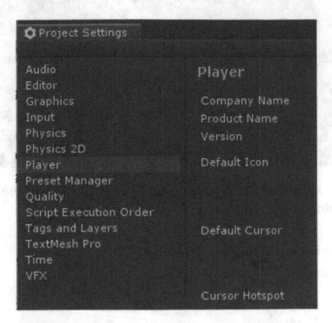

Figure 1-3. *The Player tab on the Project Settings dialog box houses VR-related properties in a Unity project*

5. Near the bottom of the Player tab, click the XR tab.

6. Select the Virtual Reality Supported check box (Figure 1-4).

   - Your installation of Unity might show additional parameters for your project's XR Settings. For example, your installation might show a check box to create support for Vuforia Augmented Reality or other head-mounted displays.

9

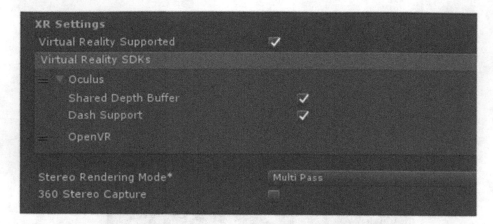

Figure 1-4. *XR settings can be found on the Player tab in the Project Settings dialog box*

7. Navigate to Main Menu ➤ Window ➤ Package
    Manager (Figure 1-5).

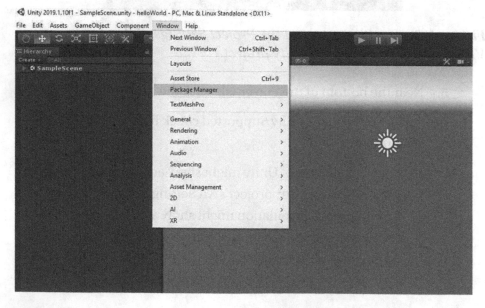

Figure 1-5. *Access the Unity Package Manager*

8. Near the bottom of the left-hand column in the
    Unity Package Manager locate the XR Legacy Input
    Helpers tab (Figure 1-6).

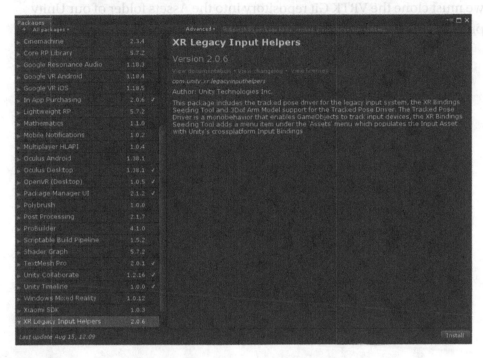

Figure 1-6. *The XR Legacy Input Helpers provide a connection
between VRTK and versions of Unity after 2018*

9. On the Legacy XR Inputs tab, click Install.

    •   You might see a button to Update or Remove
        components in your Package Manager window.
        Whatever your scenario, confirm your project
        contains the most recent version of Unity's XR
        Legacy Input Helpers.

Installing VRTK

Finally, we need to install VRTK into our Unity project. To accomplish this, we must clone the VRTK Git repository into the Assets folder of our Unity project. Follow these steps to do this:

1. In the default Unity layout the Project window is a hierarchy of your project's folders at the bottom left of the application. From the Project window navigate to the Assets folder in your operating system's Finder or File Explorer. A simple way to do this is to right-click the Assets folder in the Unity Project window and select Show in Explorer or Finder (Figure 1-7), depending on whether you use Windows or Mac OS, respectively.

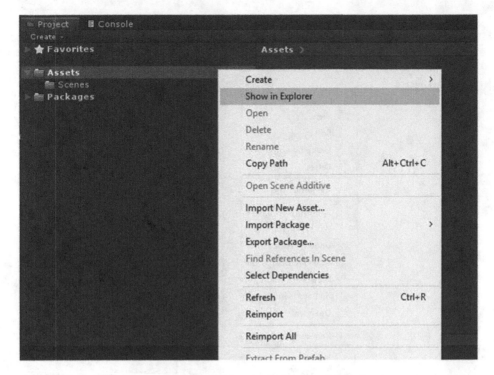

Figure 1-7. *Open the Assets folder in Windows Explorer*

2. From File Explorer, double-click the Assets folder to open it.

3. Right-click or Crtl+click in the Assets folder and select Git Bash here (Figure 1-8). If this option does not appear in the shortcut menu, then refer to the resources for installing Git on your operating system.

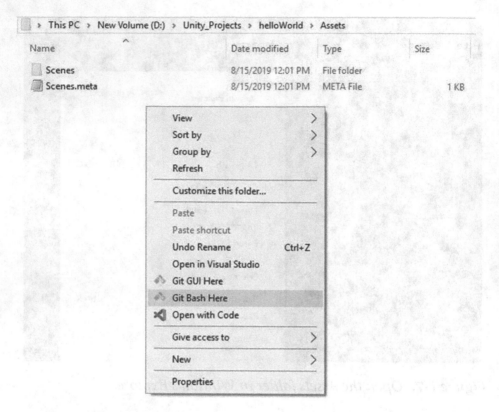

Figure 1-8. *Open Git Bash in the Assets folder from Windows Explorer*

4. A Git Bash command prompt / terminal window opens.

5. Enter the following text into the Bash and press Enter
    (Figure 1-9):

    git clone --recurse-submodules https://github.com/
    ExtendRealityLtd/VRTK.git

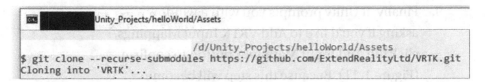

```
                              /d/Unity_Projects/helloWorld/Assets
$ git clone --recurse-submodules https://github.com/ExtendRealityLtd/VRTK.git
Cloning into 'VRTK'...
```

Figure 1-9. *Cloning into the VRTK GitHub repository from the Git Bash terminal*

6. In the Bash, type `cd VRTK` and then press Enter.

7. Enter the following text into the Bash and press Enter (Figure 1-10):

    ```
    git submodule init && git submodule update
    ```

```
                              /d/Unity_Projects/helloWorld/Assets
$ cd vrtk

                              /d/Unity_Projects/helloWorld/Assets/vrtk (master)
$ git submodule init && git submodule update_
```

Figure 1-10. *This is an example from the Git Bash terminal on Windows 10 of completing the VRTK GitHub repo clone*

8. Return to the Unity project where Unity will import and compile the new files. If you had difficulty executing any of the steps for cloning the VRTK application into your Unity project, then visit the VRTK GitHub page for more detailed instructions (`https://github.com/ExtendRealityLtd/VRTK`).

9. Finally, if Unity prompts you with a window
    asking if you'd like to Add VRTK Input Mappings,
    click the Add Input Mappings button to confirm
    (Figure 1-11). Because this step will become
    important for a future exercise in which we connect
    user actions to events in our VR scene, feel free to
    select the Do not prompt again check box.

Figure 1-11. *Clicking the Add Input Mappings button creates the input mappings required by VRTK*

Running the Example Scene

When you are ready to proceed, run the VRTK example scene prepackaged with the application's files. To do so, continue with the instructions provided by the VRTK GitHub page, which I've copied here:

1. Open the VRTK/Samples/Farm/Scenes/
    ExampleScene scene (Figure 1-12).

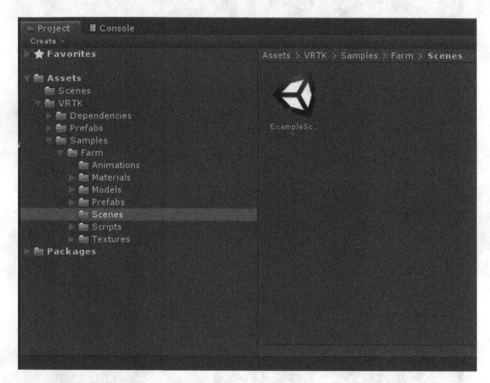

Figure 1-12. *VRTK provides a sample Unity scene to demonstrate its assets*

2. Enable Maximize on Play in the Unity Game view control bar to ensure no performance issues are caused by the Unity Editor overhead.

3. Play the scene in the Unity Editor (Ctrl+P).

4. The scene should automatically play within any Unity-supported XR hardware.

5. Explore the farmyard and enjoy!

If you've successfully set up Unity and installed VRTK, then the example scene included with the VRTK files should look similar to Figure 1-13. If your scene appears different, check the version number of VRTK you have installed. Because you are likely using a more recent version than me at the time this book was written, any distinctions between your example scene and mine could be a result of VRTK updates since its version 4 release in March 2019.

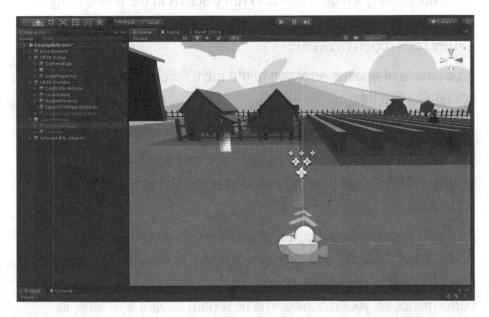

Figure 1-13. *Running the VRTK example scene in your Unity project verifies that that setup is complete*

Help! I Got Too Many Error Messages!

If, while trying to run the VRTK example scene in Unity, you received a number of error messages, congratulations! You're officially on your way toward becoming a VR developer. Errors are frustrating, I know. Believe me, I know. But errors are also opportunities to learn more about what is broken, why it is broken, and, most important, how to fix it. An example of one error you received might appear something like this:

```
XR: OpenVR Error! OpenVR failed initialization:
Installation path could not be located!
```

The solution to this error is to download Steam and SteamVR on your computer, as OpenVR requires both to function. You can read more about Unity's requirements to run OpenVR in the online Unity documentation at `https://docs.unity3d.com/Manual/VRDevices-OpenVR.html`.

An example of another error you might have received could appear something like this:

```
XR: OpenVR Error! Hmd Not Found Presence Failed!
```

The solution to this error is to confirm that your head-mounted display (HMD) is connected to your computer and that its drivers are up to date.

As many possible errors exist as there are VR systems supported by Unity, at least. MacOS and Windows, too, not to mention the specifics of your personal installation of an operating system, can affect Unity's performance on your machine. The best path toward solutions, in my experience, is to first reference the official Unity XR resources at `https://docs.unity3d.com/Manual/XR.html`.

Second, check the documentation for your specific VR system. OpenVR and Oculus, for example, both have Unity integration packages available to download. Developing for mobile VR devices might require installing tools unique to Android. Later in this book, in the chapters addressing user input, we dive more deeply into VR SDKs and integration packages. In addition to the link for Unity's OpenVR resources included earlier, here are more for Unity's use with other VR systems:

Oculus: `https://docs.unity3d.com/Manual/VRDevices-Oculus.html`

Google VR: `https://docs.unity3d.com/Manual/googlevr_sdk_overview.html`

Windows Mixed Reality: `https://docs.unity3d.com/Manual/wmr_sdk_overview.html`

Finally, although OpenVR is supported on both Windows and MacOS platforms, running OpenVR on a machine with MacOS has its own hardware requirements:

Unity OpenVR on a macOS requires the Metal graphics and 64bit application target, OpenGL is not supported.

OpenVR supports macOS 10.11.6 or later, but is optimized for macOS 10.13 High Sierra or later. (*Unity Manual*, `https://docs.unity3d.com/Manual/VRDevices-OpenVR.html`)

If you received any of the errors I mentioned or others that I did not, please do not be discouraged. I cannot emphasize enough how common feelings of frustration are during this process. If you feel overwhelmed, walk away from the computer and forget about this book for a few hours or even a day. My journey into VR programming has taught me the following lessons.

The Internet is an amazing resource for helping you find others who have experienced the same challenges you face and details of how they overcame them.

The unconscious mind untangles knots without our knowing and may be best left to its own timeline for problem solving.

Endeavor on. Improvement is promised. Knowledge is guaranteed.

While playing VRTK's example farm scene you will notice a user interface that allows you to toggle between a UnityXRCameraRig and a SimulatedCameraRig. In the next chapter we will learn the difference between these virtual cameras and how to incorporate them into an original scene of our own design.

Summary

If you've reached this portion of the chapter, it likely means you've successfully set up Unity, Git, and VRTK on your computer. That is no small achievement. I'm sure you experienced challenges, frustration, and in some cases, anger. Congratulations on seeing your way through!

Because VRTK version 4, Unity version 2019, Visual Studio 2019, and VR as a medium, as a whole, are so relatively new in the world of creative development, errors will abound; irritation will mount; and exhaustion will threaten. As a predominantly self-taught VR developer, I know these experiences intimately. However, it is no secret that there has been no greater time in human history to become an engineer of imagination. The tools, although at times buggy, exist, and the creative minds behind their design and execution have done much to pave the road ahead for us well. Yes, things might get bumpy, but the path forward, blazed by pioneers a generation before, is real, and you are on it. By completing this chapter you have proven to yourself that you are ready for the next step.

In this chapter you learned that the fundamental tools for VR development we will need are Unity, an IDE, Git, and VRTK. You learned how to download, install, and set up these tools on your local machine. You cloned a GitHub repository into a machine on your computer, and you ran the VRTK example scene to test whether you set up your tools correctly.

In the next chapter we begin creating a virtual scene of our own design using the tools we have set up on our machines. Because an immersive experience serves as a window into another world, we will begin our first scene with an introduction to virtual cameras in the VR development pipeline.

CHAPTER 2

The Virtual Camera

In Chapter 1, you left off running the sample scene prepackaged with VRTK. Although the VRTK demo scene is pretty nifty, it might not have been what you imagined the immersive power of VR could fully create.

This chapter will reacquaint you with the Unity and VRTK setup processes and provide you with the knowledge of how to move beyond blocks in a virtual space. We're going to get introduced to VRTK and set up a 3D, VR-enabled Unity project; connect the VRTK interface; connect our head-mounted display to a virtual camera; and create an application that will put our user into a photorealistic, immersive space!

In this chapter you will do the following:

- Learn the meaning and importance of high dynamic range (HDR) images to VR design.

- Change the settings for a default Unity Skybox asset.

- Download and import HDR images into a Unity project.

- Place a virtual camera in a photorealistic 360-degree environment.

- Place and manipulate a 3D object within an HDRI Skybox.

© Rakesh Baruah 2020
R. Baruah, *Virtual Reality with VRTK4*, https://doi.org/10.1007/978-1-4842-5488-2_2

Lights, Camera, Render!

I came to Unity and VR with the experience of a filmmaker. Movies and TV were much more familiar to me than 3D graphics or computer programming. However, it wasn't long before I felt comfortable creating my own VR apps in Unity. The key to Unity's accessibility to professional developers and novices alike, in my opinion, is its similarity to movies. You don't need a master's degree in fine arts to understand that movies and TV shows come about from pointing cameras and lights at subjects. With that intuitive understanding under your belt, you're already well on your way to becoming a Unity developer.

By using the language and concepts of a medium so familiar to many of us, Unity makes it possible for almost anyone to get their first VR scene up and running in minutes. Here's how simple the premise of Unity is: Every project starts with a scene. Every scene starts with a light and a camera. Instead of actors, we call the subjects of our scenes game objects. That's it! Everything else is dressing on the mixed green salad.

Of course, things can get much more complicated very quickly if you'd like. But presumably you're not here to learn how to make a AAA game for an Xbox in a weekend. Although Unity can indeed help you accomplish such a task, you and I are going to focus on VR applications beyond gaming. Yes, we will use elements and principles of game design in our exercises, but Unity and VRTK are so powerful in concert precisely because they make creating VR accessible to everyone, not just tech-savvy gamers or programming savants.

Not to worry, though, because by the end of this book you will have the knowledge you need to jump-start an even deeper dive into the promises of Unity as a game engine. If that's not your aim, that's fine, too! You'll still reach the last page of this book with the skills you need to confidently prototype whatever VR experience you can imagine. That's a lofty promise. I beg you to hold me to it!

Getting Started

To begin, first make sure you have completed the 'getting started' guide and are able to run the VRTK demo scene. When you are comfortable with the steps in that process, proceed.

Open a new 3D project in Unity. If you have not already, and you intend to test your application on a VR headset of your own, download the necessary files as per the instructions from your headset provider. Most popular headset manufacturers have a section of their web site where they explain how to integrate their tools into Unity. Make sure you have gone through the setup requirements for your device of choice. For example, creating scenes for the Oculus platform might require you to download the Oculus features from the Unity Package Manager, or the Oculus Integration package from the Unity Asset Store. Similarly, developing a scene for SteamVR might require you to install the necessary OpenVR files. Refer to the documentation on the web site of your headset provider for platform-specific requirements. If you prefer to develop and play-test your VR scenes without the use of a head-mounted display, remember that VRTK conveniently provides a simulated camera rig that allows us to test our VR project without a headset connected to our computers.

To set up our first exercise of this chapter, I'll review the procedure for creating a VR project in Unity and importing the VRTK files through your operating system's Git Bash. You can find a more detailed, illustrated description in Chapter 1.

Review: Setting Up a VR Scene in Unity and Importing VRTK

You might be saying to yourself, "I already did this. Why do I have to do it again?" To be honest with you, the most difficult part about learning to use VRTK for me was becoming comfortable with its setup process.

Because VRTK version 4 is so new, it's not fully integrated into the Unity ecosystem yet. It's so convenient as a VR prototyping framework, though, that I have good reason to believe its setup process will be streamlined over time. Until then, however, the number of steps it takes to get VRTK up and running with Unity can be a bit confusing. In my experience, the best practice for becoming comfortable with creating a project with VRTK is just that—practice! I'll hold your hand through the setup of a VRTK Unity project once more, and within a short amount of time I'm certain you'll be able to conduct the process yourself. Until then, it's once more into the breach.

1. Create a new 3D Unity project and navigate to Edit ➤ Project Settings ➤ Player. Under XR, click the Virtual Reality Supported check box. If the headset on which you plan to test your scene is not already listed, click the + icon. Select the headset system of your choice.

2. Next, navigate to the Assets folder of your project in your file explorer. In File Explorer or Finder navigate to and open the Assets folder. Here, you will need to make sure you have installed Git on your computer. If you have, right-click in the Assets folder and select Open Git Bash Here. A terminal or command prompt window will open. Copy and paste the following text:

    ```
    git clone --recurse-submodules https://github.com/
    ExtendRealityLtd/VRTK.git
    ```

3. Press Enter and navigate to the newly created VRTK directory by typing:

    ```
    cd VRTK
    ```

This is command line syntax to change into the VRTK directory. Press Enter again and type or paste the following:

```
git submodule init && git submodule update
```

4. Press Enter. You will see a progress bar countdown in your terminal window. Your computer is downloading the files required to run VRTK in your Unity application.

5. When the download is complete, return to Unity. As soon as you are back in Unity another progress bar should appear. This progress bar tells you that Unity is processing the files you downloaded from Git. Click OK on the prompt that appears.

6. Because VRTK is so new and the most recent 2019 edition of Unity is still relatively new, there's one more step we need to complete. Navigate to Window ➤ Package Manager. On the bottom left of the Package Manager window, click the XR Legacy Input Helpers tab. On the bottom right, click Install. This action downloads the remaining files required to facilitate the connection between Unity and VRTK.

When the install is complete, return to your default layout in Unity. Make sure you have a new empty scene open in the Project Hierarchy. When a new scene opens in the Project Hierarchy, Unity adds a main camera and directional light by default (Figure 2-1).

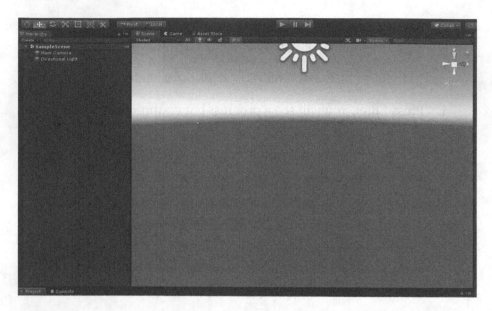

Figure 2-1. *This is the default starting state of a new Unity scene*

In your Project window, navigate to the CameraRig folder beneath VRTK/Prefabs. From the CameraRig folder, select the UnityXRCameraRig prefab (Figure 2-2).

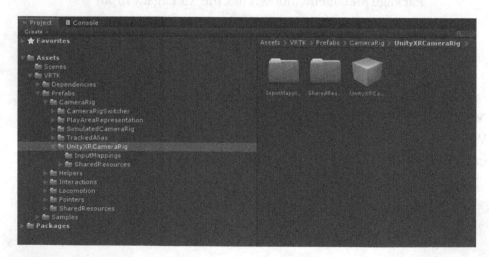

Figure 2-2. *The UnityXRCameraRig prefab is shown in the VRTK folder structure*

Drag this object into your project's Scene Hierarchy. Make sure the Unity Camera Rig stands on its own in your Project Hierarchy and not as a child object (Figure 2-3). You can tell if an object is the child of another object if a small triangle appears next to the parent object. The Unity Camera Rig should be its own object with its own children beneath it.

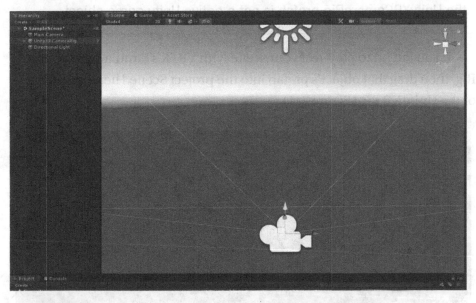

Figure 2-3. *The UnityXRCameraRig is shown instantiated in a scene*

Why Is My UnityXRCameraRig Game Object Blue?

In the Scene Hierarchy, you might have noticed that the UnityXRCameraRig is blue, and the Main Camera object is not (Figure 2-3). Blue game objects indicate the object is an instance of a prefab.

In Unity a prefab is a game object that has been designed independent of the scene to which you apply it. If you create a custom game object consisting of its own unique materials, textures, and child game objects, for example, you can drag the parent object into the Assets folder in your Project window to save it as a prefab. A prefab acts as a template from which you can create copies of a game object to populate your scenes.

The UnityXRCameraRig object is a prefab created by the makers of VRTK. Unlike the Main Camera object that appears in a default scene, the UnityXRCameraRig prefab is not a native Unity game object.

If you intend to play-test your scene with VRTK's Simulated Camera Rig, then drag that object's prefab into the project Scene Hierarchy instead of the Unity XR Rig (Figure 2-4).

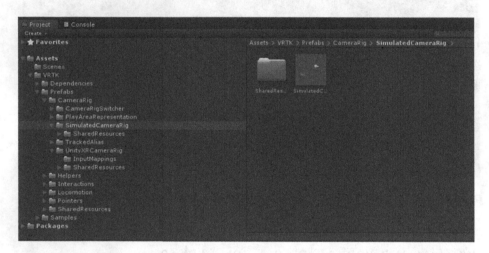

Figure 2-4. *VRTK's SimulatedCameraRig object mimics a VR system on a monitor*

Let's give our scene a test! Press the play button at the top of the Unity application. Make sure the Unity Camera Rig button is toggled in the top right corner of your game screen, if you plan to use your own head-mounted display. If not, select the simulated camera rig.

Uh-oh. Did you get an error? If you did, it might read something like this: "There are [more than 1] audio listeners in the scene" (Figure 2-5).

Figure 2-5. *A warning message is shown in the Unity Console*

This error means more than one game object with an audio listener is active in the Scene Hierarchy. Each camera game object has an audio listener component attached. Hosting more than one active camera in a scene prompts Unity to notify you that only one audio listener can exist in a scene. We can prevent this message from appearing in our console by hosting only one camera object in the Scene Hierarchy. In your Scene Hierarchy, delete the default main camera provided by Unity. You can either select the object and press Delete, or right-click/Ctrl+click the object and select Delete from the shortcut menu that appears. It is okay if you keep both the Unity XR Camera Rig and the Simulated Camera Rig in your hierarchy. However, only one camera object can be toggled on in the scene at a time. If you plan to test your scene using the simulated camera, then you will have to toggle off the Unity XR Camera Rig. If you plan to test your scene with the Unity XR Camera Rig attached to a headset of your choice, then you will have to toggle off the Simulated Camera Rig.

To toggle the state (on/off) of a camera object, select the camera object in your project hierarchy. At the top of your Inspector window, you will see the name of the camera object preceded by a check box (Figure 2-6). If the check box says Static to its right, then that is the incorrect check box to mark for your camera's on/off state. Instead, look to the left of the camera object's name; there you will see a check box without a label. Selecting this check box marks your camera object as on and clearing the check box toggles your camera object off. A game object unchecked in the Inspector appears grayed out in the Scene Hierarchy. Make sure the check box is selected only for the camera object you plan to use for your testing process. Remember, if you're using an external, head-mounted display like the Oculus Rift, toggle the Unity XR Rig to on. If you are using the built-in VRTK Simulated Camera Rig, toggle only the Simulated Camera Rig object to on.

Figure 2-6. *A cleared check box to the left of a camera object's name in the Inspector window means the camera object has been turned off for the scene*

Now, run your scene. In the Console window of your Unity application the error message you received previously should not appear. If you still see the same error message regarding multiple audio listeners, and you have made sure only one camera object is activated in your scene, then stop your scene from running. At the top of your Console menu, select Clear on Play (Figure 2-7). If you are unable to locate the Console window in your Unity layout then navigate to Main Menu ➤ Window to select the Console window to show.

Figure 2-7. *Selecting Clear on Play in the Unity Console resets the errors and warnings that notify you of something that might need your attention*

Enabling the Clear on Play feature for your Console window will clear your Console window of errors and warnings every time you stop and restart your application for testing. Of course, the errors and warnings will persist on each restart of the scene if you leave them unaddressed.

Run your scene again. If no errors regarding duplicate audio listeners appear in your Console window, then you're ready to move on to play-testing your app. Press the Play triangle at the top of the Unity application window to start your scene. Press the Stop button when you are finished.

Congratulations, you did it! You integrated a camera into your VR scene. Now, let's take this exercise one step further to introduce you to the tools you need to create an experience of your own.

Because this book is meant to introduce you to VR experiences beyond games, each exercise focuses on a single use-case that might have an application in your daily life. Each exercise addresses a scenario in a particular industry to demonstrate the versatility of VR. It is the aim of these exercises to provide you with the knowledge of Unity and VRTK to quickly prototype whatever immersive experience you can imagine.

Exercise 1: GlobeHopper

In this exercise, we are going to address the following use-case.

Priyanka just returned from a vacation to the U.S. Southwest, where she took a 360-degree panoramic photograph on her camera phone. She was so enamored with the scenery she hopes to share it with her friends.

Unfortunately, seeing the photo on a phone doesn't capture the emotion she felt standing on the peak in the desert. Let's pretend we're Priyanka and that we want to create a 360-degree immersive experience from the photo we took on our trip.

The Panorama

As with preparing a delicious meal, the success of our immersive experience depends almost entirely on the quality of our ingredients. Some camera phones allow users to capture a 360-degree panoramic photo natively, whereas others require additional hardware, software, or both. My phone, for example, only allows me to capture 180-degree panoramic images. Of course, in VR, where our canvas is completely immersive, presenting a user with only half of a 360-degree environment isn't a successful recipe for good VR content.

To follow along with this exercise, feel empowered to use your own original 360-degree panoramic image, or feel free to use the assets included in the repository for this book. You can also make use of the assets available to download through the Unity Asset Store, which you can reach directly through the Unity Application (Figure 2-8).

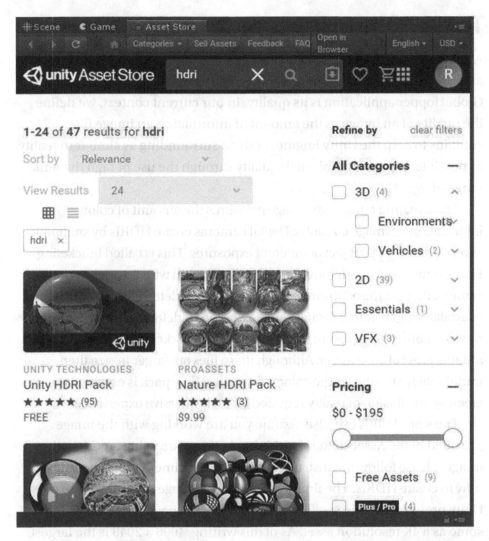

Figure 2-8. *Located as a tab in the same window as your Scene View in the default Unity layout, the Unity Asset Store gives you immediate access to thousands of items you can include in your scenes*

I have included three different 360-degree images in the Assets folder for this project at the GitHub URL. http://www.apress.com/source-code. You are free to use these images for this exercise, but if you plan to use them for your own purposes please review the licensing terms provided by the original artists.

The 360-Degree Image vs. the HDRI

A 360-degree image simply describes the orientation of our photo asset. What truly makes a 360-degree image useful for inclusion in our GlobeHopper application is its quality. In our current context, we define the quality of an image as the amount of information an image file contains to help the Unity Engine render a surrounding as similar to reality as possible. We achieve this high quality through the use of high dynamic range images (HDRIs).

The dynamic range of an image measures the amount of color information an image contains. Digital cameras create HDRIs by snapping several frames of a subject at different exposures. This is called bracketing. For example, when your parents took a photograph with an analog, manual camera, they set the exposure level for the subject determined by the level of available light. Today, digital cameras, some by default, capture several photos at different exposure levels ranging from darkest to brightest at a single press of your finger. Although these files are larger in size than traditional JPEG images, the color information they pack is essential to creating the illusion of reality required for an immersive experience.

The steps in this exercise assume you are working with the images provided in the Assets folder for this book. If you are using an original image, please follow the instructions from your camera manufacturer on how to create HDRIs. The final settings for the image we import into our Unity project as an asset will be a 4096 × 2048 image. This is known by some as a 4K resolution asset. As of this writing, 4096 × 2048 is the largest file format allowed by Unity for skymap images. The Unity best practices guide suggests using an image no larger than 2048 × 2048 because that is the maximum size handled by many graphics cards.

The Cubemap

Photographs are two-dimensional, of course. So how are we going to use them to effectively wrap a three-dimensional space? Enter the cubemap. A cubemap is a folding pattern that arranges a set of two-dimensional images into a three-dimensional geometry (Figure 2-9). Unity wraps a cubemap version of our 360-degree HDRI as a texture around a skybox material. Although there are advanced ways you can create a cubemap of your own, Unity provides a convenient feature to handle the manipulation for us. Let's give it a try!

Figure 2-9. *A cubemap is a collection of 2D images that can be arranged into a 3D representation of a space*

Let's start from the very top, as if we're going to make a recipe from scratch, so we can reinforce what we've already covered about integrating VRTK with our Unity project.

Create a new Unity 3D project. Name the project GlobeHopper and save it in a file destination of your choice. It is important that you are able to navigate to the saved destination of your project later in this exercise so note the file path if you must.

Now that we have our 3D project created, let's make it interactive by importing VRTK. Navigate to the Assets folder of your GlobeHopper project in your File Explorer or Finder. Double-click the Assets folder to make sure you are within the directory GlobeHopper/Assets. If you see a folder labeled Scenes, you are in the right place.

After you're sure you've installed the Git client on your computer and have navigated to the inside of your GlobeHopper Assets folder, right-click in File Explorer and select Open Git Bash Here.

A command prompt will appear with a blinking cursor. Type the following commands into your Git Bash command window where the cursor blinks. After each line, press Enter before typing the next command.

```
git clone --recurse-submodules https://github.com/
ExtendRealityLtd/VRTK.git
cd VRTK
git submodule init && git submodule update
```

For future reference, you can always find the steps to import VRTK at the VRTK GitHub page: https://github.com/ExtendRealityLtd/VRTK.

Return to Unity and wait as Unity compiles the VRTK scripts you just cloned from GitHub.

If a pop-up menu appears that says "The VRTK Example Scene requires additional Unity Input Axes to be defined," then click the Add Input Mappings button at the bottom of the menu. If you did not install the VRTK input mappings at this point, it's okay. We review them in more detail in Chapter 7.

If you haven't already, also be sure to update the Legacy XR Inputs in the Unity Package Manager to make sure VRTK is fully compatible with your current version of Unity.

The third and final step for our project setup is to confirm that our VR settings are correctly set in our project. To do this, navigate to Edit ➤ Project Settings ➤ Player. On the Player settings tab, navigate to Other Settings and make sure the Scripting Runtime Version is set to .NET 4.x Equivalent, and the Api Compatibility Level is set to .NET Standard 2.0 (Figure 2-10). If you are running Unity on a Mac, then select Mono as your scripting back end. If you are using Windows, select the IL2CPP back end. If you are unsure which scripting back end applies to your project, refer to the Unity web site for further information.

Figure 2-10. *Details regarding the scripting runtime of your project can be found on the Player tab of the Project Settings window*

Under XR Settings, select the Virtual Reality Supported Check box. If you do not see your Virtual Reality SDK listed, click the + button on the bottom right of the Virtual Reality SDK menu and select the device for which you intend to build your experience. If the SDK for your headset does not appear in the list, then visit your headset manufacturer's web site for specific information on how to connect your headset's SDK to Unity. If you continue to have trouble finding your headset listed as an option, then confirm the build settings of your project (Menu ➤ File ➤ Build Settings (Ctrl+Shift+B) are set to PC, Mac, & Linux Standalone; Universal Windows Platform; or even Android if targeting mobile VR devices like the Oculus Go. If you are targeting Universal Windows Platform in your Build Settings Unity might only give you the option IL2CPP as your scripting back end, which is fine. Check the Build Settings section of the Unity documentation for further reference. When this step is complete you can close the Player Settings window. You might see some yellow exclamation marks in your Console window. As long as none of them are red, you can click Clear at the top left of your Console window and proceed.

Now, we drag our UnityXRCameraRig object from our Project window into our Scene Hierarchy and delete our default camera object. As always, if you do not have a headset mounted to your computer you can select VRTK's SimulatedCameraRig instead of the UnityXRCameraRig prefab.

Finally, press the Play triangle at the top of your Unity project. If you are using an external headset, move it around to verify that the Unity Game Window tracks your headset's movement. If you are using the VRTK simulated camera rig, you can confirm your setup works by following the onscreen instructions for manipulating the viewfinder on your virtual camera.

As is, our default scene in Unity is pretty plain. All it is is a camera, a light object mimicking the sun, and a blue sky called a Skybox (Figure 2-11). Let's see what happens if we swap out that sky for a more immersive representation of the real world.

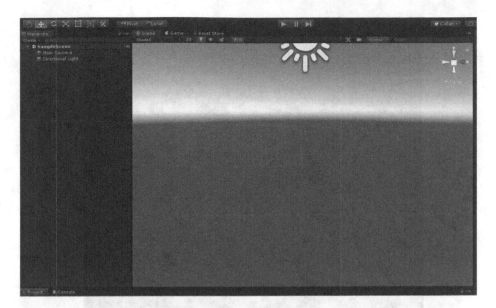

Figure 2-11. *The default state of a new Unity scene contains only a camera object and a directional light object*

In the Project window of your GlobeHopper project, right-click the Assets folder and select Create ➤ Folder. Let's name this new folder Images. Double-click the Images folder to open it. If you've downloaded the assets from the repo associated with this exercise, then navigate to the location of the `rocky_dawn_4k.hdr` file. Drag and drop `rocky_dawn_4k.hdr` into the Images folder you created in your Unity Project. If you downloaded HDRI content from the Unity Asset Store, the file extensions of your assets might be `*.exr` and `*.mat`. Although the file formats are different, the data they represent are the same.

Click once on the file name in your Project window. The file's details appear in the Inspector window to the right of your scene view in the Default Unity Layout. We'll learn more about Unity Textures soon. For now, we will leave the Texture Type of our `rocky_dawn` image asset at its default settings. Its Texture Shape, however, we will change from 2D to Cube (Figure 2-12). Recall that Unity converts our 2D environmental images into a 3D representation by reconfiguring the image into a six-sided cubemap.

43

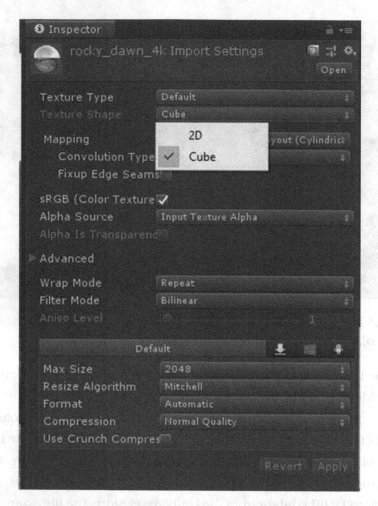

Figure 2-12. *Changing the texture shape of an HDRI to Cube reformats the image into a cubemap*

After you change the Texture Shape from 2D to Cube, new parameters appear in your Inspector. One of them is labeled Mapping. Using the drop-down menu change the Mapping value from Auto to 6 Frames Layout (Cubic Environment). Leave the remaining values in the Inspector at their defaults (Figure 2-13).

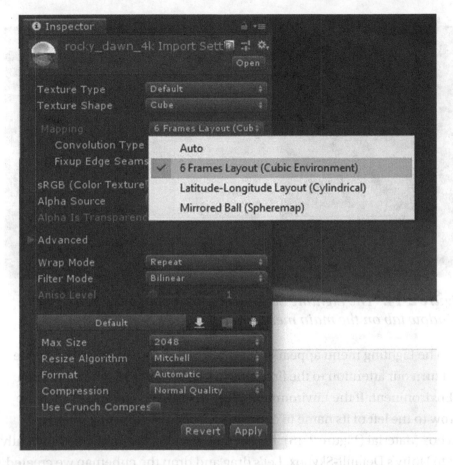

Figure 2-13. *The Mapping property of an HDRI asset includes options for transforming the image's layout*

We've got our cubemap for our environment, so now what? Now, we have to replace Unity's default sky with our own image. Let's navigate to the Skybox settings and see what we can change. In the Unity menu select Window ➤ Rendering ➤ Lighting Settings (Figure 2-14).

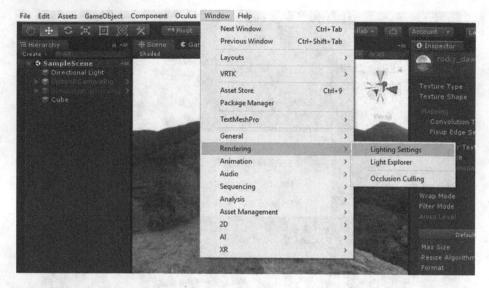

Figure 2-14. *The Lighting Settings menu can be found through the Window tab on the main menu bar*

The Lighting menu appears with three tabs at its top. We select Scene and turn our attention to the first category listed on the Scene tab, which is Environment. If the Environment drop-down list is collapsed, click the arrow to the left of its name to expand its properties. The first is labeled Skybox Material (Figure 2-15). Excellent! The value for this field is currently set to Unity's Default-Skybox. Let's drag and drop the cubemap we created from our Images folder in our Project window into the Skybox Material field of the Lighting menu.

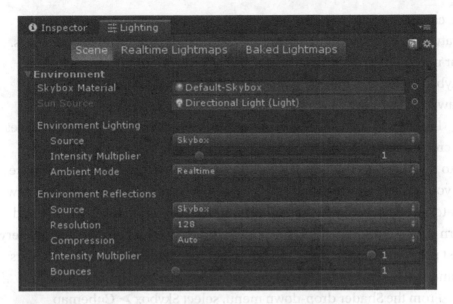

Figure 2-15. *Settings for a scene's Skybox can be found on the Lighting menu*

Uh-oh. What happened? Nothing? Good! When you dragged your Rocky Dawn image into the Lighting window, Unity gave you the "not allowed" symbol of a circle with a line through it. What gives?

Well, remember when we set the Texture property of our Rocky Dawn image to a Cube? Unity, as a 3D engine, uses a graphics pipeline common to all 3D asset programs, and in that pipeline there are three unique (although interdependent) categories that inform the way an object looks in 3D space. One is the Texture property, which helps us to render the difference between textures such as sand and brick, for example. Another is the Shader property, which primarily defines the way our objects interact with light in our virtual space. Different shaders can transform the same object from a highly reflective mirror to a muddy, matte puddle of sludge. The third property is an object's Material. Personally, I find it helpful to imagine a property's Material as the fabric pulled over the chicken wire skeleton of an object, called its mesh. It is a material to which we can add texture to transform a cylinder from an aluminum pipe to a bratwurst. We'll play much more with these parameters in later exercises. For now, though, let's create a Material to replace our current default Skybox material, a new material onto which we will project our Rocky Dawn texture asset.

Let's repeat the process we performed to create a folder for our images to create a folder called Materials in our project's Asset folder. Navigate into the Materials folder you created, right-click in the empty folder space of your Project window, and select Create ➤ Material. Let's name our new material mySkybox. After renaming your new Material asset, select it and turn your attention to the Inspector window to view its properties. The very first property listed in the Inspector is labeled Shader. Unity defaults to its Standard shader, but let's see if we can find something more specific.

From the Shader drop-down menu, select Skybox ➤ Cubemap (Figure 2-16). Beneath the Rotation property of our material there is a property called Cubemap. To its right is a thumbnail window that allows us to select the cubemap we'd like to project onto this material via the Skybox/Cubemap shader. Click Select in this window, and a new window will appear listing the assets that fit the criteria to act as a cubemap on our new Skybox material (Figure 2-17). Select the rocky_dawn_4k file. In the preview window at the bottom of the Inspector, we see what our Skybox will look like in our scene. Click in the preview window and drag the image left, right, up, and down. Well, it's definitely a six-sided cube! Let's add mySkybox to our Skybox Materials field in the Lighting menu (Hint: Window ➤ Rendering ➤ Lighting Settings).

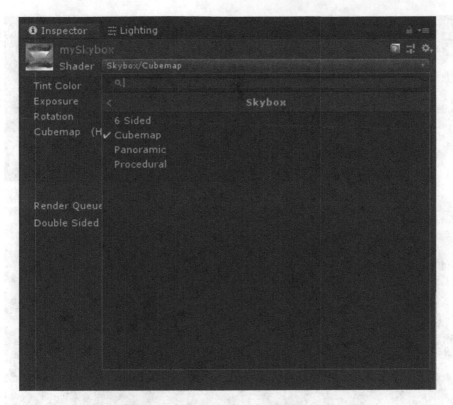

Figure 2-16. *The Skybox/Cubemap shader includes four options from which to choose*

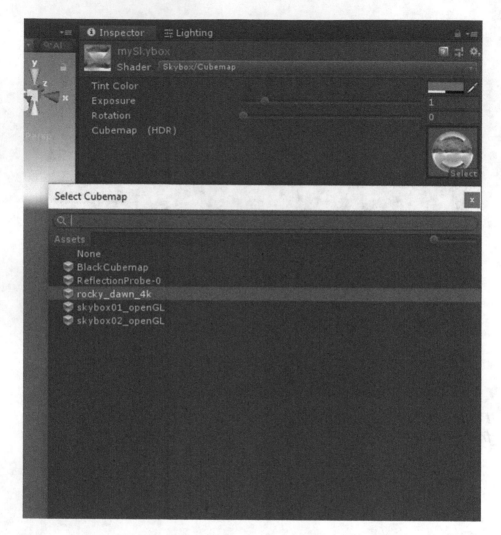

Figure 2-17. *Clicking Select on the Skybox Shader menu allows you to choose an HDRI for your scene's cubemap*

Now, when we drag our new mySkybox material into the box presently occupied by our Default-Skybox material, we receive a + sign that lets us know we can proceed (Figure 2-18). Let's test this out!

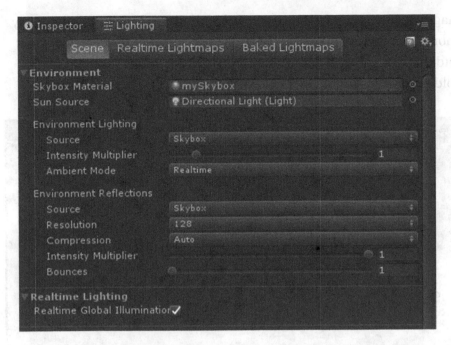

Figure 2-18. *Changing the shader of our HDRI to that of a Skybox allows us to drag and drop the asset into the Skybox Material object field on the Lighting tab*

Close the Lighting settings window. If you're play-testing on an external headset make sure the UnityXR Camera Rig is the only camera in your Scene Hierarchy on the top-left of the Unity Default Layout. Further, verify that the check box to the left of the UnityXR Camera Rig game object is selected in the Inspector when you highlight the UnityXR Camera Rig in the hierarchy. If you're using the VRTK SimulatedCameraRig, then make sure it's the only camera game object activated in your Scene Hierarchy. Ready? Press Play and enter your immersive, photorealistic world.

Welcome back! How did it go? Oh no, it's not right? I'm sorry for leading you astray (not really). We'll iron out all the wrinkles right now, I promise.

If you play-tested the GlobeHopper app in the previous step you noticed that our six-sided cubemap is quite literally a six-sided cube (Figure 2-19). Well, that might work if we have a cubemap comprised of

51

images of the inside of a box or a near-featureless room, but it's definitely a nonstarter for an immersive experience intended to re-create the great outdoors. Let's amend our texture settings to get things Goldi (as in Goldilocks—"just right").

Figure 2-19. *A 360-degree HDRI is shown converted into a six-sided cubemap and applied as a texture to a Skybox material*

In the Unity Project Explorer, navigate to the rocky_dawn-4k asset you saved in your Images folder. Select the asset, and in the Inspector window change the value of the texture's Mapping property from 6 Frames Layout (Cubic Environment) to Latitude-Longitude Layout (Cylindrical) (Figure 2-20).

We'll leave the other settings at their defaults. Click Apply in the Inspector window to save the changes we made to our texture's Mapping type. Now, let's try things again, shall we?

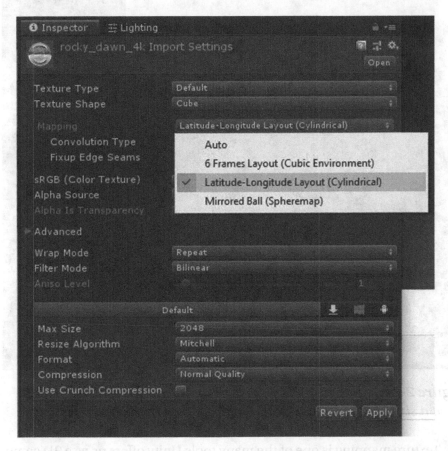

Figure 2-20. *Changing the Mapping property of an HDRI redefines how Unity will wrap the image around a scene*

Confirm your camera settings are to your preference in your Scene Hierarchy, and press Play.

Hey, that's much better, isn't it (Figure 2-21)?

Figure 2-21. *Changing the texture mapping of a 360-degree HDRI from a six-sided cube to a globe creates a convincing Skybox asset*

Texture mapping is one of the many tools Unity offers us as a 3D game engine to quickly create photorealistic, immersive experiences. It took humans until the Renaissance to master the complicated mathematics that create the illusion of not only depth, but also curved space. Unity does the same for us in a matter of seconds and a few clicks of a mouse. For further practice, try swapping out our desert setting at dusk for the other HDRIs included in the GlobeHopper repo.

Summary

A convenient way to imagine the makeup of a default Unity scene is through the language of movie-making. Each Unity scene begins with a camera, a light, and a background—called a Skybox. By importing the VRTK Unity XRCameraRig prefab or the SimulatedCameraRig prefab into our scene, we develop the ability to connect the virtual camera in our scene to our user's movements.

Because of its intuitive layout and drag-and-drop features, Unity makes it easy for developers to quickly jump into manipulating the appearance of our scenes. A quick, straightforward process like changing the Skybox material of a Unity scene can transform a mundane experience into something novel.

In this chapter you learned how to import a virtual camera into a new Unity scene; how to toggle the state of a virtual camera object in the Inspector window; the definition of HDRIs and their value to immersive experiences; the importance of the Mapping parameter on an HDRI texture to the creation of an original Skybox; how to transform an HDRI from a 2D texture into a cubemap through the image's Texture Shape property; that textures like HDRIs must exist on a Material object for Unity to recognize it as a potential Skybox; how to access the Lighting Settings window; and how to swap the Skybox material for a scene.

Before we move on to learning about creating truly interactive experiences with Unity and the VRTK, let's try one more thing in our GlobeHopper app to whet our appetite for things to come. As is, our GlobeHopper project doesn't feel very dynamic. The only thing that moves in the scene is our user's point of view. The next chapter introduces the concepts of game objects, components, and scripting in Unity. Together they provide a rich foundation from which we can create immersive experiences that combine the real with the virtual.

CHAPTER 3

Game Objects, Components, and an Introduction to C# Scripting

In Chapter 2, we created a simple VR experience called GlobeHopper, in which we placed a user in the middle of a 360-degree still image. It's all well and good that as Priyanka in our user story we created a way to share a 360-degree photograph from our trip out to the U.S. West. What if we wanted to heighten our immersive, static photo with something more virtual, though?

In this chapter you will do the following:

- Add a 3D virtual object to your scene.

- Write code to animate the object in your scene.

© Rakesh Baruah 2020
R. Baruah, *Virtual Reality with VRTK4*, https://doi.org/10.1007/978-1-4842-5488-2_3

By the end of this chapter you will know how to do the following:

- Add a 3D object to a Unity scene.

- Use a code editor to create scripts that control the behavior of, and interaction between, game objects within the scene.

- Add scripts to game objects as components to incite action.

Components as Attributes

Unity arranges its scenes with building blocks like movies. Each scene in Unity begins with a camera, a light, and a background, called a Skybox. Another name for movies is motion pictures. Traditionally, movies are images that change over time. Moving frame by frame through a projector, images create the illusion of movement. Unity, too, changes frames over time to create the appearance of motion. What's left for us, as developers, to determine is how we'd like to execute the movement we desire.

One way to create motion in our Unity scenes is through the use of scripting. Scripting is the act of composing code in a code editor to instruct a computer to perform a series of tasks. Together, the tasks comprise a program. In Unity, we program by using an IDE like Visual Studio to write code that manipulates objects in our scenes. Part of the magic of Unity is its ability to connect code we write in an IDE with visual objects we place in the Scene view of the Unity Editor. The foundation of this process is the relationship between code and game objects called components.

Components are the attributes we can add and remove from game objects to influence how they both appear and act. If the foundation of a Unity scene is a camera, a light, and a Skybox, then its floors, walls, ceilings, and roof are the game objects with which we populate a scene and the components with which we ascribe them. By creating a script in C#

using an IDE and connecting it to a game object in our scene, we uncover the powerful ability to influence how our game objects behave. Attaching scripts as components to game objects is the marble arch through which we pass to create dynamic, interactive, immersive experiences in Unity.

Exercise 2: Animating Virtual Objects in a Scene

In this exercise we are going to add a spinning 3D cube to the GlobeHopper scene we created in Chapter 2. The steps that follow will help you complete the project.

Step 1: Adding a 3D Object, Cube

To begin, add a cube to the scene.

In Unity, in the Scene Hierarchy for our GlobeHopper project, right-click and select 3D Object ➤ Cube (Figure 3-1). With the 3D cube selected, turn your attention to the Inspector window. Beneath the name of the game object there is a property called Transform (Figure 3-2). Properties listed beneath Game Objects in the Inspector are called components. Remember how we equated game objects with the actors in our scene placed beneath a directional light and in front of a camera? Well, components are what distinguish our game objects from each other. Continuing our film set analogy, a component to a game object would be similar to the relationship between an actor and their costume, name, or motivation—really anything that marks Fred Flintsone as unique from Barney Rubble. Components are the qualities of our game objects.

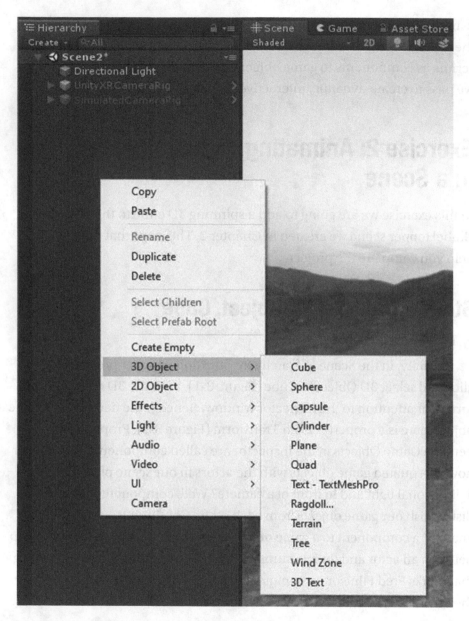

Figure 3-1. *Add a 3D object to a scene from the Scene Hierarchy*

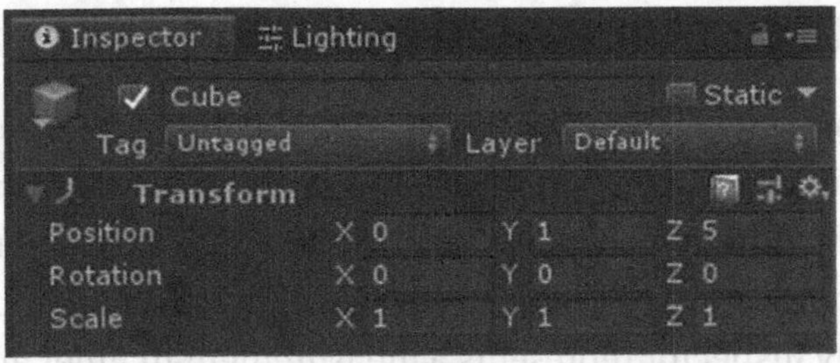

Figure 3-2. The transform component of a game object contains properties for its position, rotation, and scale in a scene

One component that all game objects have by default in Unity is a transform. A transform component tells the computer where a game object sits in 3D space, its size, and which way it faces. Let's manipulate the transform of our 3D cube object. Move the Position setting of our 3D cube transform 1 unit up on its y axis and 5 units over on its z axis, leaving its x axis value at 0.

What Are x,y, z Coordinates?

Unity uses an x, y, z coordinate plane to determine the location, size, and position of objects in virtual space. By default, the virtual camera in a Unity scene faces the positive direction of the z axis. The x axis represents space to the left and right of the camera in its default state. The y axis is the camera top and its bottom.

A convenient way to remind yourself of Unity's world axes is to make an L shape with your left index finger and thumb. Extend your left middle finger away from you. Your thumb is Unity's x axis, your index finger is Unity's y axis, and your middle finger represented Unity's z axis.

Step 2: Editing the Rotation Parameter

In this section, we will be editing the rotation parameter of the cube's transform component. Beneath the Position parameters on your 3D cube transform is the Rotation property. Let's set the x and z parameters of the Rotation property to 45 (Figure 3-3). The transform's Rotation value, 45, in the Unity Inspector represents a measurement in Euler angles. Internally, Unity interprets game object rotation through measurements in quaternions. However, it is more intuitive for us, as humans, to visualize rotation through Euler measurements. The reason why, although interesting, is immaterial to our aim in this exercise.

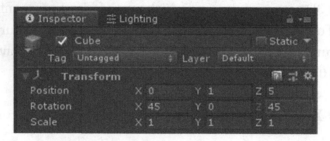

Figure 3-3. *Set the X and Z values of the cube's Rotation property on its transform component to tip the cube in the scene*

Changing the x value of a transform's rotation spins the game object around its x axis. To help you visualize this, imagine sticking a barbecue skewer through the cube along its x axis and spinning it. Along whichever axis you skewer your game object is the axis around which the game object will spin. The skewer, of course, is the axis for which you change rotational values. After you've changed the cube's transform rotation and position it should look like a white diamond hovering in the near distance relative to your scene's camera (Figure 3-4).

Figure 3-4. *Altering the X and Z rotation values of a cube's transform spins the cube relative to those axes*

If you were to play your scene now, you'd see the same 360-degree panoramic image of the desert, but now there's a cube statically hovering before you. That might be interesting in and of itself, but let's give the cube a bit of movement so we can really get an idea of what Unity can offer us.

Game Object + Component + Script = Action

Now, I need to warn you that we're about to handle some code. If you have experience with object-oriented programming (OOP) languages like Java or C++, then transitioning to C# will feel comfortable. It's okay, too, if you've never programmed a line of OOP code in your life. To start, we're going to take things nice and easy. I will do my best to spare you a lot of the more tedious, basic details many programming books force you to digest before helping you execute something interesting.

If you haven't already, now is the time you should set up Visual Studio Community or Visual Studio code on your local machine. Unity version 2019.2.4f1 includes Visual Studio 2019 Community Edition. On the Unity web site you will find simple, straightforward instructions for how to install the necessary packages to sync Unity with an IDE. Once you've completed the setup and integration of Unity and Visual Studio you can follow the remaining steps of this lesson.

Step 3: Creating a C# Script

As we did with our Image and Materials folders, let's create a new folder in our Assets folder and name it Scripts. Navigate into the Scripts folder in your Project window and right-click. From the Create menu, select C# Script (Figure 3-5). Name the new script CubeSpinner. Double-click the CubeSpinner script asset. If you successfully installed Visual Studio and its Unity integration files, then double-clicking the script will automatically open Visual Studio.

```
using UnityEngine;

public class CubeSpinner : MonoBehaviour
{
    // Start is called before the first frame update
    void Start()
```

```
{

}

// Update is called once per frame
void Update()
{

}
}
```

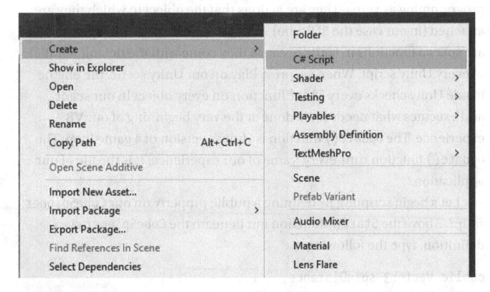

Figure 3-5. *Right-click or Ctrl+Click in the Project window to bring up the Create menu in Unity*

There are three features of a Unity C# script that are relevant to us at this point in our learning curve. The first is the name of our script. Notice that in our script CubeSpinner is followed by a colon and the word MonoBehaviour. This syntax tells us is that our CubeSpinner class inherits from the MonoBehaviour class. All this means to us, right now, is that our CubeSpinner script will act as a component on our game object.

The premise fits nicely into our film set metaphor. On a movie set, a script is what tells the actor what to do in a scene. Our CubeSpinner script, as a component of our 3D cube game object, will tell our cube what to do in our scene. It's that simple!

There are two words beneath the title of our script. One is Start and the other is Update. The parentheses and curly braces that follow the words tell us that these are functions. The functions Start() and Update() are the second and third default features of a Unity script that interest us at this point in our story. I find it helpful to think of functions in programming as verbs. They are actions that the object to which they are attached (in our case the 3D cube) will perform. Start() and Update() are special functions in Unity because they come with the default template of every Unity script. When we press Play on our Unity scene, the engine inside Unity checks every Start function on every object in our scene and executes what needs to be done at the very beginning of our VR experience. The Update() function is Unity's version of a game loop. The Update() function runs every frame of our experience. It is the life of our application.

Let's begin scripting by defining a public property on our CubeSpinner script. Above the Start() function but beneath the CubeSpinner class definition, type the following:

```
public Vector3 spinDistance;
```

Your script should look something like Figure 3-6. Save your script in Visual Studio and return to Unity.

```
1        using UnityEngine;
2
3      ⊟public class CubeSpinner : MonoBehaviour
4       {
5          public Vector3 spinDistance;
6
7          // Start is called before the first frame update
8      ⊟   void Start()
9          {
10
11         }
12
```

Figure 3-6. *This is an example of what your C# code might look like in Visual Studio*

Step 4: Adding the Script as a Component to the Cube

Select your cube game object in the GlobeHopper Scene Hierarchy. In the Inspector, click Add Component. Select Scripts and navigate to your CubeSpinner script (Figure 3-7). Alternatively, you can conveniently drag and drop the CubeSpinner script from the Project window onto the cube's Inspector window. Because we told Unity our CubeSpinner script is a MonoBehaviour, the Unity Editor understands we would like to attach it to a game object as a component.

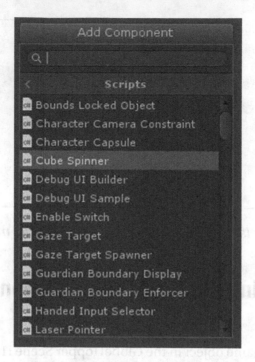

Figure 3-7. Select Add Component ➤ Scripts in the Inspector to add a script to a game object in your scene

After you've added the CubeSpinner script as a component to the 3D cube in our scene, you will see that the property Spin Distance appears in our Inspector. This is what declaring a public property in our Unity scripts accomplishes. You'll also notice that there are three values currently set to zero: X, Y, and Z. Those look familiar, don't they?

If we return to our CubeSpinner script in Visual Studio we notice that before spinDistance we include the word Vector3. In programming this is called a data type. It tells Unity that not only do we want our spinDistance property publicly available in the Inspector, but we also want it to have x, y, and z values—the values of a Vector3 data type.

What's the Big Deal about Data Types?

C# is an example of a statically typed language. Statically typed languages require us, the developers, to know what type of value we are asking our computer's memory to hold. For example, if we want our computer to reserve enough memory to store an English word in a variable, then we assign our variable a data type of `String`, which in itself is a collection of strung-along 1-byte `char` data types.

Some values require more memory from our computers than others. An `integer` data type, for example, asks for 4 bytes (32 bits) of memory from our computer. A `Double` data type asks for 8 bytes. Defining the number of bytes our program requires as we compose it allows the compiler of our IDE to determine the resources a computer will need to execute our program. With these decisions made at the time of its compilation, a program can run more efficiently on another machine. Computationally demanding applications like VR often compile from statically typed programming languages like C# and C++.

You might recall from high school physics or math that a vector is a line with length and direction. For us, in Unity, we can simply think of a `Vector3` as a collection of x, y, and z coordinates. Sometimes those coordinates will represent a game object's position in space; other times—like now—they will represent the values of angles. Recall that we set our x and z values in our transform rotation property to 45. All this meant was that we tilted our cube 45 degrees along the x barbecue skewer and 45 degrees along its z barbecue skewer. Therefore, we can think of the x, y, and z values of our cube's rotation as a `Vector3`—a single data type that holds three discrete values that correspond to points in an x, y, z coordinate plane.

Data Types: Quaternion vs. Vector3

If you're interested in the nuances of motion geometry in 3D graphics and animation, I encourage you to explore further online the topics of quaternions and Euler angles. Their definitions and roles under the hood of Unity are beyond the scope of this book, but understanding their distinctions might help you with greater VR mastery.

A helpful resource I have found online is a web site called Euclidean Space by Martin John Baker. The following URL leads to a page that explains in detail the value of quaternions over Euler angles in 3D programming: `http://www.euclideanspace.com/maths/geometry/rotations/euler/`.

Step 5: Calling a Function in the `Update()` Method of the Script

There's one last task we need to accomplish in our code before we can play-test our `CubeSpinner` script in our GlobeHopper desert scene. Because we want our cube to spin in our scene, our computer needs to draw the pixels of the cube every frame to create the illusion of its movement. Because we need Unity to execute this action every frame, we place the instructions in the `Update()` function.

Within the curly braces of the `Update` function in the `CubeSpinner` script, type the following:

```
gameObject.transform.rotation = spinDistance * Time.deltaTime;
```

Visual Studio will underline the right side of the expression with a red, squiggly line notifying you that the code you've written will not compile. This is an error, and we address it shortly. In the meantime, seeing the code in this manner will help us better understand what we aim to accomplish, how we can accomplish it, and why we might need to try something differently in our program.

In the preceding code we use what some programmers call dot notation to change the rotational direction of our cube every frame. A period, or dot, after an object allows us to access traits we've stored inside that object. For example, by using dot notation after gameObject, we've instructed Unity to navigate to the transform component within the gameObject. In Unity, we use the generic term gameObject to refer to whatever game object to which we've attached the script as a component. Because we've attached our CubeSpinner script to the 3D cube game object, gameObject in our script refers to our 3D cube. Using dot notation tells Unity to grab our 3D cube (our gameObject), reach into its transform component, and inside the transform component grab the rotation property.

Using the equals sign (=) sets the value of the property on the left to the value of the expression on the right. An expression, in coding, simply means a phrase that reduces to something, like an equation. The expression we've used is this:

```
spinDistance * Time.deltaTime;
```

We already know the variable spinDistance is the variable that we're going to set in our Inspector. Time.deltaTime is a bit more abstract. Again, we've used dot notation to access a property within the Time object. Technically, the Time object is a class provided by the UnityEngine code library, which we begin our scripts by using. No actual Time object exists in our project. Like life, though, Time exists in our VR app as a concept. We're able to access properties on the concept of Time in our script as if it were an object like our cube's transform. Pretty meta, huh?

The property we've accessed through dot notation on our Time class is a static float data type called deltaTime. Intuitively, you might understand this to mean "the change in time," and you'd be correct! The deltaTime property on our Time object simply calculates how many seconds have elapsed since the last update—which we know occurs every frame of our app's runtime. The value we set for our Spin_Distance Vector3 variable will rotate our cube that many degrees per frame.

Because the logic for our expression seems to compute, why then does Visual Studio's compiler disagree? The Transform class in Unity has a public property called rotation. This is the property we are trying to set. However, the data type for the rotation property in the Transform class is one called Quaternion. The physics of quaternions is too complex to cover in this book. For our purposes, it is just helpful to know that unlike a Vector3 data type, which holds three values, a Quaternion data type holds four values. Internally, Unity calculates an object's rotation using quaternions for reasons that have to do with computation complexity.

Unfortunately, quaternions are difficult for many of us mere humans to intuitively understand. To help us manipulate the rotation of objects without the mental overhead of quaternion calculation, Unity provides a function in its Transform class called Rotate. The Transform.Rotate() method accepts a Vector3 data type as a parameter. A Vector3 data type in the Transform.Rotate() method represents Euler angles, values that are more intuitive for many users to understand. Using an extension of Euler's formula, named for the Swiss mathematician Leonhard Euler, Unity converts the Euler angles we feed into the Rotate() method as a Vector3 data type into a quaternion value under its hood. Although Visual Studio will not allow us to implicitly convert a Vector3 data type, which is what our spinDistance variable represents, into a Quaternion data type, it will allow us to perform the conversion using Unity's Transform.Rotate() method. Because the error message we receive in Visual Studio reads:

```
Cannot implicitly convert type 'UnityEngine.Vector3' to
'UnityEngine.Quaternion'
```

We require Unity's Rotate() method to convert our equation into a Quaternion value our gameObject's Transform component can store as a value for its rotation property. Therefore, we change the code we wrote in our Update() function in our CubeSpinner script to the following:

```
gameObject.transform.Rotate(spinDistance * Time.deltaTime);
```

However, we can simplify the expression even more. Because we will connect our CubeSpinner script as a component on the object whose transform we want to rotate, we can forgo the use of the term gameObject. Unity will know to which Transform component we are referring. The final version of our CubeSpinner script's Update() function, then, looks something like this:

```
transform.Rotate(spinDistance * Time.deltaTime);
```

You can see both the incorrect and correct versions of the method in Figure 3-8.

```
CubeSpinner.cs*  ⊟  ✕
Assembly-CSharp                                          CubeSpinner
    1      using UnityEngine;
    2
    3    ⊟public class CubeSpinner : MonoBehaviour
    4      {
    5          public Vector3 spinDistance;
    6
    7          // Start is called before the first frame update
    8    ⊟    void Start()
    9          {
   10
   11          }
   12
   13          // Update is called once per frame
   14    ⊟    void Update()
   15          {
   16              // INCORRECT CODE
   17              gameObject.transform.rotation = spinDistance * Time.deltaTime;
   18
   19              // CORRECT CODE
   20              gameObject.transform.Rotate(spinDistance * Time.deltaTime);
   21
   22
   23          }
   24      }
   25
```

Figure 3-8. *The completed version of the CubeSpinner C# script is shown in Visual Studio*

That's it! Save your script in Visual Studio and return to Unity. Wait for Unity to update the changes we've made to our CubeSpinner script.

Step 6: Setting the Spin Distance Parameters on the Script Component

Now, let's set the spin distance value for our cube in the Inspector. With the 3D cube game object selected in our Scene Hierarchy, move your mouse to the Inspector. Within the CubeSpinner script component, set the x and y values of the Spin Distance Vector3 to 100 each. For now, leave the value of z at 0 (Figure 3-9). Save your scene, set your cameras, and press Play!

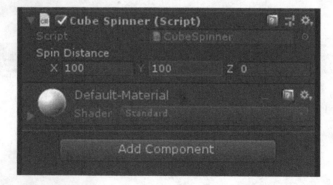

Figure 3-9. *Setting the X and Y parameters of the Spin Distance property in the CubeSpinner script component provides the Unity game engine the distance to rotate the object per frame*

Pretty cool, huh? With just two lines of code we put a virtual spinning cube in our 360-degree desert panorama. If you run the scene again, notice the way the light reflects off the spinning cube (Figure 3-10). In this example, we used only the default texture, material, and shader for the primitive Unity cube object. Just imagine what we could create with slightly more complex design elements. Are you excited yet?

Figure 3-10. *Placing the Directional Light game object in line with a Skybox image's sun strengthens the sensation of immersion in a scene*

If not, you are a tough crowd. But there's much, much more for us to uncover in Unity and VRTK.

Summary

In this chapter and the previous one we created a VR application that places a user in a photorealistic, three-dimensional space. By adding a virtual, animated cube to the scene we took a small step toward composing a VR experience. In this chapter, you also wrote code using an IDE to create a public property in a C# script, attached an original script to a game object as a component, and called a function in the Update() method of a Unity script to execute a frame-by-frame action.

Not bad for a chapter's worth of work! Yet, so far, we've only experienced what it's like to be a disembodied camera floating on a rocky mountain alongside a spinning white cube. Most VR headsets these days come with hand controllers. In Chapter we will learn how to get our hands involved in our virtual scenes and interact with our virtual world.

CHAPTER 4

Doin' Thangs: Input, Events, and Action

If this was a book just about developing in Unity, you'd find an exercise here asking you to wire up a button that responds to a user input with some kind of action. That would be cool, and you'd feel good about your understanding of such an elegant process. However, later, when you sit down to create your own VR experience, you would find that there are many more events you have to publish and subscribe to than you realized. Further, defining each one would send you deep into tinkering with code. Plenty of developers can confidently do this with nothing but Red Bull and a neck pillow, but we are more interested in getting our apps up and running quickly so that we can rapidly prototype and share our experiences. This is why VRTK suits our needs nicely.

In this chapter you will learn the following:

- How VRTK works in concert with Unity.

- About the Unity Event System.

- The role of events in C# and Unity.

- The fundamentals of functions in coding.

- The value of Generic data types.

© Rakesh Baruah 2020
R. Baruah, *Virtual Reality with VRTK4*, https://doi.org/10.1007/978-1-4842-5488-2_4

- The types of collections C# offers to store data.

- The definition of a class.

- How events operate to create communication in code.

VRTK, Please Stand Up

Oculus's VRTK 4 press release describes VRTK as "a decoupled approach to providing solutions to common problems faced in building for spatial computing." What is a decoupled approach? The press release elaborates: "Everything is available at edit time so you know exactly what is going on before you run the scene."

This is great for us because it means VRTK will handle most of the tedious scripting in Visual Studio required to execute complex although routine spatial computing tasks.

VRTK accomplishes this abstraction (a popular term in computer programming that means separating machine code from intuitive, human-friendly interfaces) by connecting to the Unity Event System.

Describing the heart and soul of VRTK and its value to us as rapid iterators, Oculus states it thus:

> *This event message passing makes it easier to decouple functionality and reuse the same logic in many different places and ways without rewriting the same code over and over again. It also means it's much easier to customize functionality without even needing to change or add any code. Pretty much every component can be updated and manipulated via changes to the UnityEvent listeners which is done via the Unity inspector.*

Now, I could show you a series of steps you could follow to connect in-experience actions with user input, but that would limit your frame of reference to only what we discuss. Instead, I spend the next section introducing you to the underlying architecture of the Unity game engine, which VRTK uses to work its magic. By understanding how event message passing occurs between Unity and VRTK, you will be empowered to use the examples we create together, not as surrogates for your own experiences, but as launchpads for your imagination.

The Unity Event System

There's a term in software composition called spaghetti code, used to describe code written hastily that no one, not even its authors, can decipher. When we encounter a bug in our software, spaghetti code can mean the difference between a half-hour problem-solving session and a three-month problem-solving session. Spaghetti code is a self-fulfilling prophecy; if you write it, it will break.

Unfortunately, it is very difficult not to write spaghetti code. Even the most rudimentary-seeming, common software applications require a harmony of moving parts. How the different parts of an application communicate with each other is the source of spaghetti code. It's also the reason Unity gives us a built-in, robust Event System.

As spatial computing developers, we are in the unique position of handling a tremendous amount of input. More than 60 times a second the software we write must allow our infrared tracking systems to compute the location of moving objects in their field of view. This dizzying collection of input, in turn, must reach destinations in our code, which in turn send output to our user. The coordination of these input and output signals is a complex enough phenomenon that an entire branch of science has emerged to study its execution in our brains. It is our role, as spatial computing developers, to re-create the synchrony of stimulus and response in our computers. No small feat!

Fortunately for us, the bright minds at Unity created a system that helps us handle the demands of this practice. Before we can make use of the Unity Event System and its cooperation with VRTK to create our own interactive experiences, though, we have to understand a little bit more about events.

What Are Events?

In our everyday life we define events as moments of significant change. If you miss the bus you normally take to the office, for example, then you've experienced an event. "What happened this morning?" your supervisor might ask as you hurry into work late. Likely, you'd say, "I missed the bus." Missing the bus was a momentous enough occurrence to have an out-of-the-ordinary effect on your day. Events are disruptions to the status quo.

In Unity, our status quo is defined by our game loop, the Update() function, which executes the code within its curly braces once every frame. You might have pondered the timeless question, "If a tree falls in a forest does it make a sound?" Well, our game loop presents an analogous query: If it doesn't have a player, is a game a game? I haven't meditated nearly enough to know the definitive answer to either question. Yet, I can say with confidence that an interactive experience is not interactive if its status quo does not change with feedback. For our purposes, an event is an action that occurs inside our program that provokes a response. Well, if an event is a cause, what then do we call its effect?

As I often do when prompted by questions above my intellectual weight class, I touch base with Microsoft's official literature to provide insight. According to Microsoft's C# documentation:

> *Events enable a <u>class</u> or object to notify other classes or objects when something of interest occurs. The class that sends (or raises) the event is called the publisher and the classes that receive (or handle) the event are called subscribers.*

Got it? Thanks, Microsoft! Let's move on. I'm just kidding. If you're anything like me (an underskilled humanities major) you might have read Microsoft's description of events, closed your eyes, and prayed for the Earth to open and swallow your weeping mind into the bosom of its oblivion. Hold off on clamoring for the sweet hereafter for now, though, because I'm going to endeavor, in the spirit of Unity and VRTK, to make events more accessible.

First, though, we have to ramp up with some basics.

Welcome to Function Junction: Population 0 or 1

In computer programming, a function is a block of code that executes an action. A block of code could execute a task as simple as multiplying a number by two, or as complicated as pinpointing your location on Google Maps. However, it is considered best practice in software composition to write functions that execute only one specific task. Here's what a multiplication function could look like in C#:

```
public int Multiplier (int x) {
        int result = x * 2;
        return result;
}
```

Our Multiplier function is simple and direct. Even by its name alone we could surmise what it does: It multiplies our input by some quantity.

Functions can be made up of other functions, too. An example of our Google Maps function could, itself, make use of several functions. In pseudo-code, it could look something like this:

```
Public void LocationFinder (your current position) {
```

- Baby Function 1: Request and return the coordinates of *your current position* from your phone's internal GPS system.

- Baby Function 2: Contact the Google Maps application programming interface (API) to request permission to access its resources.

- Baby Function 3: Submit the coordinates for *your current position* to the Google Maps API.

- ...

- Baby Function *n*: Load a new window in your phone's browser to show *your current position* on Google Maps.

```
}
```

On the one hand, functions operate like recipes; they present a sequence of tasks that together complete an operation. On the other hand, functions also execute those tasks. Therefore, a function is not only a recipe from a cookbook, it's also the chef who whips the ingredients together! Now, imagine if we had a sequence of functions that, together, identified the ingredients our dish will need, went to the market to purchase those ingredients, prepped the ingredients, cooked them, set the table, and served the food. Hopefully, by now, you can imagine the amazing, yet simple, power of functions.

Inputs, Outputs, Parameters, Arguments, and Results

I like to think of a simple function, one that executes one task only like our Multiplier function, as a little machine in a box. Like a pasta maker, it takes input, performs an operation, and returns an output—deliciously fat fettuccine!

The inputs for a function are its parameters. Its output are its result. Input: dough. Output: fettuccine. Input: lettuce, tomato, cheese, bread, bacon. Output: BLT. In our Multiplier() function:

```
public int Multiplier (int x) {
    int result = x * 2;
    return result;
}
```

The input was an integer of value x. Its output was the product of our input multiplied by the number 2. We stored the value of the multiplication operation into a variable, which we called result. By returning the variable result, which holds the integer product of x * 2, we've complied with our function's instructions to output an integer for every input, x.

We could further abstract our Multiplier() function by defining it to take two inputs instead of one.

```
public int Multiplier(int x, int y){
    int result = x * y;
    return result;
}
```

Now, we can use our Multiplier() function to find the product of any two integers not just x and 2. If we choose the integers 3 and 5 as our inputs then our output will be 15. The integers 4 and 12 will yield the integer 48. Whereas the parameters of a function define the types of information it can accept as inputs, the arguments of a function are the specific inputs a function takes when it is called. For example, x and y are parameters, but 3 and 5, and 4 and 12 are arguments.

Method Signatures and Overloading

Every function has a signature. As is the case for us humans, so it should be in the software programs we compose: A function should have a unique signature. There might be more than one Sarika Washington in a spin class of 25 people. Yet, each Sarika Washington will have a signature unique to them. The signature of a function is not limited to its name or the body of its code block. The signature of a function includes its parameters.

For example, let's say we are writing software for an animal cloning farm. The operator of the farm has asked us to write a function that will take as an input one rabbit and return as an output two rabbits. Well, we already wrote a Multiplier function at our last job, so let's just use that again and take the rest of the day off!

We call our Multiplier function and pass into it our parameter of the original bunny.

```
Multiplier(bunny);
```

Uh oh, we got an error. Our program won't compute. What happened?

```
public int Multiplier(int x){
    int result = x * 2;
    return result;
}
```

Notice that our original Multiplier function took in the data type int as its parameter. The int preceding the function's name tells us the function will only return an output that also has the data type int. Int stands for integer, and that's what our input was in our original function—a positive, whole number.

`Multiplier(2)` would therefore return the integer 4.

A bunny is not an integer, though; a bunny is, well, it's a bunny. We could write another version of our `Multiplier` function to better suit the needs of the animal cloning farm.

```
public Bunny Bunny_Multiplier (Bunny bunny1) {
       Bunny bunny_2 = bunny1.Copy();
       return bunny_2;
}
```

By changing the return type of the `Multiplier` function from integer to Bunny and its input parameter from integer to Bunny, we've created a second `Multiplier` function with the same functionality as our original but a totally unique signature. In object-oriented languages like C#, functions of the same name can be written to take different parameters as long as certain criteria are met. This is called overloading a function, an example of which was our original `Multiplier()` function. One version of it accepted one input, and another version of it, with the same name and return type, accepted two inputs. If we try to pass an integer into our bunny `Multiplier` we're going to get an error, like we did when we tried to pass a bunny into our integer `Multiplier`. Because we've changed the return data type from an integer to a Bunny, we've had to change the name of the function, too, from `Multiplier()` to `Bunny_Multiplier()`. If we did not, the compiler in our code editor would have given us an error.

Generics and Collections

Because creating functions with many overload parameters requires us to write out each method's signature, making a function with many options for overloading can become tedious. As developers are an inherently lazy bunch, the bright minds of programmers past created the concept of generics to minimize the amount of work required to write methods with a lot of options for overloading.

Generic methods are like prefabricated houses. Every house has a door, three bedrooms, two bathrooms, a kitchen, and a living room. The interior and exterior design of each house, however, can be as unique as its inhabitants decide. One might only have beanbags for chairs; one might take inspiration from a very specific time period in 18th-century France. Although the structure and purpose of each house are the same, its contents are distinct.

In C#, generics avoid the tedium of creating repetitive method signatures for different numbers and kinds of input by allowing us to write a method only once and declare its input parameter, or parameters, with the symbol <T>, which stands for any data type. For example, instead of writing a multiplier function that duplicates integers, bunnies, potatoes, floats, strings, and chestnuts, we can write one multiplier function that accepts as its input a generic collection of objects.

```
collection <T> Multiplier(collection<T> objectsToMultiply, int
factor)
{
      new collection<T> multipliedObjects;
      foreach (var object in objectsToMultiply)
      {
            for (int i = 0; i <= factor; i++)
            {
                  var copiedObject = object.Copy()
                  multipliedObjects.Add(copiedObject);
            }
      }

      return multipliedObjects;

}
}
```

This code allows us to pass into a `Multiplier` function a collection of any kind of object, from bunnies, to integers, to hot dogs, and so on. The character T between brackets < > tells our IDE's compiler to figure out what the data type is at compile time. The data type of T will be determined by the manner in which the user of our code (if it's not us) will implement the `Multiplier` function. If the user passes a collection of Bunny objects into the `Multiplier` function, then the compiler will understand <T> to represent a Bunny data type.

In addition to generics, the preceding code uses some concepts that might be unfamiliar to you. As they are fundamental to programming, I'll explain them briefly. Many entry-level programming books spend chapters on these concepts, but I'm confident you'll understand them quickly. The first concept that might be unfamiliar is the `foreach` keyword. `Foreach` is a type of loop in C# that allows us to iterate over a collection of objects. For every object in a collection, the `foreach` loop will apply the logic of its code block, the syntax between its curly braces.

A second keyword with which you might be unfamiliar is the keyword `var`. The keyword `var` allows us to create an object in our computer's memory with the promise that the compiler will understand its data type in due time. Because the collection we pass into the `foreach` loop has been defined as generic in the `Multiplier` function's parameters, neither we nor the compiler know what kind of data the object will be. Not until the compiler peeks into the collection will it know its specific data type. At that point it will understand to what data type it should assign `var`.

A third keyword you might not completely understand is the `for` loop. The `for` loop is fundamental to programming; it is valuable to know how a `for` loop works to accomplish even the simplest of tasks in VR design.

Essentially, the for loop sets a counter for the number of times to perform the task within its code block. To define the parameters of a for loop, follow these steps:

1. Define the variable i as an integer and set it to the starting value of your counter, which is usually 0.

2. Define the upper limit of the counter by setting a ceiling past which i cannot increase. In the preceding example, I set the ceiling of my variable i to no higher than the value of the factor parameter passed into the Multiplier function. I instruct the compiler of this ceiling by declaring i can only be less than or equal to the value of factor (<=).

3. Increment the counter by adding 1 to the variable i with the syntax ++.

The final term you might not recognize from the generic Multiplier method signature is the term collection. C# does not consider collection a keyword; its use is not prohibited in other contexts of a C# program. The concept of collections fits conveniently into the broader use of generics. You might not have much interest in creating generic functions at this stage of your VR development process, but it is likely that you'll encounter generics when dealing with data structures to hold information as you seek to manipulate it. C# includes a library of generic collections like Lists and Dictionaries, which are keywords that offer all kinds of benefits for classifying data for more convenient search, sort, and retrieval. To create a List for a data type you simply define the data type you'd like to hold when you create the list using the new keyword.

Creating a List

```
List<Bunny> bunnyList = new List<Bunny>();
```

Creating a Dictionary

```
var bunnyDictionary = new Dictionary<Bunny, Food>()
{
        { JennyHopper, Carrots},
        {BarbaraBounce, Lettuce}
};
```

The bunnyDictionary collection, defined here, holds a table of Bunnies stored by the bunny's name and their favorite food. The schema for a Dictionary object is the dictionary's key, in this example Bunny, and the key's value, in this example a type of Food. Together, the components that define a dictionary are called its key/value pairs.

Creating an Array

A final point I'd like to emphasize on the topic of generics and collections addresses the common programming data structure called an array. I have avoided using List and Dictionary collections in the code for this book. However, you will encounter at least one example of an array. In C#, arrays are like lists in that they are a collection of objects with the same data type. The difference between the two is that an array must be defined with a finite length that cannot change. A list, for example, can expand to fit any number of objects as long as the computer has memory to spare. An array, on the other hand, cannot hold any more objects than it was created to hold. Instantiating, or creating an array object of the Array class looks like this:

```
int [] array = new int[3];
string [] stringArray = new string[5];
Bunny [] bunnies = new Bunny[4];
```

We define an array by establishing the data type of its contents; identifying that the object is an `Array` through the use of square brackets [ ]"; naming the array; using the `new` keyword to create the array; and finally setting the number of indexes in the array by placing its length within square brackets. Like a list, an array can store a collection of any data type as long as it is defined to do so. Although the length of a list is inhibited only by the amount of memory available, it can expand to hold more elements easily. Unlike a list, an array cannot be added to indefinitely. The cost of arrays is their finite size, but their benefit is faster performance during operations that access a specific element or search through an ordered collection. Because runtime performance is so important to resource-intensive applications like VR experiences, storing collections in arrays might be preferable for your design.

Havin' Class

In our bunny `Multiplier` we used the phrase (`Bunny bunny_1`) as our function input, or parameter. Of course, no data type Bunny exists prepackaged in a code editor like Visual Studio. Whereas fundamental data types like integers, decimals, and letters (called `chars` and `strings`) exist by default in most (if not all) code editors, more unique data types like Bunny do not. Fortunately, the pioneers of OOP created an easy way for us to make our own data types. These original data types we call classes.

If Bunny is a data type we created with our own Bunny class, then a single representation of that class is called an instance of that class. Sisters Jenny Hopper and Rina Hopper are both unique instances of the Bunny class. They are bunnies and as such their data types, in our example, are Bunny. Just like 1 is an integer and 5 is a different integer, Jenny Hopper is a bunny and Rina Hopper is a different bunny. Both are bunnies, but both are not the same bunny. Bunny is a class. Rina and Jenny Hopper are objects, instances of a class.

What does this have to do with functions in software composition? Well, look again at the signature of our Bunny Multiplier method:

```
public Bunny Bunny_Multiplier (Bunny bunny_1) {
    Bunny bunny_2 = bunny_1.copy();
    Return bunny_2;
}
```

The signature of our Bunny Multiplier tells us that we can use it to clone any bunny, not just a bunny called bunny_1. Whereas our parameters define the signature of a method's general inputs, arguments define the specific inputs of a method's execution. For example, if we wanted to test our Bunny Multiplier by cloning Jenny Hopper, then we would pass Jenny Hopper into our Bunny Multiplier as its argument.

```
Bunny_Multiplier(Jenny Hopper);
```

What we'll get in return is a copy of Jenny Hopper. Whereas bunny_1 defined the input parameter of our bunny Multiplier function, Jenny Hopper defines the input argument we pass into the bunny Multiplier function when we want to use it.

Functions, data types, parameters, arguments, and return types are the building blocks of composing software. To explain the details of their roles in programming is not only beyond the scope of this book, it's also beyond the scope VRTK. VRTK exists to handle a lot of the intricacy (and complications) that arise from writing functions that call other functions to return data types for still more functions. The principles we covered in this chapter are all we need to get started adding interactivity between our users and their virtual environment in Unity and VRTK.

Two Events Walk into a Bar …

… and the bar shuts down because a thread lock occurs.

So far, here is what we have covered:

- VRTK is an interface that passes event messages back and forth with the Unity Event System.

- The Unity Event System is a built-in system provided by Unity that handles the communication between events and their outcomes.

- Events are any change to a program's status quo, such as a user's input.

Now, let's put it all together to better prepare us to launch into our exercise. First, though, let's recall Microsoft's definition of events from the previous section:

> *Events enable a <u>class</u> or object to notify other classes or objects when something of interest occurs. The class that sends (or raises) the event is called the publisher and the classes that receive (or handle) the event are called subscribers.*

Now, let's isolate the first sentence:

> *Events enable a class or object to notify other classes or objects when something of interest occurs.*

By now we have a general understanding of how a class is a blueprint for an object and an object is an instance of a class. In our Animal Cloning Farm example, Bunny was our class and Jenny Hopper was an object of our Bunny class. If we look back at our Bunny Multiplier function block:

```
{
     Bunny bunny_2 = bunny1.Copy();
     return bunny_2;
}
```

Copy() represents a function (or verb) we are performing on our object bunny_1.

Now, what if the illegal animal cloning farm's operator approaches us and says, "Listen, buddy, that bunny Multiplier gadget you created is great, but I need a way to keep track of all the copies of rabbits I'm making. My books are a mess!"

We can put our criminal employer's mind at ease by using an event in our program to notify another part of our application that a bunny copy has been made.

Sure, we could finagle our Bunny Multiplier to include a variable that increments by one every time we make a clone of a rabbit, but that will get very messy very quickly. We always want to keep our functions from performing more than one task. This principle becomes more important when you learn that functions cannot return more than one result. Our bunny Multiplier already returns a cloned bunny object. To amend our function for it to return an integer that tracks the count of our clones, too, is a bad move. Although it is possible, it is most definitely not encouraged.

The most powerful antidote to spaghetti code that we have at our disposal is the KISS mantra. You may know the acronym to stand for "Keep it simple, stupid." However, I prefer an iteration I got from software engineer Eric Elliott: "Keep It stupid simple." The most stupid simple solution to our cloning operator's request is an event.

In our cloning application we could create a class called Counter. Our Counter class could have a property in it called Number of Clones. Every time our bunny Multiplier calls the function bunny_1.Copy() we could send an event to the Counter class telling it to increase the value of its Number of Clones property by one. If we did so we will have executed Microsoft's definition of an event:

- Events enable a <u>class</u> or object (in our scenario the Bunny_Multiplier function in our Bunny class) to notify other classes or objects (our Counter class) when something of interest occurs (a bunny is cloned).

- The class that sends (or *raises*) the event is called the *publisher* (our Bunny class) and the classes that receive (or *handle*) the event are called *subscribers* (our Counter class).

As Unity developers we don't need to concern ourselves with more than this. The Unity Event System handles the plumbing that connects all our publishers and subscribers, of which there are many in an application designed to respond to a user's physical presence. All we need to concern ourselves with is telling Unity what event should go where. Unity's Event System will handle the rest!

Summary

This chapter was a breather to get you ready for the dance ahead. Although heavy on theory and light on practice, the fundamentals put forth in this chapter will better prepare you to see through the magical abstraction of interfaces like VRTK and Unity. This chapter covered the makeup of a C# function, the distinction between classes and objects in OOP, the value of generics in C#, the types of collections generics make possible, the role events play in communication between classes in a script, the responsibility of the Unity Event System to coordinate event-passing in our programs, and the functionality VRTK provides as an interface between the developer and the Unity Event System.

The underlying code of a game engine like Unity is very complex, but understanding how the inputs of a user and the outputs of our program communicate will better determine what you create in your application and, most important, why a piece of code either works or does not. Ahead, we put the theory behind us and jump into the action, literally. Through the use of VRTK Action scripts we can easily create interaction between a user and our VR experience without touching the underlying architecture of the Unity Event System. In Chapter 5, however, we'll ease into the waters by creating an interactive exercise in the manner of the old school—through the use of a keyboard.

CHAPTER 5

Keyboard Input as Action

In Chapter 4 we laid the groundwork for better understanding the Unity Event System and its integration with VRTK. For me, it's helpful to think of events as messages sent between classes and objects to notify different components of a program that a change has occurred. Because user input into our VR applications alters the state of the program, it, too, is an event. As an event, user input fits nicely into the list of responsibilities handled by VRTK as an interface for the Unity Event System.

Traditionally, in platforms such as web development, user input has taken the form of keyboard strokes or a mouse click. Because VR aims to remove the user from the context of their computers and workspaces, we, as its developers, must take into account newly possible forms of communication. The movement of a user's head, hands, and body; the press of a button; the pull of a trigger; or the utterance of a phrase replace more conventional means of input on which the computer programming community has built its paradigms of interaction. Communicating through one's body with a virtual experience is a relatively recent phenomenon, and as such introduces new complications. Further, user interaction design patterns and antipatterns are still being discovered.

Before we begin creating interactive experiences tied to contemporary VR hardware, we first focus our attention on the most classic medium of human–computer interaction—the keyboard.

© Rakesh Baruah 2020
R. Baruah, *Virtual Reality with VRTK4*, https://doi.org/10.1007/978-1-4842-5488-2_5

In this chapter you will do the following:

- Create primitive game objects in the Unity Inspector.

- Change the color of game objects through material components.

- Create a C# script to change the size of a game object.

- Connect a transformation of a 3D model to user input through the Unity Input class.

Exercise: An Interesting Calculation of One's Interest in Calculating One's Interest

I once heard someone say that the hardest thing about teaching young adults the importance of financial literacy is communicating the power of compound interest. As you might know, compound interest is the phenomenon of value increasing exponentially over time. It is the premise behind foreclosed houses and buoyant retirement accounts. For example, $100 compounded by 10% for 30 years turns $100 into more than $17,000. Keep taking the 10% you earn each year out of your account, however, and you'll only have $4,000 after 30 years. Compound interest is a fundamental tenet of accruing wealth.

Yet many people forego saving money in favor of short-term outcomes. Of course, dozens of factors inform a person's ability to save, but what if we could come up with an interactive VR app that makes the math of calculating compound interest—with its decimal places and percentages—simple enough for a grade-schooler to understand?

User Story

Kavya is a third-grade teacher, and she'd like to create a VR app to help her students understand the concept of compound interest. Money is still too abstract for them to grasp, and their developing minds still struggle with long-term planning. Kavya wants to create a VR app that will use the immediate, alluring appeal of chocolate cake to demonstrate the gains of foregoing short-term gains for even more goodness in the long run.

In this exercise, as Kavya, we will do the following:

- Import a 3D model into our Unity scene.

- Create a script to calculate compound interest.

- Connect our script to both a user input and a game object.

By the end of this exercise you will better understand the big picture of the UX input/output cycle and be able to apply basic interaction between a user and your scene.

Step 1: Create a Project

To begin let's open a new Unity 3D project and call it Interest_Calculator. To set the platform for which we want to build our application, navigate to File ➤ Build Settings (Ctrl+Shift+B). For this exercise, select either PC, Mac, & Linux Standalone or Universal Windows Platform. Each platform provides parameters for its build settings, such as target device, architecture, build type, and so on. Because these parameters depend on each developer's unique aim, I can only share with you the settings I will use for my Windows 10 PC running an Intel i-7 CPU.

My Build Settings

Platform: PC, Mac, & Linux Standalone

Target Platform: Windows

Architecture: x86_64 (You can check whether your machine is 32-bit or 64-bit via `https://www.computerhope.com/issues/ch001121.htm`).

Compression Method: Default

If you'd like more detailed information about Unity's Build settings, refer to the "Build Settings" section of Unity's online documentation, available at `https://docs.unity3d.com/Manual/BuildSettings.html`.

After defining our Build settings, we navigate into Edit ➤ Project Settings ➤ Player to set our game settings to VR supported. As we've done in previous exercises, select the VR SDK of your choice. Further, on the Other Settings tab, set the following configuration parameters:

- Scripting Runtime Version: .NET 4.x Equivalent

- Scripting Backend: Mono / IL2CPP (depending on your OS)

Then from a Git Bash terminal window you open inside your Assets folder, clone the VRTK Git repo into your project.

- Navigate to the project Assets/ directory.

- Git clone with required submodules into the Assets/ directory:

```
git clone --recurse-submodules https://github.com/
ExtendRealityLtd/VRTK.git
```

- Change to the newly cloned directory: `cd VRTK/`

- `git submodule init && git submodule update`

- The Unity software will now import and compile the new files.

Because VRTK is an evolving API, changes might occur to the underlying source code. If you have trouble cloning the repository into your Assets folder, visit the ExtendRealityLtd GitHub page (https://github.com/ExtendRealityLtd) for up-to-date documentation and troubleshooting tips.

Upon returning to Unity, if you're met with the VRTK Manage Input Mappings prompt, click Add Input Mappings. For the penultimate step of our boilerplate VRTK setup, update the legacy XR inputs from the Unity Package Manager, if you are running a version of Unity from 2019 or later.

Finally, if you are using a third-party VR SDK such as the Oculus Rift, navigate into the Unity Asset Store (Window ➤ Asset Store) and download and import the SDK package specified by your VR HMD provider. Because I am developing for the Oculus Rift, I download the Oculus Integration SDK. Depending on your setup, you might be asked to upgrade plug-ins. Confirm all updates and, if necessary, allow Unity to restart.

Step 2: Set Up the Scene

After we import and install the VRTK tools and our input resources, let's navigate into our VRTK\Prefabs\CameraRig\UnityXRCameraRig folder (Assets ➤ VRTK ➤ Prefabs ➤ CameraRig ➤ UnityXRCameraRig). Drag and drop the UnityXRCameraRig game object from the Project window into our Scene Hierarchy. Let's take this moment to also save our scene by pressing Ctrl+Shift+S and naming it Scene1 in our Assets/Scenes folder. Press Play to test your setup.

A Quick Look at the UnityXRCameraRig

What is this UnityXRCameraRig that we pulled into our Scene Hierarchy? First, in our hierarchy, it appears blue, whereas other game objects like Main Camera and Directional Light are gray. A blue game object in the Scene Hierarchy indicates a prefab, which is a reusable asset. Because it is a prefab, we can use the UnityXRCameraRig object in any VRTK-enabled scene. If it was not a prefab then we would have to reconstruct the game object each time we would like to use it.

To the right of the UnityXRCameraRig prefab in the Hierarchy is a caret (>). Hovering over the caret with our mouse, we learn that clicking it will reveal more information about the prefab asset. Clicking the caret opens a new Scene View of the prefab and a new Hierarchy window displaying the prefab's child game objects. As the UnityXRCameraRig has no shape in its Scene View, we can deduce that the object is prefabricated with abstract components. Highlighting the UnityXRCameraRig parent object in the prefab's Hierarchy reveals its components in the Inspector window.

The Inspector window shows the components attached to a game object. As with all game objects, the UnityXRCameraRig contains a transform component, which contains the data of its position, rotation, and scale in a scene. The UnityXRCameraRig parent object also contains two VRTK-specific C# scripts attached as components. The first is the `Unity XR Configurator` script, which hooks into the UnityEngine's XR code library. The second is the `LinkedAliasAssociationCollection` script, which is part of the system VRTK creates to enable us to design for a variety of VR systems. We will explore C# scripting and the `LinkedAliasAssociationCollection` script, specifically, in more detail later.

Finally, the UnityXRCameraRig prefab contains three child game objects: `HeadAnchor`, `LeftAnchor`, and `RightAnchor`. These, too, we will dive into more deeply in the chapters ahead. For now, it is sufficient to understand that the UnityXRCameraRig prefab, as a game object provided by the VRTK framework, frees us to design an immersive experience without regard to a specific underlying VR SDK, such as the Oculus Rift, HTC Vive, Google Daydream, or others. Like VRTK as a whole, the UnityXRCameraRig serves as a universal adapter, of sorts, that allows us to create one experience for many headsets.

Step 3: Add Game Objects

Recall that we can only have one camera object active in a scene at a time so let's disable our default Unity Main Camera, if you have not already. While we are in the hierarchy, let's also add some simple game objects to help us prototype our scene. First, let's add a floor. Right-click in the Scene Hierarchy and select 3D Object ➤ Plane. Right-click the plane object and select Rename. Rename the plane Floor. We'll leave the plane's transform default settings as they are.

Second, let's add a little table. Again, right-click in the Scene Hierarchy and navigate to 3D Object ➤ Cube. We'll leave the cube's transform settings in their default state. Right-click to select the cube and from the shortcut menu, select Rename. Rename the cube game object Table. Make sure your table has a Box Collider component attached to it. To confirm, select the cube in the hierarchy and check its components in the Inspector (Figure 5-1).

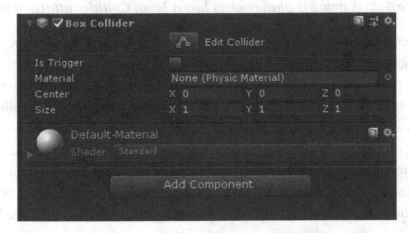

Figure 5-1. *A new 3D cube has a Box Collider component attached to it*

If you don't see a Box Collider component, you can add one by clicking Add Component and searching for Box Collider. Confirm, too, that your plane object has attached to it a component called Mesh Collider (Figure 5-2).

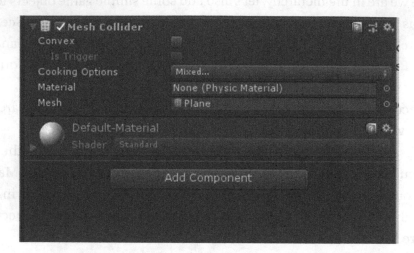

Figure 5-2. *A new 3D plane object has a Mesh Collider attached to it*

A collider component gives a game object a boundary that can keep other game objects with colliders from passing through it. However, colliders can also allow game objects to pass through them. In the latter case, colliders operate as triggers. A game object passing through a collider that is a trigger can incite an action in the program in response to the object's transgression into the collider's boundary. An example would be an action of collecting coins in a game as the player passes through the coin; the coin's collider would serve as a trigger tripped by the player. We will work more intimately with colliders as triggers in Chapter 8, where I discuss user interaction with game objects.

Step 4: Change the Color of a Game Object

By default, our box and our plane will have the same white color Unity provides as its default material. If you'd like to change the color of an object, remember that materials are components we wrap around an object's mesh to create surface. Right-click in the Assets folder in the Project window and select Create ➤ Folder. Name the folder Materials. Open the new folder, right-click in the Project window, and select Create ➤ Material. Highlight the new material and locate the heading Main Maps in the Inspector (Figure 5-3).

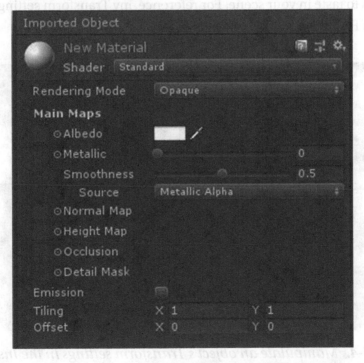

Figure 5-3. *A material component's color can be edited in the Inspector*

The first property beneath Main Maps is Albedo, next to which is a color selector. The Albedo parameter of a material object's Main Maps property allows you to set the color of a material. Click the rectangle to open a color selector. Select the color you'd like to apply to the floor in our scene. When you have selected a color, rename the material to the color you selected by selecting it once in the Project window, and, when its title is highlighted, type the name of the color and press Return.

Finally, drag the material from the Project window onto the Floor object in the Scene Hierarchy to set it as a material component on our plane game object. If you'd like to change the color of the cube as well, follow the steps you performed to create the material for the plane.

In the transform component of each game object you can manipulate the x, y, and z parameters of the transform's location property to place the items to taste in your scene. For reference, my Transform settings are shown in Figure 5-4.

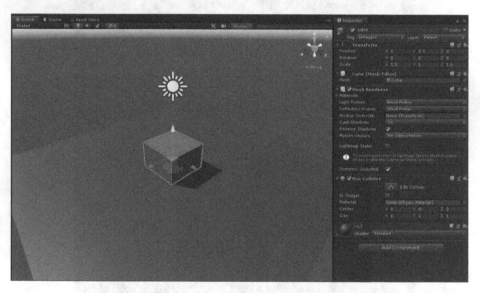

Figure 5-4. *Manipulate an object's Transform settings in the Inspector*

At this point in the exercise your Scene Hierarchy should include the following active objects:

- Directional Light
- UnityXRCameraRig
- Floor
- Table

Step 5: Create a C# Script

Recall that game objects are the actors in our scenes, poised before cameras and beneath lights. Scripts are components we attach to game objects to dictate the behavior we'd like them to display during the execution of the Unity game loop. We are going to create a script that calculates interest for our project, and we will need a game object on which to attach it as a component.

In the Project Hierarchy create a new empty Game Object and name it CalculatorController. In your Project window create a new folder beneath Assets and name it Scripts. Inside your new folder, right-click and select Create ➤ C# Script. Name the script Calculator. Double-click the script to open it in Visual Studio (or whatever code editor you have chosen to download).

Step 6: Write Code in Your IDE

In Visual Studio beneath the title public class Calculator : MonoBehaviour and before the Start() function, add the following code:

```
public GameObject cube;
public float interestRate;
```

```
Transform cube_transform;
Vector3 currentVolumeVector;
float cubeLength, cubeHeight, cubeWidth;
```

Beneath the Update() function and before the final closing brace (})
of the class, declare a new function called CalculateInterest() with a
return type of void.

```
public void CalculateInterest(){

}
```

Write the following code between the curly braces of the
CalculateInterest() function:

```
Transform transform = cube.transform;

float cubeLength = transform.localScale.x;
float cubeWidth = transform.localScale.z;
float cubeHeight = transform.localScale.y;

cubeLength *= interestRate;
cubeHeight *= interestRate;
cubeWidth *= interestRate;

transform.localScale = new Vector3(cubeLength,
cubeHeight, cubeWidth);

float newVolume = cubeLength * cubeHeight * cubeWidth;
Debug.Log("New Volume: " + newVolume);
```

This is neither the most efficient nor most elegant script, but it
clearly demonstrates the fundamentals you will need to create C# scripts of
your own.

The intentions of the script are twofold. First, we grab properties of
the game object we would like to influence in our script and store those
properties in our script so we can manipulate them. We accomplish this

intention by defining variables and setting them to the properties of the game object we'd like to manipulate:

```
Transform transform = cube.transform;

float cubeLength = transform.localScale.x;
float cubeWidth = transform.localScale.z;
float cubeHeight = transform.localScale.y;
```

Second, we manipulate the properties we've stored by using the *= operator, which, in English, translates to "equals itself multiplied by." Like this:

```
cubeLength *= interestRate;
cubeHeight *= interestRate;
cubeWidth *= interestRate;
```

Third, we reattach the updated properties to the game object to be reflected back to us in the scene:

```
transform.localScale = new Vector3(cubeLength,
cubeHeight, cubeWidth);
```

Because we will be manipulating the volume of our game object, we will manipulate its length, height, and width. We access the values of those properties within the game object's transform. If you select a game object in the Unity Scene Hierarchy, you will see in the Inspector a component called Transform with three properties: Position, Rotation, and Scale. We can access the x, y, and z values of these properties in our scripts using dot notation. Dot notation enables us to access the properties of a class, such as GameObject. Because x, y, and z are properties of a transform, for example, we can "dot" into the Scale property of an object's transform with the dot notation transform.localScale.x where x is the axis to affect. We dot into the localScale property because that is the public property available to us as developers on the Transform component. You can learn more about Transform properties in the "Transform" section of the Unity documentation, available at https://docs.unity3d.com/ ScriptReference/Transform.html.

Near the top of our class we declared variables we would need throughout our script. These include the length, height, and width of our game object as float values:

```
public GameObject cube;
public float interestRate;

Transform cube_transform;
Vector3 currentVolumeVector;
float cubeLength, cubeHeight, cubeWidth;
```

We declare these variables with the data type float because we will use them to create a Vector3 data type, which only accepts floats as its parameters.

Unity's Definition of a Vector3 Data Type

This structure is used throughout Unity to pass 3D positions and directions around. It also contains functions for doing common vector operations.

https://docs.unity3d.com/ScriptReference/Vector3.html

In our CalculateInterest() method we multiply the game object's length, width, and height by the interestRate amount we specify later in our editor (that is the purpose of a public, or Serialized property in a Unity script). After we calculate each value by the interest rate, we place those x, y, and z values into a new Vector3 object, which we then reassign to the game object's Scale property of its transform:

```
transform.localScale = new Vector3(cubeLength,
    cubeHeight, cubeWidth);
```

CHAPTER 5   KEYBOARD INPUT AS ACTION

You can imagine the whole operation as akin to accepting a car into a mechanic's garage. In this example, the game object we intend to manipulate is the car and our script is the garage. We remove the parts of the car we would like to work on by storing them in variables in our script. We then perform the work that must be done on those parts and reassemble them before reattaching them to the vehicle.

Creating a New Object Instance of a Class

To create a new Vector3 object with the coordinates of our cube's updated dimensions, we use the syntax of the new keyword to invoke the Vector3 constructor:

```
new Vector3(cubeLength, cubeHeight, cubeWidth);
```

As indicated by the input parentheses following the name of the Vector3 structure, the constructor of an object is a function method of a class. Classes define the requirements of their input parameters as part of their constructor's signature. Because the Vector3 constructor requires three float values, we can instantiate a new Vector3 object by passing three float values into its constructor.

The new keyword prepares our compiler to set aside enough memory to store the object of the data type we intend to create. Because three float values, each requiring 4 bytes of memory in our computer, comprise a Vector3 object, the new keyword preceding a Vector3 data type constructor requests 12 bytes of memory from our system.

As our final step in Visual Studio, add the following code between the curly braces of the Update() function:

```
if (Input.GetKeyDown(KeyCode.Space))
{
        CalculateInterest();
}
```

Because the Update() function runs once every frame of our game, the code we just wrote will listen for an event from the user. That event will be the pressing of the spacebar on the keyboard. If and when the event takes place, our Input EventHandler will execute our CalculateInterest function.

According to Microsoft documentation, an EventHandler "represents the method that will handle an event when the event provides data." The data provided by the EventHandler in our example is of type Bool—true or false. If our user presses the spacebar, the condition of the IF statement becomes true and our EventHandler fires a message to run the CalculateInterest() function. In the language of our Bunny_Multiplier example from Chapter 4, the Input.GetKeyDown() function is the publisher and the CalculateInterest() function is the subscriber.

Make sure you saved the changes to your script in Visual Studio to see them reflected in Unity.

Step 7: Compile Our Code by Returning to Unity

When we return to Unity, the application compiles the changes we've made to our script. For scripts to interact with objects in our scene, our scene must be able to find those scripts. A common pattern in Unity software composition is to create a Controller game object to make our scripts available to our scene as a component of a game object.

Select the CalculatorController object in the hierarchy and, in the Inspector, drag and drop the Calculator script from the Assets/Scripts folder in the Project window onto the Inspector. Alternatively, you can click Add Component in the Inspector and search for the `Calculator` script.

Step 8: Activate Our Script by Attaching It to a Game Object in the Scene

Once we have attached our `Calculator` script to our `CalculatorController`, we can select our `CalculatorController` object in the hierarchy and inspect its properties. In the Inspector we see our `Calculator` script attached as a component on the game object and beneath the script two empty fields: Cube and Interest Rate (Figure 5-5).

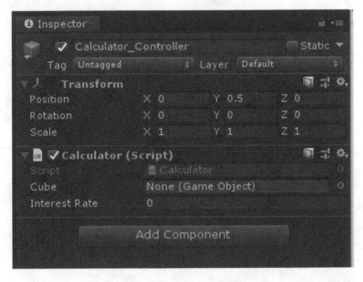

Figure 5-5. *The public properties created in a C# script appear in the Unity Editor's Inspector window*

Step 9: Define the Game Object That Responds to the User's Input

Because our field says Cube, let's create a 3D cube in our Hierarchy window (right-click, then select 3D Object ➤ Cube). With the cube highlighted in the hierarchy, drag (don't click) the mouse over the Scene window. Press the w button to display the movement handlebars and use them to place the cube at a position slightly above the table game object.

When you've done so, add a Rigidbody component to the cube by selecting Add Component in the Inspector and searching for Rigidbody (Figure 5-6). Make sure you do not select a 2D Rigidbody because we are working in three dimensions.

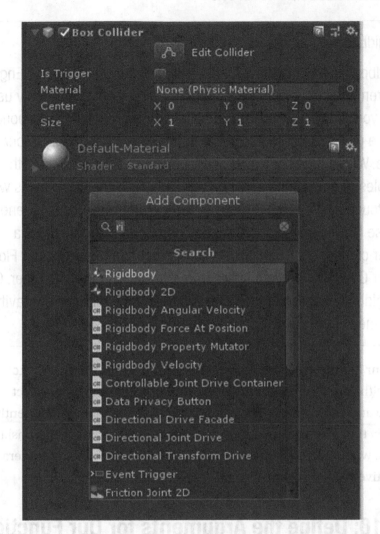

Figure 5-6. *Add a Rigidbody component to a game object in the Inspector*

On Rigidbodies

A Rigidbody is a component that is a part of the Unity Physics Engine. It is a remarkably powerful component that will be a commonly used tool in your Unity developer toolbox. In short, a Rigidbody component allows a game object to interact with the physics of gravity in our scenes. With a Rigidbody attached, our cube object will follow the principles of gravity and settle on our Floor as if the two objects were really touching. Our Floor, however, will not not move in our scene because it does not hold a Rigidbody component. It only holds a Collider component. The colliders of the two game objects, our Floor and our Cube, will prevent either from passing through the other. Only the Rigidbody applied to the Cube will follow the dictates of gravity in our scene.

If your table and cube objects share x and z `transform.position` values with your UnityXRCameraRig game object, then Shift+Select the table and cube objects in the hierarchy to select them dependently. With only the table and cube objects selected, you can use the translate shortcut, w, to slide both objects further in front of the virtual camera in the positive z axis direction.

Step 10: Define the Arguments for Our Function

With our cube set, let's drag and drop it from the hierarchy into the Cube property of our `Calculator` script on our `CalculatorController` game object (Figure 5-7). To do so, select the `CalculatorController` object in the hierarchy to display its components in the Inspector.

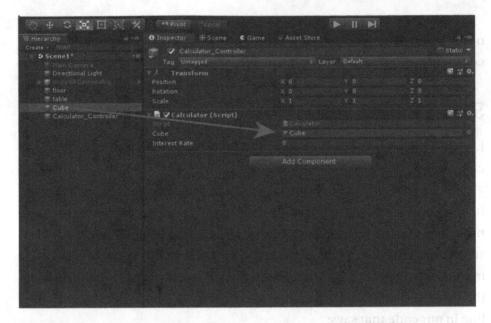

Figure 5-7. *Connect a game object to a script component's public property*

To begin, let's set our interest rate at 1.06 (Figure 5-8). This setting will allow our script to increase the volume of our cube by 6% every time the user presses the spacebar.

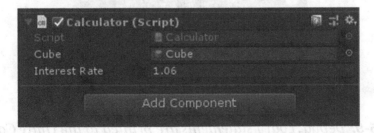

Figure 5-8. *Manually enter the value for the rate at which you'd like the Cube object to grow*

Each press of the spacebar simulates another year of interest on our principle, our inflating cube. This is the fundamental premise of compound interest implemented in VR!

Step 11: Play-Test

Let's test the project out. Press Play and hit the spacebar to watch your cube grow.

After play-testing your scene, navigate to the Console window of Unity. In it you will see printed the dimensions of the cube's new volume each time the spacebar was pressed (Figure 5-9). Calling Debug.Log in a C# script prints the arguments of the Log() function to the Console window in the Unity Editor. The arguments we passed into the Log() function print the volume of the Cube object after each inflation. This is the result of the line in our code that says:

```
Debug.Log("New Volume: " + newVolume);
```

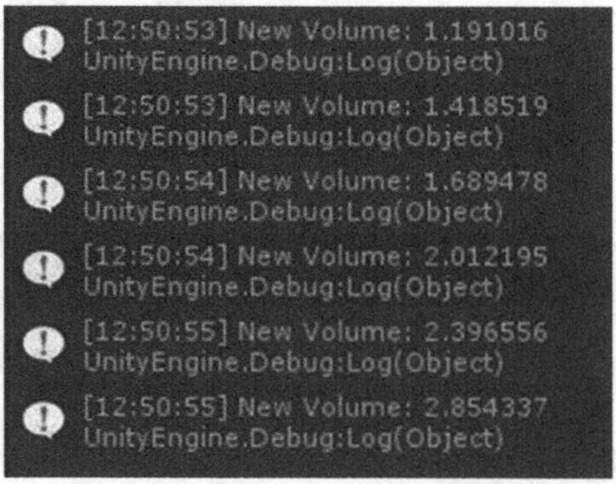

Figure 5-9. Debug.Log() statements are printed to the Unity Console

Debugging in the Console

Writing to the console through Debug.Log is a common and effective way to test if certain values in your script are responding in the way you expect. The + in our Debug statement signifies string concatenation. This simply means that while the words between the quotation marks in our Debug statement are a string and rendered to our Console window verbatim, the variable newVolume will appear as the content of its value. If newVolume also appeared in quotation marks then the variable's name would be written to our Console window instead of its value. String concatenation joins the value of strings to create sentences, whereas the + operator means something very different between numeric data types. Between numeric data types, + of course means addition.

Step 12: Replacing Our Cube Game Object with a 3D Model

To resize a game object in your scene view window, you can use the Scale tool by selecting its icon in the toolbar (Figure 5-10). Alternatively, you can use the resizing keyboard shortcut r.

Figure 5-10. *The Scale tool is highlighted on the Unity Editor toolbar*

Of course, our script is called Calculator, not Cube Calculator. We can magnify the size of any game object we would like. It doesn't matter that our `Calculator` script property reads `Cube`. If you'd like, you can access the exercise's project folder on the book's GitHub repository to download the 3D "Chocolate Cake" asset created by the 3D artist 3DMish (Figure 5-11). More 3D art by the same artist can be found at the URL of their Sketchfab portfolio, `https://sketchfab.com/3d-models/chocolate-cake-10e1714` `54c1148be96e684fcf3b48d3b`.

Figure 5-11. *"Chocolate Cake" by 3DMish is used in accordance with the Creative Commons 4.0 license*

To use the asset, simply drag it into your Assets folder in Unity, place it in the hierarchy of the scene, adjust its dimensions to taste, and drag and drop it into the Cube field on our Calculator script in the hierarchy.

Seeing double? The cake model might include a virtual camera of its own as a child object (Figure 5-12). If that is the case, then you will experience two unique points of view in your VR headset. To remedy this, toggle the cake's camera child object to Off by highlighting the child object in the Scene Hierarchy and clearing the check box to the left of the camera's name in the Inspector.

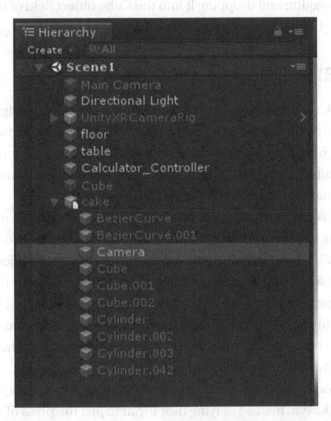

Figure 5-12. *If a 3D object created by another artist includes a camera object as a child, then deactivate it to prevent more than one audio listener from appearing in the scene*

Again, make sure to add a box collider and Rigidbody to the cake object so that it remains on its table.

Step 13: You're Done!

Congratulations! As Kavya, you've just successfully created a VR app your students can use to better visualize the concept of compound interest. If a cake doesn't convey the message effectively in your opinion, you can swap the object out with whatever item or shape you believe is more appropriate by simply dragging and dropping it into the Cube object field of the `Calculator_Controller`'s `Calculator` script component.

Summary

In Chapter 4, we waded into the waters of how we can create original functions to tap into the robust Unity Event System. In this chapter, we floated a bit further from the shore as we began to explore the input system built into Unity. The exercise we completed serves as a good introduction to the most basic fundamentals of user–Unity interaction.

In this chapter you learned how to resize and translate game objects in a scene using menu commands and keyboard shortcuts. You also created new materials, changed their color, and added them to game objects. You created a C# script that alters the transform properties of a game object; you connected game objects to scripts through public properties; you exposed public class properties in the Unity Editor for efficient testing; you called the `Debug.Log()` command to write to the Unity Console; and, finally, you used the Unity `Input` class to handle keyboard input to call a function.

In the next chapter we will build on the Interest Calculator application we made as Kavya. Instead of tying user input to just the press of the spacebar, however, we will introduce the features of VRTK that empower us, as developers, to create more than one input for the same event—one through the keyboard and the other through a VR touch controller.

CHAPTER 6

Controller Button Inputs as Actions

So far, we've set up virtual cameras in our scene that connect to the user's head-mounted display. We've also added interactive game objects to our scene and wired them up to user input through the keyboard. But this is VR. We're not here to use keyboards. We want to use touch controllers.

Keyboards are old school, but coordinating user input through VR applications, which are very much new school, can be challenging to the point of frustration. In this section we are going to build on our Cake Calculator Unity project to add input management through VRTK. Through a series of steps, we will transform our Cake Calculator into an application that accepts user input through both the keyboard and our VR controllers.

In this chapter you will learn how to do the following:

- Install a third-party VR SDK.

- Add a third-party VR camera rig to a scene.

- Use the VRTK TrackedAlias game object.

- Use the VRTK Button Action component.

- Connect VR controllers to VRTK controller prefabs.

- Create VRTK proxy actions.

- Chain actions using the VRTK Boolean action component.

© Rakesh Baruah 2020
R. Baruah, *Virtual Reality with VRTK4*, https://doi.org/10.1007/978-1-4842-5488-2_6

VR SDK Integration Packages

Before we move on, there's a little bit of housekeeping I need to address. So far, we have limited our engagement with our VR hardware to the head-mounted display. In the following section we will begin connecting our VR controllers to the VRTK interface. To do this, you must download and install the Unity integration package for your device from the Unity Asset Store. Read more about the requirements of your VR SDK in the Unity online manual.

- Unity Manual Entry for Getting Started with the Oculus SDK: `https://docs.unity3d.com/Manual/VRDevices-Oculus.html`

- Unity Manual Entry for Getting Started with the OpenVR SDK: `https://docs.unity3d.com/Manual/VRDevices-OpenVR.html`

- Unity Manual Entry for Getting Started with Google VR: `https://docs.unity3d.com/Manual/googlevr_sdk_overview.html`

- Unity Manual Entry for Getting Started with Windows Mixed Reality: `https://docs.unity3d.com/Manual/wmr_sdk_overview.html`

The Tracked Alias

As a framework, VRTK provides a library of prepackaged objects and functions that simplify our prototyping tasks in Unity. The UnityXRCameraRig is an example of a VRTK prefabricated game object that acts as a layer between us and the complexity of Unity's inner workings. Another such game object is VRTK's TrackedAlias prefab.

The purpose of the VRTK Tracked Alias game object is to coordinate two or more inputs that execute the same event. In Chapter 5, we created an event handler through the built-in Unity Input class. In this chapter, we perform the same action. However, instead of passing a user's keystroke into the Unity Input System, we will pass the press of a button on a touch controller.

Step 1: Drag and Drop the Tracked Alias Prefab into the Hierarchy

If you created a project for the original Interest Calculator exercise, then for this exercise you can simply copy Scene1 and rename it Scene2. A keyboard shortcut to copy an asset is to highlight it in your Project window and press Ctrl+D. Once you've created a duplicate, double-click Scene2 to open it in the Hierarchy window.

After we've saved our new scene and confirmed the installation of our integration package, we must import the VRTK Tracked Alias object into our scene. In the Project window, select Assets ➤ VRTK ➤ Prefabs ➤ CameraRig ➤ TrackedAlias ➤ TrackedAlias (Figure 6-1). The VRTK TrackedAlias game object acts as a mediator between us and Unity's Input Manager. I like to think of the TrackedAlias game object like a power strip or USB hub. It's a single object into which we can plug different wires to execute the same task.

125

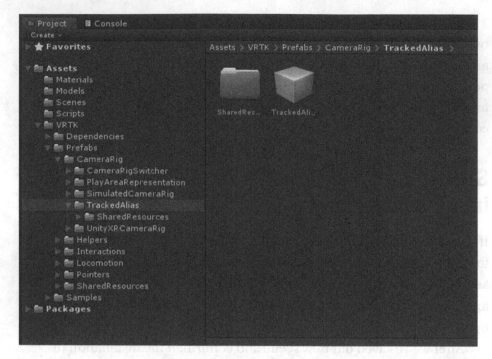

Figure 6-1. *VRTK includes a TrackedAlias prefab game object to help coordinate between scripts and XR inputs*

Step 2: Connecting Our Touch Controllers to VRTK

Because we turned on VR support for our project in the Unity Project Settings when we began the Interest Calculator exercise, the SDK for our VR headset is already running in our scene. Now, we can use the VRTK TrackedAlias object to connect our controllers to our Unity scene. To do this we simply need to add the VRTK Interactor prefab as a child object of our TrackedAlias object in the Scene Hierarchy.

Navigate to the VRTK Interactor prefab in the Project window: Assets ➤ Prefabs ➤ Interactions ➤ Interactors ➤ Interactor (Figure 6-2). Drag and drop the Interactor object from the Project window into the Scene Hierarchy as a child of both the LeftControllerAlias child game object and

RightControllerAlias child game object beneath the Aliases game object within the TrackedAlias game object (Figure 6-3).

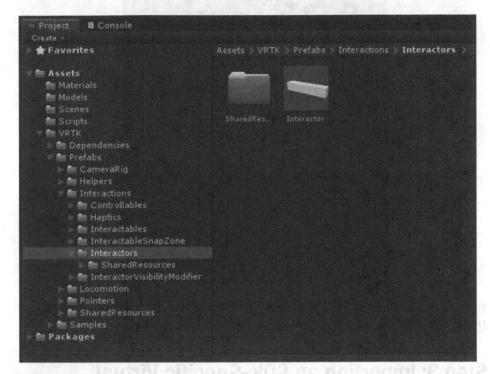

Figure 6-2. *VRTK's Interactor prefabs provide a quick way to track a user's hand movements*

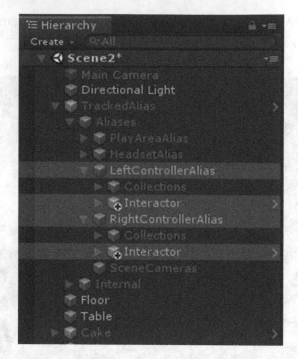

Figure 6-3. Add the VRTK Interactor prefabs to the TrackedAlias to track left and right controller movement

Step 3: Importing an SDK-Specific Virtual Camera Object

Until now, we've relied on the UnityXRCamera rig as our interface for a virtual camera. However, now that we have introduced SDK-specific touch controllers (specific, in my case, to the Oculus Rift) we must bring our SDK's camera object into the scene.

Beyond the UnityXRCameraRig

If you're asking yourself why the UnityXRCameraRig game object can't continue to serve as a surrogate for our head-mounted display, it might be helpful to consider that our VR system is more than the sum of its parts. Yes, a VR system is a headset, controllers, and a tracking system, but the interaction of its components in concert creates the fluidity of a single machine. For example, many headsets contain spatial anchors that coordinate with the positional tracking of their accompanied touch controllers. To have controllers active in our scene without a shared headset might cause conflicts in the messaging between Unity, VRTK, and the third-party VR SDK.

To replace the UnityXRCameraRig in our Scene Hierarchy, we first locate the SDK camera object with which we will replace it. Locate the folder for the VR integration system you installed within your Project window's Asset hierarchy. Because I installed the Oculus Integration Package, to locate my Oculus camera object, I navigate to the Project window and select Assets ➤ Oculus ➤ VR ➤ Prefabs ➤ OVRCameraRig (Figure 6-4). All figures in this chapter pertaining to an SDK-specific camera rig will portray the Oculus rig. However, VRTK supports many different brands of headsets.

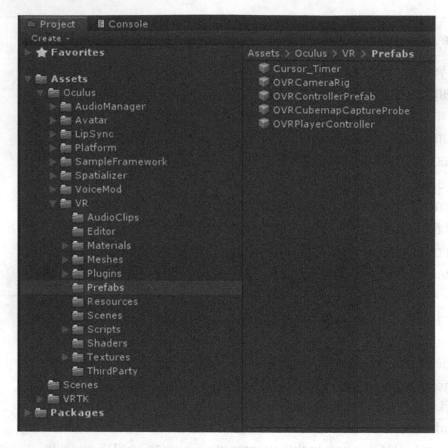

Figure 6-4. The virtual camera object specific to your head-mounted display can be found inside the SDK integration package downloadable from Unity

Drag the SDK camera object into the Scene Hierarchy (Figure 6-5).

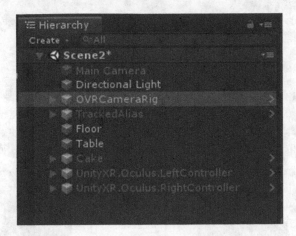

Figure 6-5. *After dragging the SDK camera object into the Scene Hierarchy, you can delete the UnityXRCameraRig object*

With the SDK camera object selected in the Scene Hierarchy, turn your attention to the Inspector window. If you are using a 6DoF headset, which offers the ability to move around a play area, set the tracking origin of the camera object in its Manager component to Floor Level (Figure 6-6). Otherwise, if you are using a 3DoF headset, which offers the ability to look around but not move through a play area, select Eye Level.

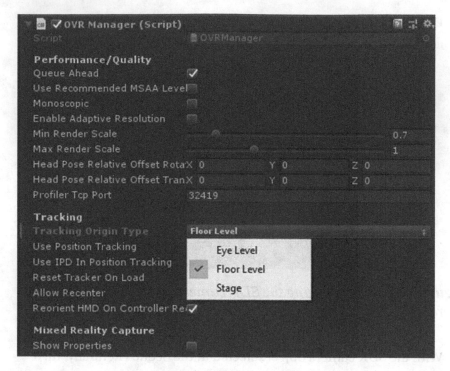

Figure 6-6. *The Oculus camera rig game object's Manager component. The camera rig for your VR system might appear differently in the Inspector*

Step 4: Connect the SDK Camera Rig with the TrackedAlias Game Object

Now that we have a camera rig object connected to our SDK in our Unity scene, it's time to wrap it in our TrackedAlias prefab so that VRTK can coordinate the messaging between Unity and our third-party SDK. To do this, first click Add Component on the SDK CameraRig object in the Inspector and search for the Linked Alias Association Collection component.

With the Linked Alias Association Collection component attached to
our SDK CameraRig prefab (Figure 6-7), we have permission to connect
it with our TrackedAlias prefab. However, we first must declare the
relationship between the elements of our SDK CameraRig prefab and our
TrackedAlias prefab. We accomplish this by defining the settings in the
SDK CameraRig prefab's new Linked Alias Association component.

Figure 6-7. *The Oculus camera rig game object with VRTK's Linked
Alias Association Collection component attached*

To define the settings in the SDK CameraRig prefab's Linked Alias component, we drag and drop the objects of our camera rig in the Scene Hierarchy into their matching object fields in the Inspector. First, let's define the PlayArea Settings on our Linked Alias Association Collection component by dragging the SDK CameraRig parent object, which includes its children by default, to the PlayArea Settings object field in the Inspector (Figure 6-8).

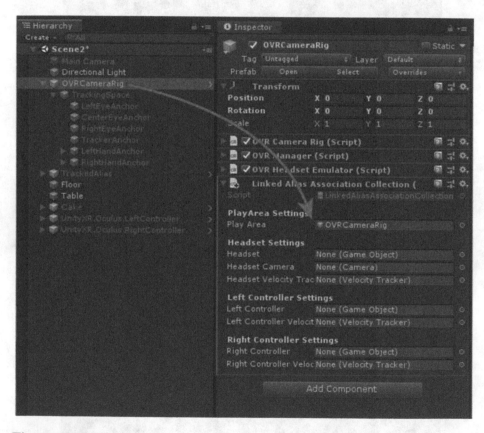

Figure 6-8. *Drag and drop the SDK CameraRig parent object to the PlayArea object field of the Linked Alias Association Collection script component*

Next, we'll define the headset and controller settings for the Linked Alias Association Collection component. Whereas the Headset property refers to the game object representing our physical headset, Headset Camera refers to the virtual camera within our headset that will translate our scene into VR. For our purposes, it is sufficient to drag and drop the SDK CameraRig's CenterEyeAnchor child object into both fields (Figure 6-9).

Figure 6-9. *For the Oculus Rift SDK, drag and drop the CenterEyeAnchor to the Headset settings of the Linked Alias Association Collection*

Similarly, we will drag and drop the LeftHandAnchor and RightHandAnchor child objects from our Scene Hierarchy into the Left Controller and Right Controller object fields in the Linked Alias Association Collection (Figure 6-10). As of this writing, VRTK does not contain velocity tracker information for certain SDK headsets and controllers. You can find more information on the VRTK web site if you are interested in exploring the feature in greater depth. For this exercise, we will leave the velocity tracker fields of the Linked Alias Association Collection component empty.

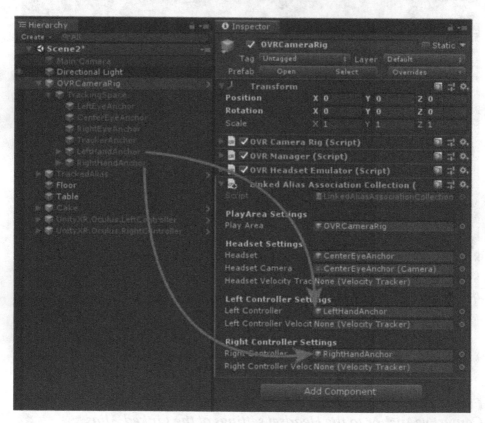

Figure 6-10. *To connect external controllers to the VRTK input mapping system, drag and drop left and right anchors to the Left and Right Controller Settings fields, respectively, of the Linked Alias Association Collection script attached as a component to the SDK CameraRig*

With the properties of our SDK CameraRig prefab defined in the
Linked Alias Association Collection component, we are finally able to
connect our headset and controllers to the VRTK TrackedAlias prefab. To
do so, select the TrackedAlias prefab in the Scene Hierarchy to open it in
the Inspector. If you are using the same project from our previous exercise,
you'll notice that we have one camera rig in our Tracked Alias Settings
Elements list, and that camera is the UnityXRCameraRig (Figure 6-11).

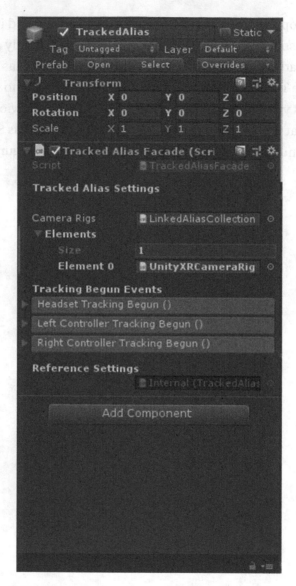

Figure 6-11. *Before adding the SDK CameraRig to the TrackedAlias Façade, there could be either zero or one camera rig listed as an element*

Because we will use our SDK's CameraRig object, we can replace the UnityXRCameraRig prefab in the Element 0 field with the SDK CameraRig prefab we set up in our Scene Hierarchy. If there are no camera rigs in the Elements list of your TrackedAlias prefab, then change the size of the Elements property by entering 1 and pressing Enter. Drag and drop the SDK CameraRig prefab from the Hierarchy into the Element 0 object field (Figure 6-12). This completes the connection between our headset's virtual camera and VRTK's TrackedAlias game object.

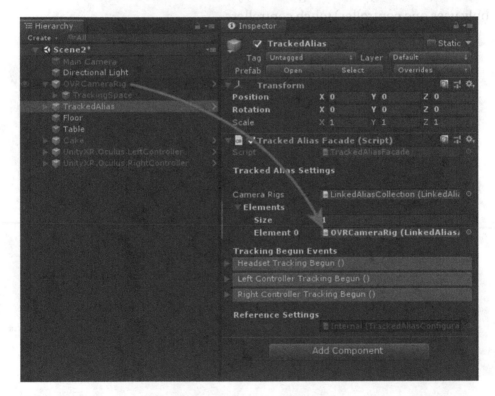

Figure 6-12. *After attaching the Linked Alias Association Collection script to the SDK CameraRig game object, we can drag and drop the SDK CameraRig into the Elements array of the Tracked Alias Facade*

Step 5: Play-Test

Press Play on your scene. If your VR HMD and tracking are set and connected properly through Unity then you will see at least one gray rectangle tracking the movement of your left and right controllers (Figure 6-13). We will address changing the default shape of these virtual controllers in a future exercise. For now, pat yourself on the back for incorporating user movement via not only a head-mounted display but also two (or one if you're using a 3DoF system like the Oculus Go, which only uses one controller) touch controllers.

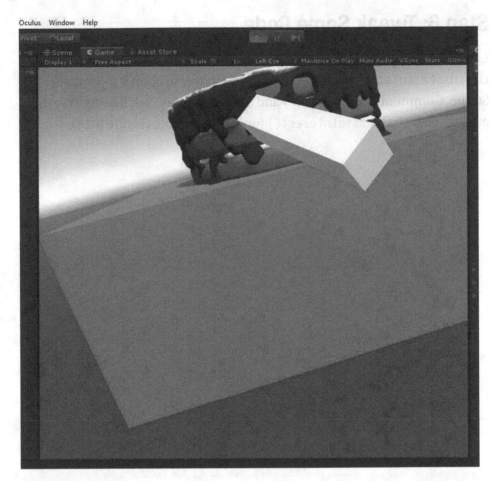

Figure 6-13. *After connecting a headset and touch controllers to the VRTK TrackedAlias game object, we see the VRTK Interactor prefabs track the motion of external VR controllers in play mode*

As of now, our controllers move within our virtual scene, but they don't really do anything. Because interaction is the soul of an immersive experience, let's turn our attention to adding a couple Unity Button Actions to our scene. First, we'll update our `CalculateInterest()` function to include a Unity Button Action connected to our spacebar. Second, we'll do the same for a button on one of our touch controllers.

Step 6: Tweak Some Code

Let's begin by making some small changes to our Calculator script. Double-click the Calculator script in your Project window to open it in Visual Studio. Comment out the Start() and Update() functions, leaving only the public void CalculateInterest() function operable (Figure 6-14).

```
3    using UnityEngine;
4
5    public class Calculator : MonoBehaviour
6    {
7        public GameObject cube;
8        public float interestRate;
9
10       Transform cube_transform;
11       Vector3 currentVolumeVector;
12       float cubeLength, cubeHeight, cubeWidth;
13
14       //// Start is called before the first frame update
15       //void Start()
16       //{
17
18       //}
19
20       //// Update is called once per frame
21       //void Update()
22       //{
23       //    if (Input.GetKeyDown(KeyCode.Space))
24       //    {
25       //        CalculateInterest();
26       //    }
27
28       //}
29
30       public void CalculateInterest()
31       {
32           Transform transform = cube.transform;
33
34           float cubeLength = transform.localScale.x;
35           float cubeWidth = transform.localScale.z;
36           float cubeHeight = transform.localScale.y;
37
38           cubeLength *= interestRate;
39           cubeHeight *= interestRate;
40           cubeWidth *= interestRate;
41
42           transform.localScale = new Vector3(cubeLength, cubeHeight, cubeWidth);
43
44           float newVolume = cubeLength * cubeHeight * cubeWidth;
45           Debug.Log("New Volume: " + newVolume);
46
47       }
48
49   }
50
```

Figure 6-14. *In Visual Studio 2017, commented out code appears in green*

No Comment

In Visual Studio, highlighting a block of code and pressing Ctrl+K, Ctrl+C comments code out. Ctrl+K, Ctrl+U comments code back in.

Save the `Calculator` script in Visual Studio and return to Unity. Allow the changes you made to your `Calculator` script to compile in Unity. After a few seconds, everything should be updated.

Because we moved the calling of our `CalculateInterest()` function from our update function, our script will not listen for our user input every frame. How will our program know when to execute our action if we removed any code that tells Unity to increase the size of our cake at the touch of a button? To the rescue, again, comes VRTK and its Unity Button Action component.

Step 7: Add a Unity Action Component

Let's create a new empty game object in our Scene Hierarchy and call it `KeyboardManager`. On this object we will attach a Unity Button Action component connected to the cake object the size of which we'd like to inflate. Select the `KeyboardManager` game object in the hierarchy. In the Inspector, click Add Component.

The component we'd like to add is the Unity Button Action component, so search for it in the Search field (Figure 6-15). Once you've attached the Unity Button Action component to the `KeyboardManager` object, you will see the script in the Inspector. Expand the Unity Button Action script component on the `KeyboardManager` to see its properties (Figure 6-16).

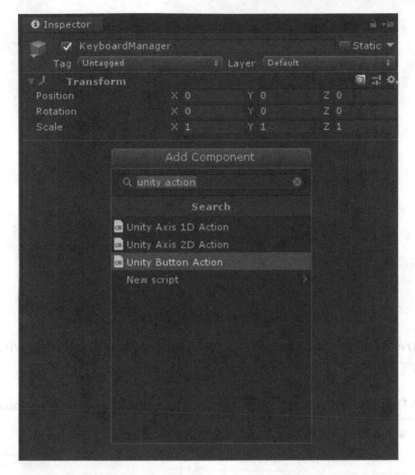

Figure 6-15. *A Unity Button Action component is a VRTK script that can be attached to a game object in the Unity Inspector*

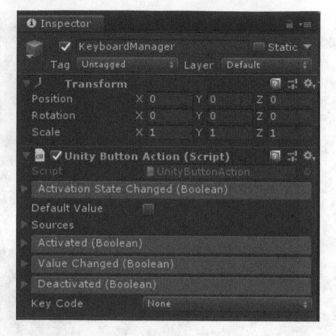

Figure 6-16. A Unity Button Action script has four events that can trigger an action

A Unity Button Action component has four events we can hook into.

- Activation State Changed notifies a subscriber that an event has gone from either on to off or off to on.

- Activated notifies a subscriber that an event has been turned on.

- Value Changed notifies a subscriber if the true/false property of an event has changed.

- Deactivated notifies a subscriber that an event has been turned off.

For this exercise we're going to focus on the Activated (Boolean) event.

Step 8: Tell Our Button Component What to Do in Case of an Event

To tell our program what to do when the user sends an event to our KeyboardManager by pressing the spacebar, we have to give it a function to fire when the event occurs. What's the function we want to tie to this event? If you guessed the action we want to fire is our CalculateInterest() function, then you are correct. Recall that we must attach scripts as components to game objects for them to operate in our scene. In the previous chapter we created a CalculatorController to hold our Calculator script. In this chapter, however, because we are going to task VRTK's TrackedAlias object with coordinating our inputs, we are going to instead attach our Calculator script to the object whose size we want to calculate—our 3D cake.

Drag and drop the Calculator script we updated at the start of this section on to the cake object in our scene. We still have to specify what the target "cube" game object will be in our script. We want it to be the cake, so let's drag and drop the cake object from the Hierarchy onto the Cube property of its own Calculator script. If you find this confusing, you can think of the cake, by assigning itself as its Cube property, saying, "I don't need a CalculatorController to grow, I can call my own function myself!" Okay, cake, if you say so, but how are you going to know when to call your own grow function? Here, our adolescent cake is a bit stumped. Let's help it out.

Select the KeyboardManager in the Hierarchy and in the Inspector click the + sign beneath the Activated (Boolean) event. An empty object field appears along with a drop-down menu that says No Function. Drag and drop the cake object into the empty object field (Figure 6-17). From the drop-down menu, select Calculator ➤ CalculateInterest(). At the bottom of the KeyboardManager's Unity Button Action component, locate the property labeled Key Code. From the drop-down menu, select Space.

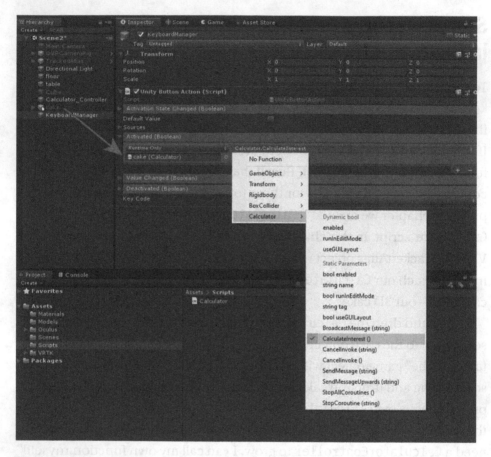

Figure 6-17. *Drag and drop the game object to which the desired subscriber action is attached into the object field of the Unity Button Action component*

We've just connected our spacebar to the `CalculateInterest()` function located in a script on our cake game object. In Chapter 5 we accomplished this by creating a function in our `Calculator` script's `Update()` method that used the Unity Input Manager's `GetKeyDown` method.

"Okay, big deal," you might be saying. "We still had to write some code. I don't get how using this VRTK interface made anything easier." Well, you'd be right. Creating a Unity Button Action still required us to create our CalculateInterest() function and attach it to our cake game object (the object whose size we aim to increase by pressing the spacebar). What if we wanted to connect another button to our CalculateInterest() function? On the one hand, we could write a new function in our Update() function that calls GetKeyDown on our right touch controller instead of our keyboard. We'd also have to do the same thing if we wanted to connect our function to a button on our left touch controller. Just like that, we've gone from writing one function to writing three. On the other hand, we can use the VRTK TrackedAlias game object to connect different inputs to a function we only have to write once.

Creating Proxy Actions and Chaining Actions

In VRTK, this is called creating proxy actions and chaining actions. To see how it works, we're going to connect our CalculateInterest() function to the A button on the Oculus touch controller.

Step 1: Connect Our Touch Controller Hardware to Their Virtual Counterparts

To accomplish this, we first need to bring in a couple references to our touch controller into our scene. Yes, we brought in Interactor prefabs in the previous exercise, but these simply applied shapes to our controllers in VR space. The VRTK interactor prefabs can't communicate with the buttons, triggers, or joysticks on our controllers. For that, VRTK offers us more specific options. Navigate to the InputMappings folder within the VRTK folder in the Project window. Select Assets ➤ VRTK ➤ Prefabs ➤ CameraRig ➤ UnityXRCameraRig ➤ InputMappings (Figure 6-18).

Figure 6-18. *Included in VRTK are prefabs that map to Oculus and OpenVR controllers*

Inside the InputMappings folder there are game objects coinciding with the VR system you've set up in your application. Because I have both Oculus and OpenVR set up on my project, I have four game objects in my InputMappings folder: two for the left and right Oculus controllers and two for the left and right OpenVR controllers. Select the controllers that apply to your application. Because I am developing for the Oculus Rift, I will choose the UnityXR.Oculus.LeftController game object and the UnityXR. Oculus.RightController game object. Drag the game object controllers best suited to your project into the Scene Hierarchy (Figure 6-19).

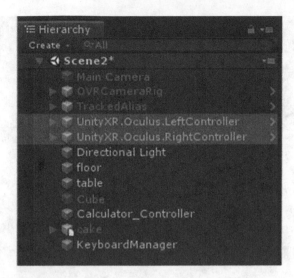

Figure 6-19. *Drag and drop the VRTK controller prefabs that match your VR hardware and SDK*

Step 2: Map a Unity Button Action Component to Our Controller

Because I want to connect the CalculateInterest() function to the A button on my Oculus Rift touch controller, I check the Unity XR Input documentation, where I learn Unity identifies the Oculus Rift A button as Button.One, which has a Unity Button ID of 0 (Figure 6-20).

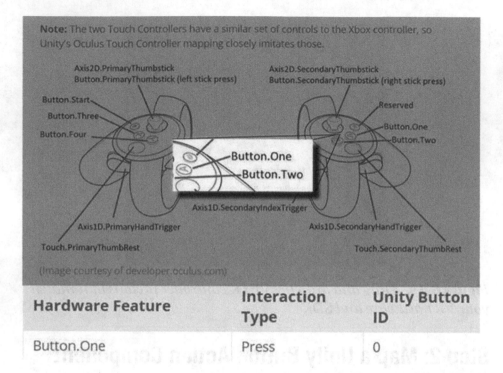

Note: The two Touch Controllers have a similar set of controls to the Xbox controller, so Unity's Oculus Touch Controller mapping closely imitates those.

Hardware Feature	Interaction Type	Unity Button ID
Button.One	Press	0

Figure 6-20. *In Unity, the Oculus Rift touch controller's A button has the hardware feature name* `Button.One`*. The Unity Button ID given to Oculus Rift's* `Button.One` *is 0. Find more at* `https://docs.unity3d.com/Manual/xr_input.html`

Do the same for whatever input you'd like to connect the `CalculateInterest()` function to. For my project, I expand the child objects beneath the UnityXR.Oculus.RightController prefab in my Hierarchy. I expand ButtonOne and find two leaves: Touch[10] and Press[0] (Figure 6-21).

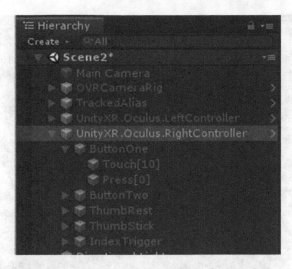

Figure 6-21. *Expanding the VRTK controller prefab in the Hierarchy reveals child objects mapped to each input*

The UnityXR controller prefab should come with a Unity Button Action component already attached (Figure 6-22). If it doesn't, add it yourself as you did earlier in this exercise with the KeyboardManager (Add Component ➤ Unity Button Action).

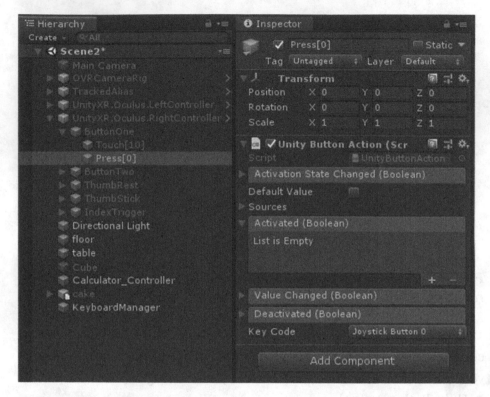

Figure 6-22. *The VRTK Input Mapping prefab game objects come with a Unity Button Action component already attached*

Step 3: Define the Action to Occur in Response to a Button Event

Because we are chaining two proxy events to the same action, let's do exactly as we did with our KeyboardManager game object (Figure 6-16). With Press[0] (or whatever XR object maps to the button of your choice on your VR system) selected, click the + sign beneath the Activated (Boolean) event on the XR controller's Unity Button Action component.

Drag the cake object, which has the `Calculator` script component
attached to it, from the Scene Hierarchy onto the empty object field
of the Unity Button Action component. Select the Calculator ➤
`CalculateInterest()` function from the Function drop-down menu. For
Key Code, leave the default setting, which should map to the XR button to
which the Unity Button Action script is attached (Figure 6-23).

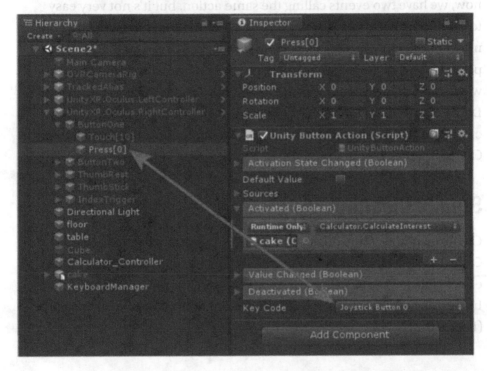

Figure 6-23. *VRTK sets the Key Code parameter automatically on the
Unity Button Action components of input mapping prefabs*

Step 4: Play-Test

Alright! We now have two unique events wired up to the same action! On
your cake game object, be sure to set the Interest Rate modifier on the
`Calculator` script component to a value like 1.06, otherwise, with the

modifier set to 0, the cake will disappear after one press of a button. Then, save the scene. When you press Play and enter your VR scene, you will be able to increase the size of the cake by pressing either the spacebar or the button you specified on your VR controller. Give it a test!

Before we hand over our project to Kavya to use with her third graders, there's just one more thing I'd like us to do to organize our project. Right now, we have two events calling the same action, but it's not very easy to discern which events correspond to which action. Sure, you and I might know what buttons do what in our Scene Hierarchy, but if we had partners on this project, they might be left confused about the changes we've made to the scene since we added the TrackedAlias VRTK object. Let's make things a bit clearer for both ourselves and everyone else by creating a game object that houses all the components involved with our CalculateInterest() function.

Step 5: Cleanup

Create an empty game object in the Scene Hierarchy and name it CalculatorManager. This object will hold all our calculator logic so it is easy to locate should we have to refactor (edit, rearrange) our code. In the Inspector, add a Boolean Action component to the CalculatorManager (Figure 6-24).

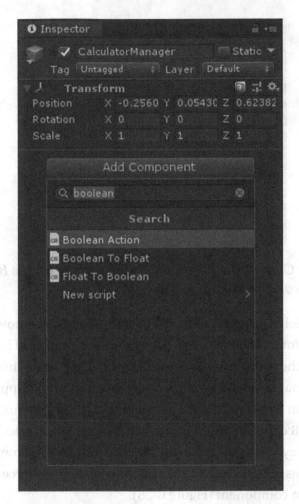

Figure 6-24. *Add a Boolean Action component to the* CalculatorManager *game object*

Like the four events attached to the Unity Button Action we listed earlier, the Boolean Action component also contains an expandable property called Sources. Expand Sources on the CalculatorManager's Boolean Action component. By default, the Size parameter of the Sources property is set to 0. Change that to 2 and press Enter (Figure 6-25).

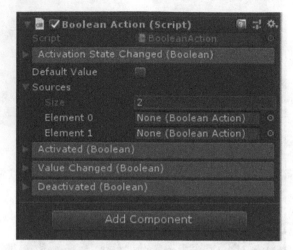

Figure 6-25. *Change the size of the Sources array on the Boolean Action script component to 2*

Two new fields appear: Element 0 and Element 1. We know that the two "sources" for our action in this project are key presses of both the spacebar and the touch controller's main button. Let's add those to the CalculatorManager's Sources property by dragging and dropping, first, the child button object to which we attached an Activation function on our UnityXR controller prefab in the Hierarchy. Second, let's drag and drop the KeyboardManager game object from the Hierarchy into CalculatorManager's Element 1 parameter beneath its Sources on its Boolean Action component (Figure 6-26).

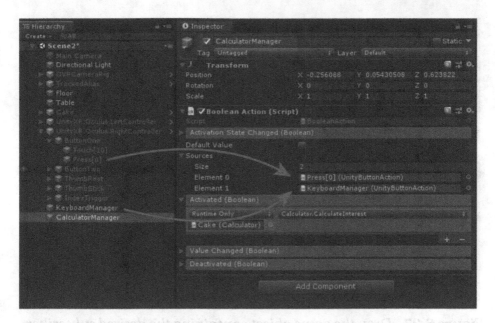

Figure 6-26. *Chain the two events defined in our scene to the same action by dropping them into the Sources parameters on the* `CalculatorManager`

Now that we know what two events call our action on our Boolean Action component, let's tell our `CalculatorManager` what function to call when either of our two event sources fire. Just like we did with the Unity Button Action component on game objects previously, click + under Activated (Boolean) on `CalculatorManager`'s Boolean Action component. Drag the cake object (with the `Calculator` script attached as a component) from the Hierarchy into the empty object field of the ActivatedBoolean event handler. Select the Calculator ➤ `CalculateInterest()` function from the drop-down menu (Figure 6-27).

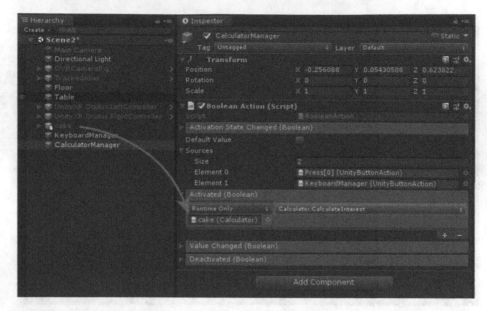

Figure 6-27. *Drop the game object containing the desired subscriber action as a script component into the game object field of the Boolean Action component on the* `CalculatorManager`

We now have our two input events (proxy actions) wired to the same action (chained action) on a single game object in our scene. Delete the functions listed below the Activated (Boolean) events on the Unity Button Action scripts of both the UnityXR controller button object and the `KeyboardManager` by clicking the - sign next to the + sign you used to add the functions (Figure 6-28). Do not delete the event you just added to the `CalculatorManager`'s Boolean Action component. After you remove the two event publishers on the controller button and the `KeyboardManager`, the `CalculatorManager` will be the only event publisher we have to fire off events to its subscriber, the cake object.

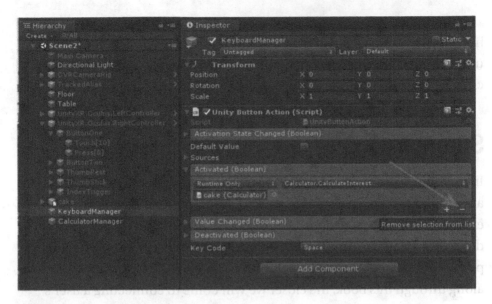

Figure 6-28. *Delete an action connected to an event handler by clicking the - icon*

When you've confirmed that the `CalculatorManager`'s Boolean Action component is the only Activated event publishing to the cake object, save your scene and play-test it by pressing both the spacebar and the controller button to inflate the dimensions of the cake. If everything is in working order, recall that you can manipulate the rate at which the cake expands by changing the Interest Rate property on the `Calculator` script we've stored on our cake object in the Hierarchy.

Play Doesn't Save

It's important to note that changes made to your scene in play mode are not saved. If you'd like to change the Interest Rate property of the `Calculator` script, it's best to stop the scene from playing, change the value, save the scene, and restart it.

161

That's that! We've passed the Cake Calculator off to Kavya, who said her students enjoyed it and have all committed to leaving their allowance untouched in a savings account until they are 65 years old. See, VR changes lives!

Summary

Interaction is the main ingredient of an immersive VR scene. Enabling a user to affect the environment around them in VR heightens an experience. It also puts more creative power in the hands of the developers. Passive experiences become active as users move from the position of viewers to actors, to players, to characters. The further we move along through this book, the closer we will come to connecting a user's consciousness with a reality that is virtual. Involving their eyes and hands are early steps toward capturing their hearts and minds.

In this chapter you replaced a UnityXRCameraRig with an SDK-specific camera rig. You also connected physical controllers to their virtual counterparts. Using the VRTK TrackedAlias object, you connected a user's controllers to a scripted event. Using VRTK Button components, you mapped this event to inputs from two different sources—a keyboard and a controller—creating proxy actions. By creating a single game manager object with a VRTK Boolean Action component, you chained these two actions to one event without writing any new code.

Although powerful and convenient, the buttons on a VR controller are only some of the input options available to users of VR. Many controllers include triggers and joysticks in addition to buttons. In this chapter we focused on boolean events that delivered on/off signals, but in the next chapter we will learn about creating Axis Actions for the triggers and joysticks on our VR controllers. Because they convey more complex data than boolean actions, trigger events allow us, as developers, to put even more power to influence the immersive environment into the hands of the user.

CHAPTER 7

Trigger Input Through One-Dimensional Axis Actions

What a mouthful, huh? One-dimensional axis actions. It sounds more complicated than it is. Hopefully, by the end of this chapter you will agree.

So far in this book we've introduced virtual cameras, 3D objects, tracking and spatial anchors, interactors, and button events. Together, those things can makeup a valid virtual experience. However, one element integral to VR—so much so that it's in the name of its controllers—we haven't discussed is touch.

In the context of the human mind, the medium through which you and I interact every day, touch is the sensation we *feel* through our skin. The world outside us, reality, excites nerves and stimulates them, creating the pressure of touch, the weight of touch, the resistance of touch, and the warmth of touch. As of this writing, we are not yet able to re-create the psychophysical sensation of touch through a consumer-grade VR system. If the concept of touch isn't even within the boundaries of achievable VR, what then do we mean when we discuss touch?

© Rakesh Baruah 2020
R. Baruah, *Virtual Reality with VRTK4*, https://doi.org/10.1007/978-1-4842-5488-2_7

In this chapter you will learn the following:

- The role touch plays in VR immersive design.

- The purpose of the VRTK 1D Axis Action component.

- The value of lighting design to VR scenes.

- The different kinds of lighting options provided by Unity.

- How to navigate through a scene in the Unity Editor using the 3D viewport and Unity hot-keys.

- How to connect VRTK's Input Mappings to VR controllers and Unity Actions.

The Psychology of Touch

Within the overlap of neuroscience and physical rehabilitation, there exists an exercise that physicians perform with patients who suffer from phantom limb syndrome (Figure 7-1). In a group of people who have undergone amputation of an extremity, a percentage experience pain in the limb they lost. Although the limb is no longer a part of their physical body, the patient *feels* pain in the limb as if it were still physically there. Because the limb does not exist, physicians conclude the pain the patients feel exists not in the limb itself, but in the mental model the patients have formed of their body. The pain, in other words, occurs in the mind.

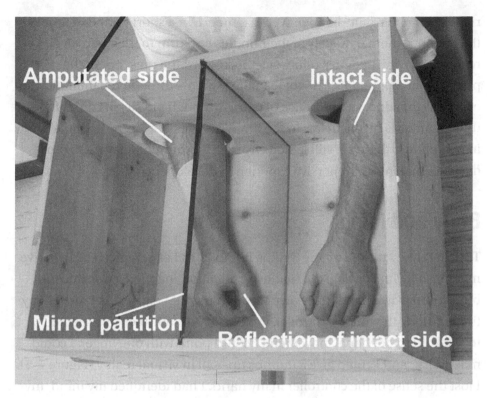

Figure 7-1. *An exercise to treat phantom limb pain in amputees provides lessons applicable to VR design. Source: Golan Levin via Flickr CC BY 2.0.* `https://www.flickr.com/photos/` `golanlevin/19290187922`

One practice designed to treat phantom limb syndrome leverages the patients' way of thinking to ease their discomfort. For example, to treat patients experiencing phantom limb pain in a left hand they lost in a motor vehicle accident, the exercise requires them to place both arms inside opaque containers. The container for the left hand has an opening through which the patients can see. What the patients see, however, is not actually there. What they see is a mirror image of their right hand broadcast through a video screen, for example. What they see appears to be the return of their left hand. As the patients move their right hand, their "left" hand moves in concert. In a short period of time, the patients' mental models of their bodies conform to their perceived reality. Once the patients' mindset shifts toward the presence of the phantom limb, therapists might lead the patients through rehabilitation exercises to reduce the presence of pain. Although physicians don't fully understand the mechanisms in the brain responsible for the patients' shift in perception, there are still lessons from the treatment relevant to our decision making as immersive experience developers.

Body and Mind

The first time I turned on my Oculus Rift in 2018 I experienced a formative mental shift. On starting, the Oculus application mapped a translucent, blue, human-like hand to my own through my VR headset. As I moved my fingers along the touch controller, the Oculus system's sensors seemed to track their individual movement. I could point with one finger, I could make a fist, and I could give a thumbs up—all in virtual reality (Figure 7-2). I lost the sense of the controller in my hand. I had identified my mind, my sense of self, with the digital representation of my body.

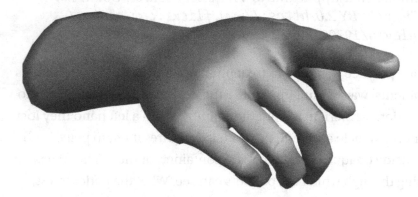

Figure 7-2. *Through the use of physical avatars, VR developers facilitate the sensation of immersion*

Other mixed reality systems, such as the Hololens 2, forgo representation completely. Inside-out tracking, which moves infrared sensors from external towers to sensors inside the headset, provides the ability to track a user's hands without controllers. It likely won't be long until both MR and VR headsets interpret the presence of a user's body without controllers at all. Unconscious association of the self with a virtual avatar might become more seamless and more natural over time.

This is the next level of media to which VR evangelists refer when they speak of this great, new technology. The most powerful, most useful feature of VR is the synthesis it catalyzes between the outer and inner self. The moment of transcendence, the moment that clicks within a virtual experience when your body leaves your mind—that is the wonder of VR. It is also the foundation of what we explore in this chapter.

The Unified Whole

If the core of VR is immersion then its antithesis is disruption. Feedback determines the quality of an immersive experience. Does what the users see conform with their expectations? We can orchestrate these expectations through visual and audio cues in our experiences. For example, a highly stylized environment might allow a user to loosen their expectations of realistic physics. A cartoonish, modularly designed, voxel-based world, however, might not prepare a user for a gritty, violent, dramatic experience. At a more fundamental level, however, we find the success of immersion within the synchrony of the brain.

Identification of wholeness, of bodyness, we feel as humans when we watch our fingers move is a fulfillment of the feedback loop between the sensory, motor, and visual cortices of our brains (Figure 7-3). I will an action, I carry it out, and I validate its occurrence. A stuttering frame rate, an unrealistic response to physics, and inaccurate input feedback are the death knells of VR. The human mind is unforgiving of false reality. Any way the movement of our users does not match the visual feedback expected by their brain will tear them out of an immersive state we hope to design them into. How, then, do we capture a user's hand movement to foster the experience of immersion?

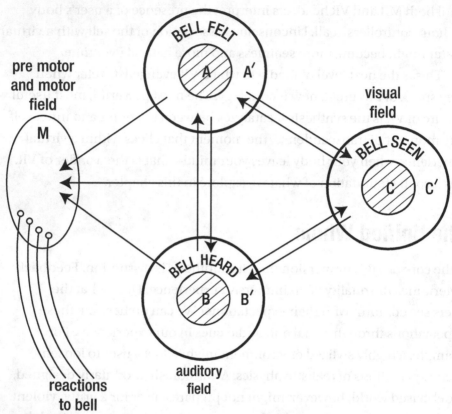

Figure 7-3. *A 20th-century interpretation of the process carried out within the mind of a rat at the sound of a bell. Source: Image from "Brains of Rats and Men; a Survey of the Origin and Biological Significance of the Cerebral Cortex" (1926, 71)*

Enter the VRTK Axis Action

According to the VRTK documentation:

> *Unity Axis Actions tie into the Unity Input Manager and emit events when a defined Input axis changes value. There are two kinds of Unity Axis Actions:*

> - *Unity 1D Axis: listens for changes on a single axis and emits a float value for the axis changes.*

> - *Unity 2D Axis: listens for changes on two axes and emits a Vector2 value combining both axis changes.*

> *A Unity Axis Action is derived from a Zinnia.Unity Action and therefore can be injected into any VRTK prefab that requires varying float data (e.g., touchpad movement).*

> *VRTK will ask via a popup window on first load of the Unity project whether to attempt to auto create some Unity axis input mappings. If this is accepted then default axis data for left and right controller touchpad/thumbsticks, grip and trigger axes will be created.*

The most important information from the VRTK documentation regarding Unity Axis Actions explains how the VRTK framework can help us introduce touch controller action into our scenes beyond simply acknowledging when a user presses a button. Triggers and joysticks are common input features on many VR touch controllers. That these input systems allow for more than simply on/off values like float (numeric decimal) values makes them powerful tools in our toolkit for the creation of immersive, VR experiences.

The Unity Input Manager exists in every Unity project in the Edit ➤ Project Settings window from the menu bar. It maps the relationships between user inputs and their impact on our applications. The Input Manager contains a list of axes and buttons available for us to connect events to in our application. The Unity Input Manager can

169

overwhelm developers new to Unity design. Changes to its settings can have far-reaching impact (both intended and unintended) on the development of our experiences. By tying into the Unity Input Manager, the VRTK framework's Unity Axis Action components streamline the development process for prototyping user interaction within our VR experiences.

Like with our Unity Button Action and Unity Boolean Action components, VRTK's Unity Axis Action component uses the TrackedAlias VRTK game object to accept input from our VR touch controllers to produce a change in our program. The only distinction unique to a Unity Axis Action from its Button and Boolean Action siblings is that it tracks a gradient of input through numbers not just an on/off state. For a simple analogy, let's look at an automobile. The ignition in our car, fundamentally, has two states: on and off. Our accelerator, however, allows us to change speed across a continuum of values. The function of a car's accelerator is like the function of a Unity Axis Action component through VRTK.

To see the purpose a Unity Axis Action component can serve in our VR apps, let's try our hand at a prototype.

Exercise: Location Scouting

Annie Svenstrup has a passion for theater. Rather than in front of the lights, however, her place is behind them. She works as a dental hygienist, but she devotes her free time to the community theater in the town where she lives. One day, Elgin Sommers, the eccentric director of this season's big production, approaches Annie to help him execute his vision for the play's stage design. He'd like to build the facade of an abandoned, decrepit inn. Before he commits the theater's budget to building the set, however, he'd like Annie to help him visualize the set's lighting to convince the donors to cut the big check.

In this exercise, as Annie, we will import a 3D model of Elgin's set. We will place virtual lights into the scene to illuminate the set. Finally, we will connect user input to the control of the lights so Elgin can impress the theater's board of directors with the veracity of his vision.

The model we will be using in this exercise is available from the project GitHub repo labeled by chapter. The model is called "Team America 2004 Miniature (photogrammetry)" by Austin Beaulier. You can find the original and more of Austin's work from their Sketchfab profile at https://sketchfab.com/Austin.Beaulier.

I'm using the model under the Creative Commons licensing agreement (CC BY 4.0). If you plan to incorporate Austin's work into your own immersive experiences, please follow the guidelines of attribution documented at https://creativecommons.org/licenses/by/4.0/.

It might be of interest to you to know that scenarios like the one I have described are, in fact, taking place in the commercial world. In 2017, Cirque du Soleil used the Microsoft HoloLens to help design sets for future performances. In 2018, hip-hop artist Childish Gambino and his team used VR and the HTC Vive to prototype "Pharos," an immersive concert experience that won its creators a prestigious award from the Visual Effects Society. Although these productions are enormous endeavors with huge teams, the tools used by their creators to grow a vision from the seeds of imagination are available to you and me.

Before we get to work with VRTK's Axis Action component, however, let's create a scene the old-fashioned way to get our feet wet with the fundamentals.

Step 1: Project Setup

An easy reference for getting a Unity VR project setup with VRTK is available at https://github.com/ExtendRealityLtd/VRTK#getting-started.

Create a new VR-supported, 3D project in Unity. If you are using Unity 2019 navigate to the Window ➤ Package Manager console and install the XR Legacy Input Handlers.

Here, we follow the now familiar step of cloning the VRTK GitHub repository into our Unity Project's Asset folder. Use the following procedure from the VRTK Getting Started documentation to clone the repo.

1. Navigate to the project Assets/ directory.

2. Git clone with required submodules into the Assets/ directory:

    - git clone --recurse-submodules https://github.com/ExtendRealityLtd/VRTK.git

    - Change to the newly cloned directory: cd VRTK/

    - git submodule init && git submodule update

3. The Unity software will now import and compile the new files.

If Unity prompts you with a window asking if you'd like to update its input mappings, click Yes. This is the window to which the VRTK documentation refers when it states:

VRTK will ask via a popup window on first load of the Unity project whether to attempt to auto create some Unity axis input mappings. If this is accepted then default axis data for left and right controller touchpad/thumbsticks, grip and trigger axes will be created.

172

Before we drag the UnityXRCameraRig and TrackedAlias objects into our scene from the VRTK prefabs folder in our Project window, let's create a demo of our scene in simple 3D.

To begin, we import our 3D model into our Assets folder. If you plan to use the 3D model of the building exterior I've provided for this exercise, you can download it from the exercise repo. Unzip the file and drag its contents into your project's Asset folder. Unity might notify you of a warning about the model's "normals" on its default mesh (Figure 7-4). If the warning appears yellow in your console you can ignore it for the purpose of this exercise. Select the model prefab that is identified by the name "model" preceded by a triangle identifying it as a parent of child objects. Drag the model into the Scene Hierarchy (Figure 7-5).

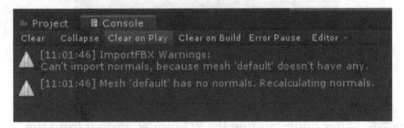

Figure 7-4. *Warning messages appear in yellow in the Unity Console window. Unlike errors, which appear in red, their presence does not prohibit the execution of a scene*

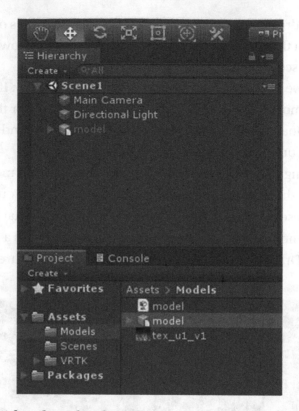

Figure 7-5. *After downloading the 3D model, drag it from the Assets/Models folder into the Scene Hierarchy*

You might notice the orientation of the model is askew in our Scene view (Figure 7-6). This can occur often when importing 3D assets because the zeroed, default positioning of the model might be determined by the asset artist on exporting from 3D modeling software such as Blender, Maya, or Cinema4D. Change the values of the parameters in the Transform component of the model to set the scene to your liking.

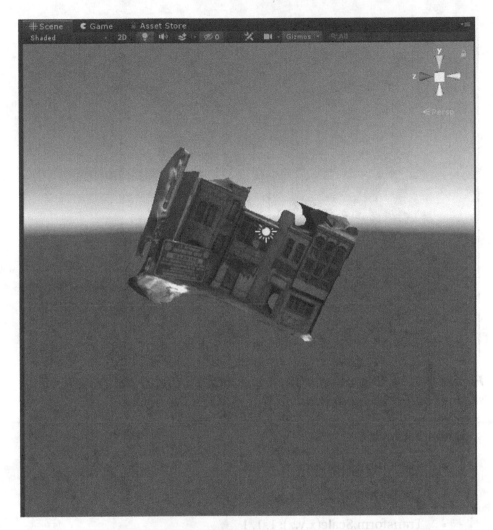

Figure 7-6. *Models might import to Unity askew because of Transform settings baked in by the model's modeling software*

If you're using the 3D model provided for this exercise, you can also feel free to copy the Transform settings I've used for the game objects in my scene, which include a plane object for the ground (Figure 7-7). Listed here are the game objects in my Scene Hierarchy and the properties I've set on their transforms.

Figure 7-7. *A screenshot of my scene after changing the Transform settings of the 3D model and adding a 3D plane object*

Main Camera

- Transform.Position(x,y,z): -0.74, 1, -10

- Transform.Rotation(x,y,z): 0, 0, 0

- Transform.Scale(x,y,z): 1, 1, 1

Model

- Transform.Position(x,y,z): 2.05, -.02, 2.68

- Transform.Rotation(x,y,z): 23, -90, 0

- Transform.Scale(x,y,z): 2, 2, 2

Plane (right-click in Hierarchy ➤ 3D Object ➤ Plane)

- Transform.Position(x,y,z): 1.02, -0.9, 1.52

- Transform.Rotation(x,y,z): 0, -90, 0

- Transform.Scale(x,y,z): 5, 1, 5

Alternatively, you can use whatever model you prefer to set your scene or simply construct your own building facade using object primitives (cubes, planes, cylinders) from within the Unity Editor. The purpose of this exercise is to learn the process of placing lights in a Unity scene and controlling the appearance of lighting through user input. As long as you follow along with the placement of lights and the scripting, the purpose of the project will not be lost on you.

Step 2: Swap the Skybox

Lighting is the primary technique we have at our disposal as Unity developers to manipulate the mood of our scene. Because the model Annie uses is of a decrepit, old inn, it doesn't feel right to Elgin, her director, that the model sits beneath a blue sky lit by the sun. Instead, Annie wants the user, on entering her scene, to feel an ominous threat of possible danger. Anything could be lurking in the night.

To create this vibe, let's swap out the default, sunny, blue Skybox in our scene with a black, starless night. To accomplish this, we simply follow the steps from Exercise 1. First, let's create a new folder in our Assets folder called Materials. In the Project window, right-click inside the Materials folder and select Create ➤ Material. Name the material black. In the Inspector, set the black material shader to Skybox/Cubemap, and set its Tint Color value to black (Figure 7-8).

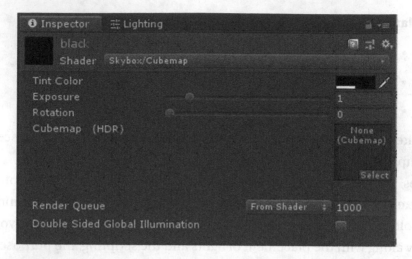

Figure 7-8. *Create a black Skybox from a material object*

As we did in Exercise 1, let's open up our Skybox properties and swap out its material. Navigate to Window ➤ Rendering ➤ Lighting Settings. Into the Skybox Material field beneath the Lighting ➤ Environment Property, drag and drop the Black material we created.

Step 3: Change the Value of the Directional Light

Speaking of light, let's add some to our scene! First, let's start by adding a little bit of moonlight. We can re-create the ambience of moonlight through the use of a Unity Directional Light. Right-click in the Scene Hierarchy and select Light ➤ Directional Light (Figure 7-9).

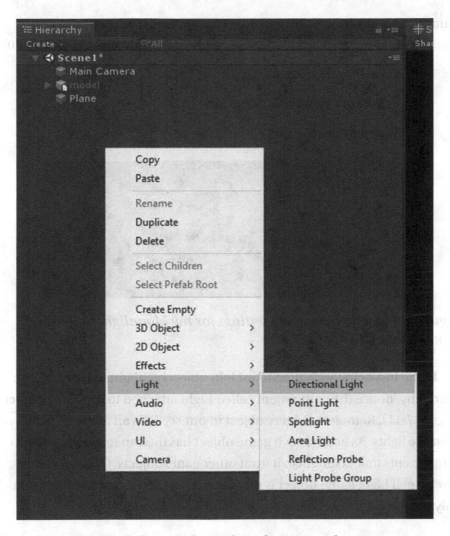

Figure 7-9. *Right-click or Ctrl+Click in the Hierarchy to create a new Light object*

Unity places a default Directional Light object in our scene. For convenience sake, if you haven't already, delete the original Directional Light object that comes as a default object with each new Unity Scene.

Name our new Directional Light object MoonLight. The following are the Transform settings I set for the MoonLight object in my scene (Figure 7-10):

- Transform.Position: 9, 11, -16

- Transform.Rotation: 37, -25, 0

- Transform.Scale 1, 1, 1

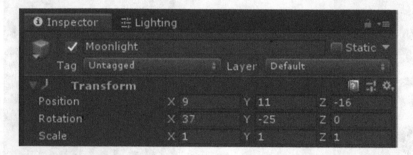

Figure 7-10. *The Transform settings for my Moonlight object are shown in the Inspector*

In the Inspector, with the MoonLight object highlighted in the Scene Hierarchy, notice the component called Light attached to the game object (Figure 7-11). Remember, every object in our scene is an actor, ironically, even the lights. As actors, each game object has the capacity to hold components that distinguish it from other game objects. Of course, a Directional Light game object is distinct from an empty game object that only holds a Transform because of its component called Light.

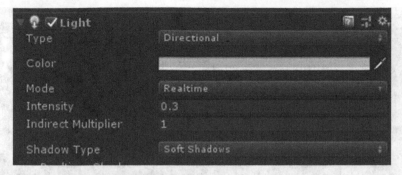

Figure 7-11. *A Light component appears by default on a Directional Light object created in the Scene Hierarchy*

Let's manipulate the settings of our Light component to better simulate moonlight. In the Inspector, confirm that the Light.Type is Directional. Using the color picker, set the Light.Color property to a cool, whiteish blue.

Let's wrap up the settings on our MoonLight game object's Light component by setting its Intensity to 0.3 and its Shadow Type to Soft Shadows. These settings, like most of the others related to the appearance and location of game objects in our scenes, are to taste. Fiddle away at the knobs until you've tweaked the appearance of the scene to your liking (Figure 7-12). You're learning Unity and VRTK to better express your creative vision, after all, so you might as well practice along the way.

Figure 7-12. *What the scene can look like with the Skybox removed, a directional light tinted blue, and soft shadows elevated on the 3D model*

Step 4: Add a Doorway Point Light

With the settings of our MoonLight object applied, let's turn our attention to another kind of light provided by Unity. In the model I am using for this exercise, a doorway sits to the right of the building's main entrance. The doorway looks as if it could lead to some kind of alley; appropriately spooky, I'd say. I'd like to apply a small light to the eave of the alleyway that the user can dim and lighten at will.

Unity offers a set of built-in lighting objects we can use to create an atmosphere in our scenes. They are a directional light, a spotlight, an area light, and a point light. There are also two options for objects called probes, but we discuss those later. In this exercise we've already worked with a directional light to mimic the soft light from our moon. Now, let's add a point light.

As we did to create the MoonLight object, right-click in the Scene Hierarchy and select Light ➤ Point Light. Name the new object Point Light and in the Scene view place the point light to appear as if it emanates from the overhang of the alley. If you are following along with the exercise using the settings I have applied to my project, you can use the following Transform coordinates to position the Point Light game object.

- Transform.Position: 2.17, 0.83, 2.63

- Rotation: 0, 0, 0

- Scale: 0.8, 0.8, 0.8

In the Light component attached to the Point Light game object confirm the Light.Type is set to Point. Set the range to a value that you feel is appropriate for the mood you're creating for your scene. Notice if you hold your mouse over the Range field, your cursor turns into a pointer with two opposite-facing arrows. When the two opposite-facing arrows appear around your cursor, you are allowed to click and hold your left mouse button to drag the field to the value you'd like to set as its parameter. I've chosen a float value of 4.45 for my PointLight.Light.Range value. Set the Shadow Type to Soft Shadows and select a warm, yellowish color to simulate the appearance of streetlights or glowing lamps (Figure 7-13).

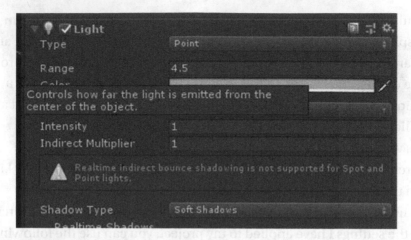

Figure 7-13. *A Point Light's Range, Color, Shadow Type, and other parameters can be manipulated in the Inspector*

By now your scene should be looking a lot more interesting than when we started the exercise. By adding three objects to our default scene—a 3D model, a directional light, and a point light—we've already created an interesting prototype for an immersive experience (Figure 7-14).

Figure 7-14. *Simply adjusting the parameters of light objects in Unity can completely alter the tone of a scene*

Step 5: Allow the User to Change the Point Light Through the Keyboard

Of course, as we've already discussed, the key to a convincingly immersive experience is—that's right—feedback! Now, we're going to create a script to empower our user to control the brightness of our doorway light.

Recall that when we introduce interactivity into our scene through an original script, we need a game object in the Scene Hierarchy on which we can attach our script as a component. By convention, we give this otherwise empty game object a name that ends with either "manager" or "controller."

185

Let's create an empty game object in our Scene Hierarchy by right-clicking with our mouse. Name the new, empty game object LightController.

Before we create our script, create a new folder in your Assets folder called Scripts. Getting into the habit of organizing your Unity projects with easily identifiable folders will help increase the speed of your prototyping over time. In the new folder, right-click and create a new C# script. Double-click the script to open it in your IDE, and add the code shown here. You can find the code for this project like the others on the exercise's GitHub page.

```
using UnityEngine;
public class Dimmer : MonoBehaviour
{
    public Light targetLight;
    public float rate = .08f;

    // Start is called before the first frame update
    void Start()
    {
    }
    // Update is called once per frame
    void Update()
    {
        Light pointLight = targetLight;
        if (Input.GetKey(KeyCode.UpArrow))
        {
            pointLight.range += rate;
        }
        else if (Input.GetKey(KeyCode.DownArrow))
        {
            pointLight.range -= rate;
        }
    }
}
```

Like the script we wrote in our last exercise, this script stores a component of a game object in a variable, manipulates the value of the variable, and attaches the component back to its object. Two things you might not recognize in our `Dimmer.cs` script are the += and -= operators. These translated into English are "equals itself plus" and "equals itself minus," respectively. In the code within the `Update()` function in `Dimmer.cs` the expressions within the conditional statements (`if/else if`) can be expressed in words as "set the point light range value equal to itself plus the value of the rate variable" and "set the point light range value equal to itself minus the value of the rate variable." The value of the rate variable is a property on our `Dimmer.cs` script component we make public to allow us to adjust it within the Unity Editor.

An Aside on Magic Numbers

Storing known values like `0.08f` (where `f` identifies the value as a data type `float`) in variables allows us to avoid a bad habit in programming called magic numbers. When developers tell you that you have a magic number in your code they are telling you that you have used a literal value, like `0.08f`, instead of a variable. Although our code would still execute if we used the floating-point number `0.08f` instead of the variable rate, the practice of avoiding magic numbers pays dividends over time. What if, for example, our `Dimmer.cs` script was but one component in a complex web of scripts communicating with each other, passing values back and forth? Under such conditions, a request from a project manager to change the rate at which our point light dims would require us to go through all of our code, changing each and every instance of the literal value `0.08f`. Using a variable like rate, instead, gives us the freedom in the future, if we choose, to change the value of the point light's rate of dimming by simply updating the value once at the moment we declare the rate variable in our script.

With the code in our `Dimmer.cs` script set, we save our changes and return to Unity. After waiting for the code to compile in the Unity Editor, attach the `Dimmer.cs` script as a component to the LightController game object in the Scene Hierarchy. Once you've attached the `Dimmer.cs` script to the LightController object, you will see two empty fields beneath the Dimmer (Script) in the Inspector. As we did with the cake object in our Interest Calculator exercise, drag and drop the Point Light object from the Scene Hierarchy on to the Dimmer (Script) Target Light field (Figure 7-15). Because we assigned the data type `Light` to this field in our script, Unity will only allow us to drag and drop a Light object into the Target Light field. Notice, too, that the value of our Rate field is already set to the 0.08 value we defined in our script. This is how we can define default values for public properties we create on objects through our scripts.

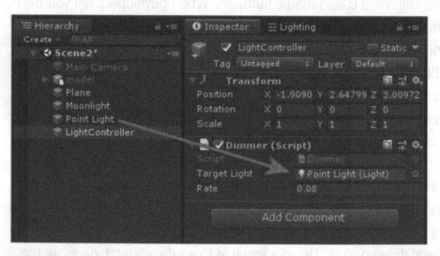

Figure 7-15. *Declaring the Target Light "public" in our C# script allows us to drag and drop the light object we'd like to control through scripting on to the script's game object property in the Inspector*

Step 6: Play-Test

Once you've set the properties on the Dimmer.cs script component attached to our Light_Controller, save the scene and give it a play. When you press the up-arrow key, the point light hanging in our alleyway should increase in brightness by a value of 0.08. Pressing the down-arrow key will diminish the brightness by 0.08. This is the work of the conditional statements we wrote in our Update() block (Figure 7-16).

```
// Update is called once per frame
void Update()
{
    Light pointLight = targetLight;

    if (Input.GetKey(KeyCode.UpArrow))
    {
        pointLight.range += rate;
    }
    else if (Input.GetKey(KeyCode.DownArrow))
    {
        pointLight.range -= rate;
    }
}
```

Figure 7-16. *The conditional statements (if/else) we wrote in the Update() function of the C# script control the intensity of a light object through user input*

An Aside on Errors

If you get an error in the Console window of the Unity project, click it to read the details. Double-clicking the error might take you to the line of code in the Dimmer.cs script where the error occurred if it is in fact the result of a coding mistake. If you do encounter an error notification connected to the code, refer back to the code printed in this book. Confirm that everything is entered as is with the same spelling, capitalization, and punctuation. Because VRTK 4 only became available for public use in March 2019 and both Unity and Visual Studio release frequent updates, the error might not be a result of anything you did. Such is the nature of developing in such a bleeding-edge space. Fortunately, as an open source project, VRTK allows users to submit errors through its GitHub page. Forums, too, keep developers abreast of the latest developments to a code base.

Step 7: Practice Moving Lights, Cameras, and Yourself Around the Scene

If you'd like more practice placing point lights in your scenes, you can find a way to place a point light within the 3D model in our scene to create the illusion that a light burns within one of the rooms of the building. You can use the toolbar above the Scene View window to manipulate the size, location, and rotation of any object in your scene. Convenient shortcut keys for manipulating game objects are as follows:

- w to display handles to move the object along an axis.

- e to display the handles to rotate an object around an axis.

- r to display the handles to change the size of the game object.

In Windows, holding the Alt key and the left mouse button in the Scene View window allows you to rotate your view around the scene. Holding the right mouse button allows you to tilt and pan across the scene. If your mouse has a button between its left and right buttons, then scrolling it allows you to zoom in and out of the scene, and holding it down and moving the mouse allows you to move vertically and horizontally in two dimensions within the scene.

Changing your view within a scene has no impact on the placement of your scene's main camera. Camera objects, like other game objects, can be moved through the buttons on the toolbar or the keyboard shortcuts laid out earlier. If, however, you would like to reposition a scene's camera to match the view you've found in your Scene window, then you can use the ever-handy shortcut Ctrl+Shift+F (in Windows) to align any game object highlighted in your Scene Hierarchy to the view currently displayed in your Scene View window. Other convenient functions to help you maneuver objects around your scene can be found on the GameObject menu (Figure 7-17).

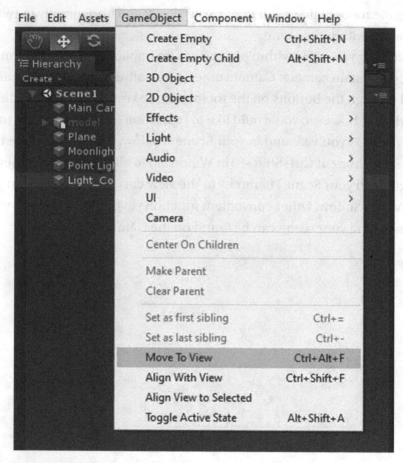

Figure 7-17. *The GameObject menu includes helpful shortcuts for maneuvering around a scene*

Step 8: Change the Value of the Rate Variable in the Unity Editor

Finally, before we move on to converting our scripted dimmer function into a Unity Axis Action component using the VRTK framework, experiment with changing the value of the Rate variable in the Dimmer.cs script component in the Unity Inspector. Remember, changing the value of a game object property while the Editor is in play mode will not save it to the computer's memory. If, however, you change the value of Rate while the Editor is stopped and then press Play, you will notice that the increment by which the alleyway point light brightens and dims changes, too. As you can see, defining malleable properties in our scripts with the `public` keyword allows us to prototype more quickly and efficiently in our editor.

Remaining in the Unity Editor as much as possible is a convenient and quick way to get ideas for our immersive experiences out of our imaginations and into a visual space. It's one thing to creatively solve the problem of what code to write to execute an action you envision in your scene, but it's another to write the code in an elegant, efficient way that allows for easy troubleshooting and smooth playback. Scripting a dimming function to respond not just to a touch controller's trigger input, but to the trigger input of any brand of touch controller that has and is yet to exist, is the fastest, easiest way to lose steam on an immersive project.

In today's fast-paced world where content ships quickly and can update within moments, getting our experiences out into the world is our goal. Although it's tempting to curate every nook and cranny of our app to make sure our code doesn't expose us as frauds, the unseemly secret of interactive applications is that we can't know how they'll work until someone interacts with them. To that end, rapid iteration is essential to VR development. The more often we can steamroll our way through the prototype of a vision, the more reps our application will get with real-life users and the more feedback we'll receive to improve it. It is for this very reason that the VRTK framework can be such a valuable weapon in your creative arsenal. Let's see how easy VRTK makes it to hook up our touch controller to a function that dims a light in our scene.

Adding a Unity Axis Action

By now, if you've completed the exercises from previous chapters and the section prior to this, then you are familiar with both connecting controller events to Unity Button Actions and manipulating float values of game objects through user input. What we have not yet addressed, however, is the process required to link user input to a parameter's float value through a VR controller. A Unity Button Action will not work because our parameter, the intensity of a point light, requires more than an off/on signal. One way we create a channel through which our VR application captures a user's controller input as a continuous float value is by implementing the VRTK framework's Unity Axis Action component.

Step 1: Add a Second Point Light

Remember how earlier I said you could have optional practice with our broken building scene by placing a point light in one of its windows? Well, I lied. It's not optional. If you've already done it, excellent! If you haven't, please do it now. Refer to the steps we followed when placing the alley light in our scene for reference.

For your convenience, here are the transform settings for the bedroom pointlight I placed in my scene (Figure 7-18):

- Transform.position: -5.43, 4.88, 4.21

- Rotation and scale set to default.

Figure 7-18. *Adding a second point light to the scene creates the effect of an occupied bedroom on the model's second floor*

Step 2: Write a Second C# Script for the New Axis Action

Now that you have a point light set up inside one of the building's windows, let's wire it up to a trigger action on our right touch controller. To accomplish this, we must use a Unity Axis Action component. Why a Unity Axis Action component? Well, buttons have two inherent states that developers use to communicate responses to yes/no, true/false questions. Triggers, as an axis action, allow us, as developers, to measure a user's input on a spectrum, for example, between 0 and 1.

After you've set up a second point light in your scene, name it RoomLight. Create a new empty game object in the Scene Hierarchy and name it LightController2. Because this game object is going to be a controller in our scene, let's add a script to it. The script connected to the controller as a component will provide the controller instructions for that which it will control. Let's create a new C# script in our Scripts folder in our Project window and name it, creatively, Dimmer2. Once you've confirmed you've spelled and capitalized the script's title as per your intention, double-click it to open it in Visual Studio.

Now that we're in Visual Studio, let's delete everything in this script and write some code from scratch. If you're feeling palpitations in your chest, don't worry; I'll be here to guide you each step of the way.

```
using UnityEngine;
```

That's the first line we write at the top of our script. It tells our script what code library to use. By telling our script to use the UnityEngine namespace we give our script access to all the classes and functions defined inside the UnityEngine namespace such as the Input system, the Event Manager system, the Physics system, and so on.

```
public class Dimmer2 : MonoBehaviour {
```

Like the first statement we typed, the class definition appears by default in the Unity script. This is the name we give our script on first creating it in our Project window. Recall that a class is a blueprint for an object. We won't be creating a `Dimmer2` object in our scene. We still, however, need the script to exist for us to access the functions (verbs, the doers) in our script. It exists to hold properties and functions for us like a container.

Notice that our class name inherits from the `MonoBehaviour` class and concludes with an opening curly brace {. What does it mean when our class inherits from the `MonoBehaviour` class? It means we can now attach the script of our class to a Unity game object as a component. The opening curly brace tells our compiler (the program that translates our more human-readable C# code into the language of our processor, machine code, through a C++ intermediate) that we are beginning the definition of a class. The next line we write is this:

```
public Light targetLight;
```

This line declares a public variable called `targetLight` that is of data type `Light`, which we gain access to through the `using UnityEngine` statement at the start of our script. Because it is public, the field will be available to us in our Unity Editor.

```
public void DimLight(float rate) {
```

Again, we use an opening curly brace. Here, however, our curly brace does not indicate the creation of a new class. Because we are already within a class called `Dimmer2,` this opening curly brace marks the opening of the code block for our function `DimLight`. The parentheses after a function's name indicate the type of input our function will take. `DimLight` will take a `float` data type. The name of our parameter is arbitrary. I've chosen the variable name `rate` because it determines the rate at which our light's intensity will increase or decrease according to the user's trigger input. Although the variable name of a parameter is arbitrary, it must remain consistent through the block of a function.

```
Debug.Log("Dimmer2 function called");
```

A value within quotation marks in a script is of data type string. In this line, I've passed a string as an argument into the Log function of the Debug class. Let's do a quick experiment. Comment out the first line we typed into our script using two forward slashes:

```
//using Unity.Engine;
```

After a moment your script will recompile. Do you see three red squiggly lines in your code as shown in Figure 7-19? If so, good! In Visual Studio, red squiggly lines tell us we have an error in our code.

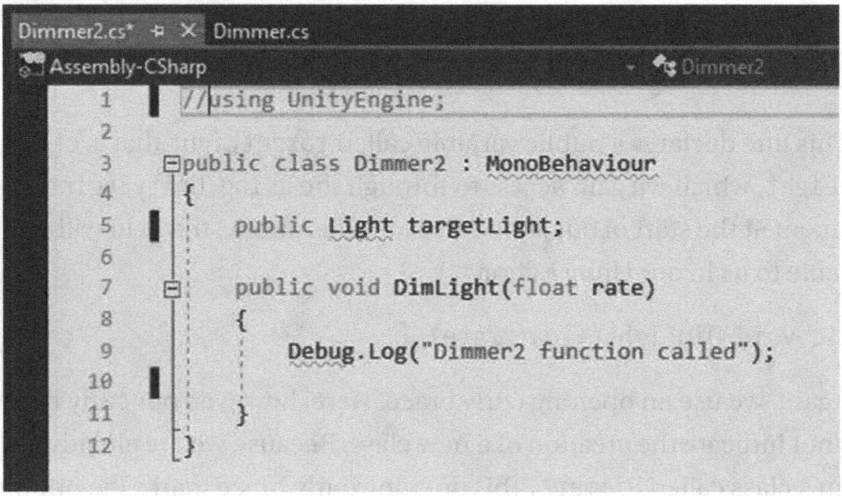

Figure 7-19. Commenting out the UnityEngine *using a statement removes the definitions for objects in its namespace, creating errors*

At the bottom left of the Visual Studio window is a menu called Error List (Figure 7-20). If you click that menu, a window appears that lists the errors the compiler found in our code.

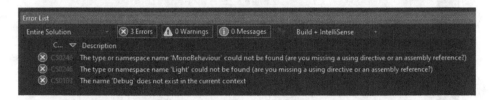

Figure 7-20. *The Error List in Visual Studio lists the errors in your code. Double-clicking an error often takes you to the specific line in the code where the error occurs*

The third error that appears in my code is this:

Error CS0103 The name 'Debug' does not exist in the current context

Now, let's uncomment our using statement by removing the two forward slashes. The red squiggly lines disappear and our Error List shows no errors. Further, in our code the words MonoBehaviour, Light, and Debug have returned to the color green (Figure 7-21). We've just learned that these three words are classes in the UnityEngine namespace. We did not have to create object instances of these classes in our script because the statement using UnityEngine does that for us.

```
Dimmer2.cs*  ⊕ ✕  Dimmer.cs
Assembly-CSharp                                      Dimmer2
  1  │  using UnityEngine;
  2
  3     ⊟public class Dimmer2 : MonoBehaviour
  4      {
  5  │         public Light targetLight;
  6
  7     ⊟        public void DimLight(float rate)
  8              {
  9                  Debug.Log("Dimmer2 function called");
 10  │
 11              }
 12      }
```

Figure 7-21. *Removing the comment marks returns the UnityEngine library to the scope of the project*

I've called the Log function on the Unity Debug class and placed it into our function so that I have some kind of visual reference that the code is executing should another error appear in my scene. Its value will become apparent shortly.

```
float intensity = targetLight.intensity;
```

Here, again, we're using a new variable to hold the value of a property on our targetLight object as if our script is a garage accepting a car called targetLight into service. We can't work directly on the car so we remove its component of interest to isolate it for manipulation. I define my new variable intensity with the data type float because that is the data type required for a Light object's intensity property. It is because Unity measures a Light's intensity with a float value that makes it a property great for us to connect to a Unity 1D Axis Action through VRTK. Recall that the distinguishing feature between an Axis Action and a Button Action is that an Axis Action can communicate values on a spectrum. Whereas the integer data type (int) can only hold whole numbers, float data types can hold decimal numbers. As a result we can measure a user's input beyond just 0 and 1; we can also capture values (to a finite decimal point, of course) between 0 and 1. Naturally, this makes perfect sense for us to use in our `DimLight` function because we are interested in not only capturing the intensity of a light at its maximum and minimum (on and off), but also in a range between.

```
intensity = rate;
```

After storing our public `targetLight` game object's intensity property in a variable of its own, we set the value of that variable, `intensity`, to the value of the argument of our function. Remember, the argument of a function is the specific value passed into the function at the time of its call. Because VRTK's Unity 1D Axis Action component will execute our `DimLight` function whenever the user presses the right trigger button on the touch controller, the rate will be whatever `float` value corresponds to the pressure with which the user pulls the trigger. This expression, therefore, sets the intensity of our `targetLight` according to the input from the user's finger.

```
targetLight.intensity = intensity;
```

Here, after we've manipulated the desired property, we attach it back to the game object from which we originally took it. In our analogy about the mechanic, this code equates to the moment we return the car's carburetor after fixing it, for example, back to the car's engine.

Finally, to complete our script, we add two closing curly braces } } to mark the end of our `DimLight` function code block and `Dimmer2` class (Figure 7-22). That's it! Let's save our script and return to Unity.

```
Dimmer2.cs  ⊅ ✕  Dimmer.cs
Assembly-CSharp                                              Dimmer2
    1        using UnityEngine;
    2
    3      ⊟public class Dimmer2 : MonoBehaviour
    4       {
    5            public Light targetLight;
    6
    7      ⊟       public void DimLight(float rate)
    8            {
    9                Debug.Log("Dimmer2 function called");
   10
   11                float intensity = targetLight.intensity;
   12
   13                intensity = rate;
   14
   15                targetLight.intensity = intensity;
   16            }
   17       }
```

Figure 7-22. *The completed program is shown for the* Dimmer2 *C# script*

Step 3: Add a Unity Axis Action Component to a Game Object

After we allow Unity to compile the changes we've made to our Dimmer2 script, we're ready to attach it as a component to our LightController2 game object. Select the controller object in the Scene Hierarchy, and in the Inspector add the Dimmer2 script as a component. Remember, you can either click Add Component and search for Dimmer2 or drag and drop the script from the Project window onto the controller object.

With our Dimmer2 script attached to our LightController2 object we can add the VRTK Unity Axis 1D Action component. With the LightController2 game object selected in the Scene Hierarchy, click Add Component in the Inspector and search for the Unity Axis 1D Action script (Figure 7-23). Notice that it has the same four events as the Unity Button Action component.

Uniquely, though, the Axis 1D Action component has a field called Axis Name. This will be the axis to which our Value Changed event will listen. What's the one-dimensional axis to which we're interested in listening? It's the right trigger button on the VR touch controller. How do we do that?

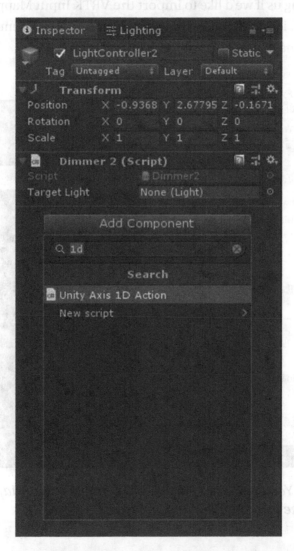

Figure 7-23. *Add a Unity Axis 1D Action as a component by clicking Add Component in the Inspector and searching for the term*

Step 4: Identify the Controller Button to Connect to the Unity Axis Action Through the Input Menu

Recall that when we imported VRTK into our Unity project, a window appeared asking us if we'd like to import the VRTK Input Mappings. If you didn't click OK, it's no problem. Simply navigate to Main Menu ➤ Window ➤ VRTK ➤ Manage Input Mappings (Figure 7-24).

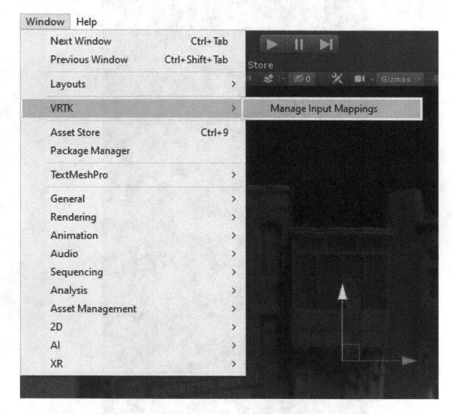

Figure 7-24. *You can access the VRTK Manage Input Mappings setting anytime through the Window menu*

When we open our Unity input settings (Main Menu ➤ Edit ➤ Project Settings ➤ Input) we see a drop-down list of all the axes to which Unity has mapped input.

Your list of inputs might look different than mine, but what's relevant to this exercise is the presence of the VRTK Axis mappings (Figure 7-25). If they do not appear in your Input list repeat the import process described in the previous paragraph.

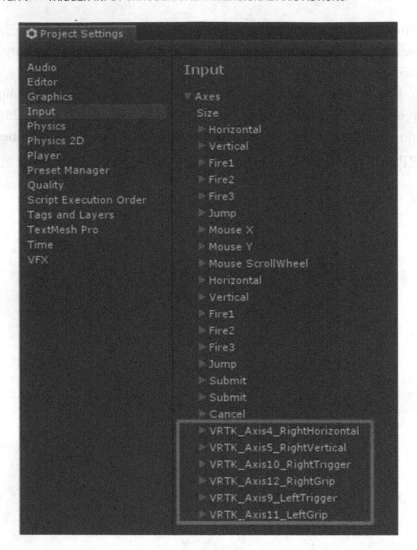

Figure 7-25. *Confirm that VRTK input mapping took place by locating the VRTK axes in the Unity Input Manager*

Let's expand the heading VRTK_Axis10_RightTrigger. You'll find a collection of fields defining the right trigger axis. Copy the value of the Name property to your computer's clipboard (Figure 7-26). Close the Input menu and return to your project's Scene Hierarchy.

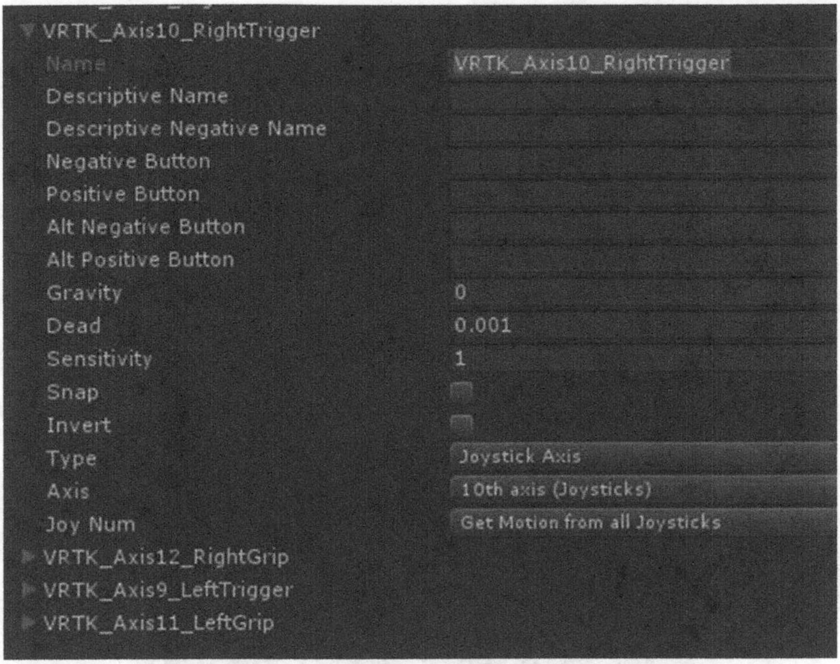

Figure 7-26. *Copy the Name value of the right trigger axis input to connect a Unity Axis Action to the right touch controller*

With your LightController2 object selected, turn your attention to the Inspector. In the Axis Name field of the Unity Axis 1D Action component, paste the name of the VRTK axis you just copied (Figure 7-27).

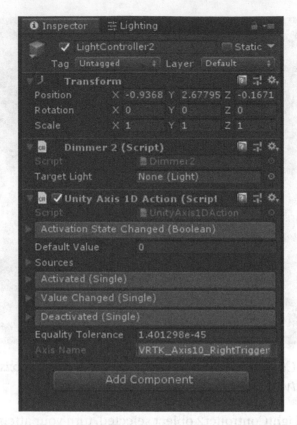

Figure 7-27. *Pasting the right trigger axis property name into the Unity Axis 1D Action component connects the trigger event to our* Dimmer2 *script*

Congratulations! You just mapped your controller game object and its attached Dimmer2 script to your touch controller's right trigger button. Now, the float variable rate we defined as a parameter on our DimLight function in our Dimmer2 script will read the value communicated by the pressure placed on your touch controller's right trigger. With our input into our Unity Axis 1D Action established, let's define our output.

Step 5: Connect the Chain of Events

Because our right trigger event will control the intensity of our room light, we want to call our `DimLight` function whenever the user's pressure on their trigger changes. To accomplish this, we'll connect our `DimLight` function as the subscriber, or listener, on our value changed event of the Axis Action component (the publisher). Click the + button on the Unity Axis 1D Action component Value Changed (Single) event. In the field that presently reads None (Object), drag and drop the `Dimmer2` script component from the same LightController2 object (Figure 7-28).

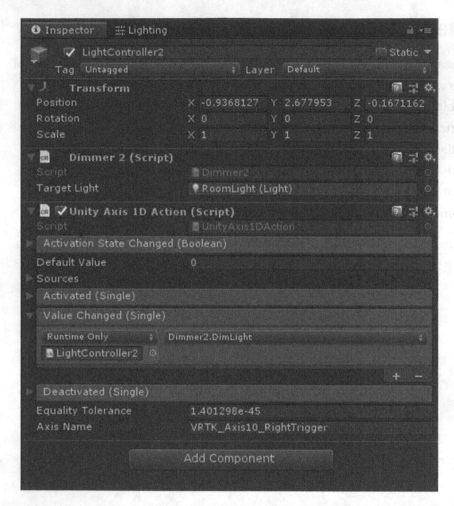

Figure 7-28. *Drag and drop the* `Dimmer2` *script component from the LightController2 object into the object property of the Unity Axis Action component*

From the Value Changed function pull-down menu select Dimmer2 ➤ (Dynamic Float) DimLight (Figure 7-29). Although there is a DimLight(float) function listed beneath the Static Parameter heading, we want to use the DimLight function beneath the heading Dynamic Float. Confirm that the `Dimmer2` script component in the LightController2's

Inspector window has a Light object from your scene identified in its Target Light field. In my scene, I placed a point light in the top left window of the building (in the negative x axis direction). I named the light RoomLight in my Scene Hierarchy and dropped it into my `Dimmer2`'s Target Light field. The Light object you select should be the one you created after placing the alleyway light in the scene. Before we move on from the controller object, confirm that you've properly named the Axis Name on the Axis 1D Action component and connected the `Dimmer2` script component to the Value Changed event.

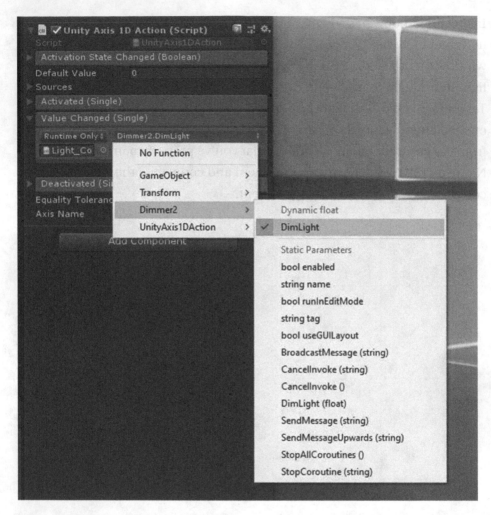

Figure 7-29. *Dragging the* `Dimmer2` *script into the Unity Axis ID Action component allows us to connect the Axis Action script to the DimLight function on our* `Dimmer2` *script*

Step 4: Add a Virtual Camera and a TrackedAlias Prefab to the Scene

Back in the Scene Hierarchy, let's add a UnityXRCameraRig object (if you plan to play-test with an external HMD) or a SimulatedCameraRig (if you plan to play-test inside the Unity Editor). Because we are listening to a trigger event from our VR touch controller, let's also drag and drop a TrackedAlias game object into our hierarchy. Increase the size of the Element property on the TrackedAlias's Tracked Alias Facade component and drag and drop the UnityXRCameraRig into the field Element 0 to complete the synchronization between the TrackedAlias game object and the UnityXRCameraRig (Figure 7-30).

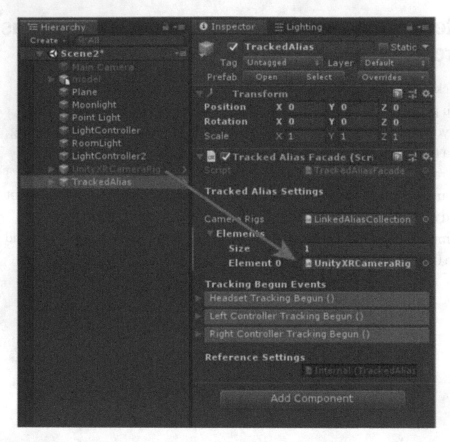

Figure 7-30. *Map the UnityXRCameraRig prefab to the TrackedAlias prefab by dragging and dropping the camera object into the Elements property of the TrackedAlias*

Finally, in the Scene Hierarchy, also confirm that only one camera game object is active. If your scene includes a default Main Camera game object, then deactivate it in the Inspector. Further, confirm the two point light objects you've added in this chapter are active, too, and connected to their respective LightControllers.

Step 5: Play-Test

That's it! Save your scene and give it a whirl!

If you play-tested your scene, did you find that when you pulled the right trigger button on your touch controller the point light you placed in one of the building's windows dimmed on and off? If not, check the Unity console for any error messages. If the Axis 1D Action did work, then your Console window should show the string we passed into the Debug.Log() function in our Dimmer2 script for every time you pulled the right trigger on your touch controller (Figure 7-31). You now have the power to create VR apps that can read the sensitivity of a user's input through touch.

Figure 7-31. *The Console window prints the string we entered into our Debug.Log() function to confirm our trigger action connects to the script we wrote*

As Annie, you just heard back from Elgin that the theater's board of directors were impressed with his immersive presentation. With a clear understanding of Elgin's vision they have no problem cutting the check required to fund the production. Congratulations, Annie! Because of you the show can go on!

The application of the tools you've learned in this exercise is, of course, not limited to dimming lights. With the knowledge you now have about VRTK, Unity, and C# scripting, you can create an assortment of actions influenced by the sensitivity of a user's input. For example, you could create an interior design tool to help a user visualize what different shades of a certain color would look like in a bedroom. You could prototype an installation and test parameters of different ambient features in a space. The possibilities are defined by your imagination.

Summary

In this chapter we covered the creation of an event handler that connected user input through both a keystroke and touch controller trigger action. The event handler, contained within a VRTK Unity Action component, published a notification to our application when the user provided a particular input. We created subscribers to these user inputs by writing functions in C# scripts that performed an operation on a property of a game object in our scene. Finally, we connected both the scripts and the game objects that served as targets for our user's actions to the VRTK Unity Action component's event handler, which we stored in our scene as components of an empty game object we called a controller.

Specifically, in the location scouting exercise, the event handler with which we concerned ourselves the most was the Value Changed event on the Unity 1-Dimensional Axis component. The Directional Light has been a consistent game object in the scenes we have created throughout this book, but in this chapter we manipulated its default settings and introduced Point Light game objects into the scene as listeners to our 1D Axis Action event. Connecting control of the Point Lights' intensities to both a keyboard input and controller input demonstrated two of the ways available to us, as developers, to capture user input. As VR aims to liberate the user from a workstation like a computer, events in our applications tied to controller input increase the immersive sensation of our experience. Further, familiarity with VRTK's Button and Axis Action components streamlines the trial-and-error methodology of iterating a VR experience. The more reusable components we can use in the design of our VR applications, like VRTK's Action components, the more quickly we can create and the more code complexity we can avoid.

So far, we've imported 3D assets into our projects; we've connected our headsets to our scenes through virtual cameras; and we've mapped changes to game objects to user input through both a keyboard and touch controller. Although the key to effective immersive experiences is dynamic feedback to a user's input, the promise of VR lies in much more than interacting with an object at a distance. We want to be able to touch a virtual object and feel as if our bodies can change our environment. That's the real high of a virtual existence; the moment our minds slip from R to VR. In the next chapter, we'll delve deeper into that through the use of VRTK's suite of tools for interaction.

CHAPTER 8

Interactors and Interactables

In the previous chapter we connected a VRTK 1D Axis Action component to the right trigger button of our touch controller. Unlike buttons, triggers communicate a continuum of data to our programs. However, many times the extra information conveyed through a range of `float` values is not only unnecessary for a VR application, but also unhelpful. Fortunately, VRTK offers a component to convert a trigger event from a collection of `float` values to a single `boolean` value of either on or off.

The Float to Bool component in VRTK is the third and final input handler we will discuss. The other two input handlers have been the Unity Button Action and the 1D Axis Action.

- A Unity Button Action connects a user's press of a button to a discrete action in our program.

- A Unity 1D Axis Action connects a user's pressure on a trigger to a continuous action in our program.

- The Float to Bool action component serves to transform a 1D Axis Action into a Button Action through the medium of a Boolean Action component.

A Boolean Action component converts the `float` values from a Unity Axis Action and connects the Axis Action to an event that has either an

© Rakesh Baruah 2020
R. Baruah, *Virtual Reality with VRTK4*, https://doi.org/10.1007/978-1-4842-5488-2_8

on or off state (Figure 8-1). For example, if we created a program that simulated the behavior of a nail gun, then we would want to convert a user's pressure on a trigger to one of two states: fire a nail or don't fire a nail. The pressure a user places on a trigger is immaterial. We'd simply want to know if they pulled the trigger on a touch controller past a certain value to activate an event that fired a virtual nail. For such a purpose, the VRTK Float to Bool and Boolean Action components perform well. The Float to Bool component will tell our program if and when a user pulls a touch trigger past a certain point; the Boolean Action component will then trip the "fire nail" event in the program's script.

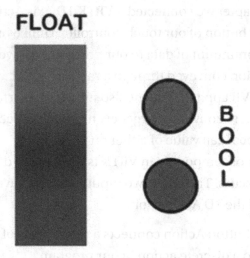

Figure 8-1. *An Axis 1D Action component captures a range of float values. A Float to Bool component transforms the spectrum of float information into one of two states: true or false*

Like many of the concepts conveyed in this text, it will be most helpful to put the theory into practice. Therefore, in this chapter you will do the following:

- Add a VRTK Interactor to a scene.

- Connect a VRTK Interactor to a VR touch controller.

- Add an interactable 3D object to a scene.

- Create the ability to pick up and move 3D objects using VRTK components.

- Add text elements to a scene that respond to user actions.

- Script actions triggered by the location of objects placed by a user.

Exercise: A Physician's Cognitive Testing Tool

Dr. Tanisha Pallavi is a practicing neurologist. She specializes in seeing patients who suffer from cognitive impairment. One exercise she uses to test a patient's reasoning abilities is a simple shape selector. She instructs a patient to pick up an object of a particular shape and place it in a bin. If the patient succeeds, she can rule out any degenerative diagnosis. However, if the patient either selects the incorrect shape or demonstrates an inability to place it in a bin, then she knows further examination of the patient's cognitive and motor skills is prudent. To help Dr. Pallavi perform the test at scale and even administer it remotely, we will create a VR app that reproduces the requirements of the examination (Figure 8-2).

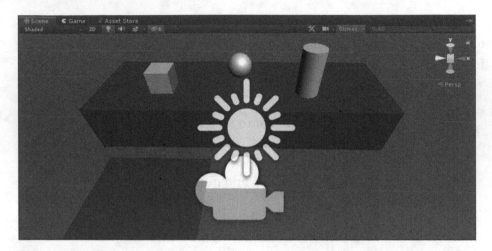

Figure 8-2. *This is a Scene view of the final prototyped testing application*

Part 1: The Scene

Part 1 of this exercise will address the visual elements of the scene, such as the dressing of our set and the appearance of our props. However, because VRTK prefabs offer functionality without the requirement of code, you can create interaction in a scene with only what we cover in Part 1. Part 2 takes us into the code behind the scene that drives the logic of the application. In concert, Parts 1 and 2 provide a complete picture of the elements that make up an interactive VR experience and the code that connects them.

Step 1: Set Up a VR-Supported 3D Project in Unity with VRTK and a VR SDK

Hopefully by now you feel a bit more comfortable setting up a Unity project with VRTK. If you still feel uneasy, refer back to the previous chapters for reference.

Step 2: Add a TrackedAlias Prefab and a Virtual Camera Rig

As we have done in previous exercises, add the TrackedAlias prefab and the virtual camera rig best suited to the needs of your system. If you are using an SDK-specific camera rig connected to an HMD, then you can forgo the UnityXRCameraRig. Refer to Chapter 6 to review linking an SDK-specific camera rig (e.g., the Oculus OVRCameraRig) to the TrackedAlias prefab.

Step 3: Add 3D Objects to the Scene for Setting

Because we are re-creating a doctor's office, let's sketch out the bare bones of the set dressing we will need. Create a plane object, and rename it floor. Create a cube object, and rename it table. Create a plane object, and rename it plane. Refer to my transform settings, shown here, to place your objects in the scene:

CameraRig

- Position: 0, 0, 0

- Scale: 1, 1, 1

TrackedAlias

- Position: 0, 0, 0

- Scale: 1, 1, 1

Floor

- Position: 0, 0, 0

- Scale: 10, 0.5, 10

Table

- Position: 0, 0.25, 1

- Scale: 3, 0.5, 1

Plane

- Position: -0.8, 0.05, -0.2

- Scale: 0.1, 0.1, 0.1

Further, you can set the color of the materials for each object to your preferences. Your scene should resemble Figure 8-3.

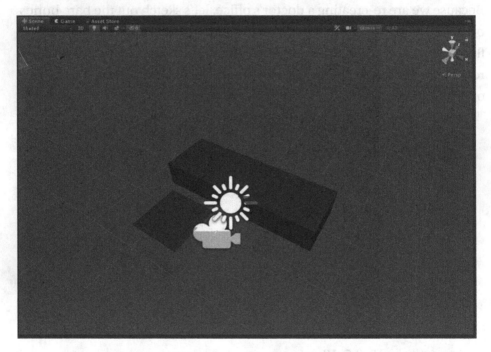

Figure 8-3.   *This is a bird's-eye view of the game objects that define the setting of the scene*

Step 4: Add VRTK Interactors to the Scene

This step connects our VR touch controllers to the VRTK interface to facilitate communication between our VR SDK and Unity. To do this, drag and drop the VRTK Interactor prefabs from the Project window to the TrackedAlias's controller aliases. Refer to Chapter 6 to review connecting Interactors to the TrackedAlias prefab.

Step 5: Set Up the Game Objects with Which the User Will Interact

Here, we do something new.

VRTK offers prefab objects replete with the necessary features to facilitate user interaction. They are called Interactables, and, if you downloaded VRTK from GitHub correctly, they are available in the VRTK folder in your Unity Project window. Navigate to Assets ➤ VRTK ➤ Prefabs ➤ Interactions ➤ Interactables (Figure 8-4).

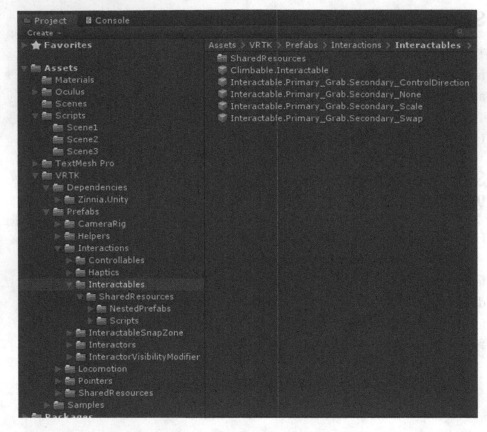

Figure 8-4. *The VRTK library offers prefab objects containing within them the logic required to create items a user can grab*

The final object interactable listed in my VRTK/Prefabs/Interactions/Interactable folder is called Interactable.Primary_Grab.Secondary_Swap (Figure 8-5).

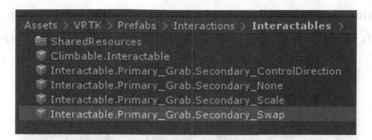

Figure 8-5. *VRTK offers interactable objects with logic suited for different actions*

Drag and drop the object three times into the Scene Hierarchy so you have three instances of the object (Figure 8-6).

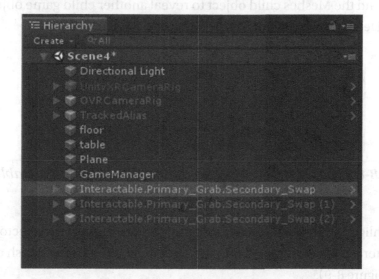

Figure 8-6. *Create three instances of interactable objects by dragging them into the Scene Hierarchy from the VRTK folder in the Project window*

Clicking the triangle to the left of one of the Interactable objects in the Hierarchy exposes its children, of which there are three (Figure 8-7).

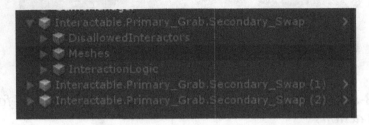

Figure 8-7. *Clicking the triangle to the left of the parent Interactable object reveals its three child objects*

Expand the Meshes child object to reveal another child game object named DefaultMesh (Figure 8-8).

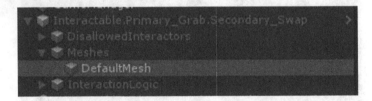

Figure 8-8. *The DefaultMesh child object of a VRTK Interactable is shown*

Highlighting DefaultMesh reveals its components in the Inspector. Each Interactable we dragged into our Hierarchy has a DefaultMesh called Cube (Figure 8-9).

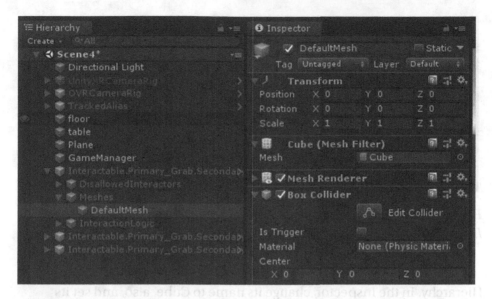

Figure 8-9. *A VRTK Interactable object has attached to it by default a Cube mesh*

Because we would like three different shapes to meet Dr. Pallavi's requirements, we will replace the default meshes of each Interactable with a unique shape.

Step 6: Set a Unique Default Mesh Property for Each Interactable Game Object

We will create three shapes to serve as the meshes for our Interactables: a cube, a sphere, and a cylinder. Because the cube mesh is the default mesh for the Interactable, we don't need to change its shape, only its size. Edit the Scale property of the cube default mesh child game object to (0.2, 0.2, 0.2). Change its name to Cube (Figure 8-10).

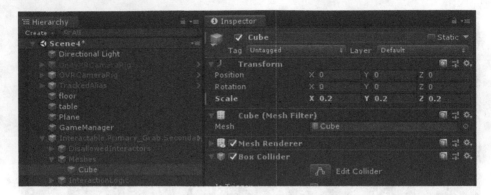

Figure 8-10. *Edit the properties of the Interactable's mesh in the Inspector*

Highlight the topmost parent object of the cube mesh in the Scene Hierarchy. In the Inspector, change its name to Cube, also, and set its Transform.Position values to (-0.7, 0.75, 0.65).

For the second Interactable object in our Scene Hierarchy, let's change its DefaultMesh to a sphere. To do so, navigate to the child DefaultMesh object of the second Interactable object in the Hierarchy. With the DefaultMesh object highlighted in the Hierarchy, turn your attention to the Mesh Filter component in the Inspector (Figure 8-11). As we noted, the default mesh filter on a VRTK interactable is a cube. To change the shape of the mesh filter, click the small circle to the right of the object field in the Mesh Filter component.

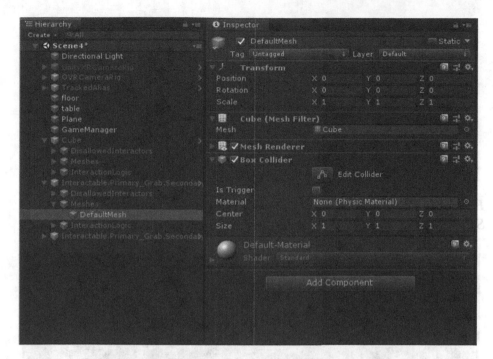

Figure 8-11. *Select the DefaultMesh child object of the second Interactable object to change its properties in the Inspector*

Double-click the Sphere mesh to add it as the default mesh on the second Interactable game object (Figure 8-12). Resize the Scale values of the DefaultMesh transform of which the Sphere mesh filter component is a part to (0.2, 0.2, 0.2), and change its name to Sphere (Figure 8-13).

Figure 8-12. *Clicking the circle with your mouse will open a new Select Mesh window*

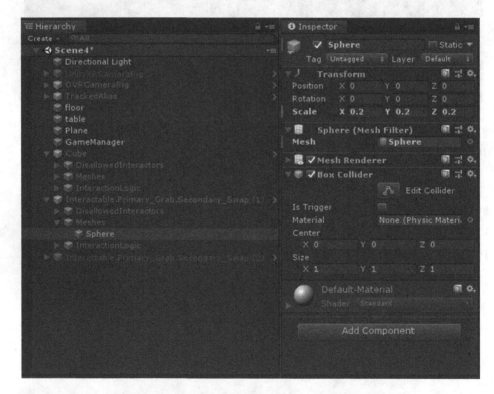

Figure 8-13. *Changing the DefaultMesh value of the second Interactable object to Sphere distinguishes its shape from the Cube interactable*

Highlight the Interactable parent object of the Sphere mesh filter, and, in the Inspector, change its name to Sphere and its Transform.Position to (0, 0.9, 0.6) as shown in Figure 8-14.

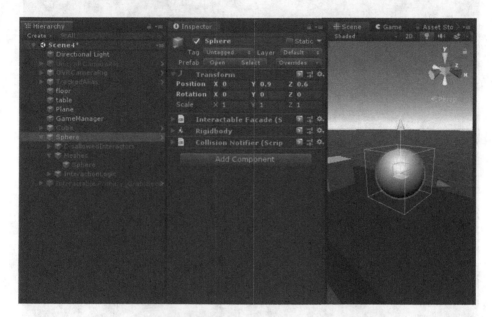

Figure 8-14. *Change the position information of an Interactable object's parent game object to prevent misalignment with its mesh child object*

For the third Interactable object in our Hierarchy, set its mesh filter to a Cylinder; rename the default mesh to Cylinder; set its x, y, and z scale values to 0.2; and rename its parent object Cylinder. Its names and properties should match those shown in Figure 8-15.

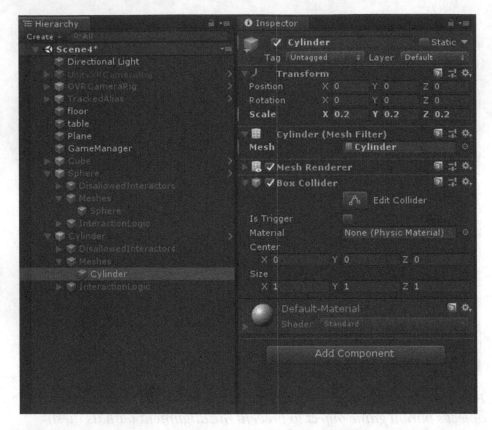

Figure 8-15. *Make sure the name of the DefaultMesh matches the name of the parent Interactable object. Otherwise, the scripting for the application will not work correctly*

Set the Transform.Position values of the parent Cylinder interactable object to (0.6, 0.85, 0.6). The properties of the Cylinder interactable object and the broader scene's view should resemble Figure 8-16.

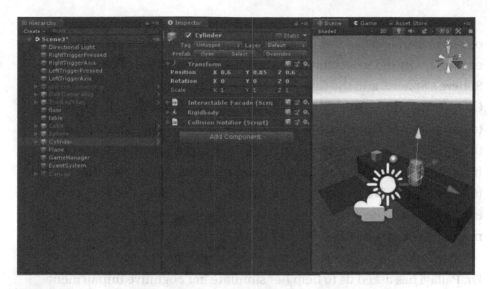

Figure 8-16. *The final Transform settings for the Cylinder interactable and an example of the Scene view after all Interactable properties have been set are displayed*

Troubleshooting: My Transforms Are All Messed Up!

If you find that the transforms for your mesh filters and parent interactable objects don't align, then you might have edited the position values of the mesh filter instead of the parent object. Because the properties of a parent object cascade down to its child and not the other way around, changing the position values on the mesh filter will not align with the position values of the parent object automatically. Because we only aim to change the scale property of the mesh filter component, we leave its position and rotation transform values at their defaults. Instead, we manipulate the transform position values of the master parent game object so that the position of all children objects remains aligned.

You might be asking yourself why we went through the work of naming our Interactable objects and their default mesh filters the same name. For example, why did we name the Cube Interactable's mesh filter Cube, the Sphere's Sphere, and the Cylinder's Cylinder? In Part 2 we will write the C# code that drives the application logic of the scene. We will need a way to compare whether the object selected by the users is the same shape as the object they were instructed to pick up. By matching the name of the Interactable shape to its mesh filter, we create two values we can compare to test equality. We create the code for this logic in Step 4 of Part 2 of this exercise. You'll know you've reached it when you come across the totally random keyword CUPCAKE.

Before we proceed, let's better understand what it is we need to do. Dr. Pallavi has asked us to help her simulate her cognitive impairment exercise. The exercise requires a patient to select an object, grasp it, and place it in a bin. So, we know one entity in our program:

- Patient

- Actions: `Grab_Object`, `Release_Object`

Second, because Dr. Pallavi will not be present for the virtual test, we will need something in our program that replaces her. What functions does Dr. Pallavi perform during the test? She begins the test, she instructs the patient which object to choose, and she evaluates if the patient responded correctly. If Dr. Pallavi were a machine, we could categorize this domain of her job during the test as follows:

- Evaluator

- Actions: `Start_Test`, `Issue_Object_To_Select`, `Determine_If_Correct`

We also need an object in our scene that performs Dr. Pallavi's function of communicating with the patient.

- Marquee

- Actions: `Write_To_Screen`

Finally, we'll need an object that captures the patient's object on release so that the program can evaluate it:

- Collector

- Actions: `Identify_Released_Object`

If we were creating a traditional 2D program, we would embellish the `Patient` class with code to define the actions the user will perform. However, because we are developing a 3D, VR application, we can avail ourselves of the GUI provided by Unity to facilitate our scripting.

Step 7: Create a User Grab Action

We have determined that the user must be able to, at the very least, grab and release game objects in our scene. Our input will be the user's press of a trigger button on the controller that simulates a grab. Our output will be the visual feedback to the user of his or her hand holding a virtual object. How, then, can we connect a user's action in the real world with an object in the virtual world?

If you expand the TrackedAlias object in the Scene Hierarchy and highlight the Interactor prefab you added previously to preview it in the Inspector, then you will see a component called Interactor Facade (Script) like Figure 8-17.

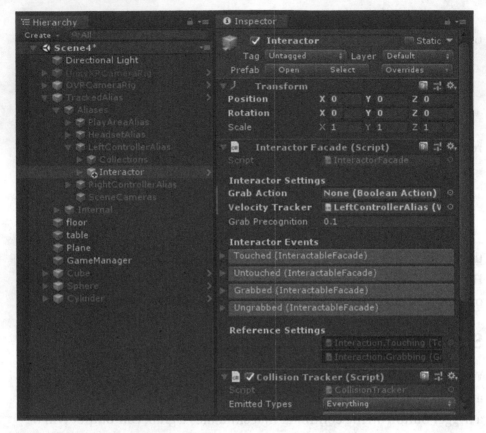

Figure 8-17. *The Interactor prefab provided by VRTK includes a Facade component, which exposes events and properties into which we can hook user actions to facilitate grabbing an object in our scene*

The Interactor Facade component has two parameters in its Interactor Settings: Grab Action and Velocity Tracker. In this exercise we only concern ourselves with the Interactor Facade's Grab Action. A Grab Action is a property unique to VRTK. Its data type is a VRTK-defined BooleanAction, which means the Grab Action property holds either a true or false value. The event wired as a publisher to the Grab Action property determines whether Grab Action represents a true BooleanAction or a false BooleanAction. What is the event for which a Boolean Grab Action listens? It is the press of the VR controller button that simulates for a user what it is like to grab an object. In this example, let's make that button the right grip trigger for an Oculus Rift touch controller.

What's a Facade?

Computer programming, like architecture, industrial engineering, and even writing for that matter, is as much an art as it is a science. Consequently, elegant solutions to complex problems are as subjective to the developer as drama is to playwrights. In short, there is no right answer. There can be, however, right answers. In scripting, a facade is a design pattern that uses one class as an interface for a subsystem of interconnected parts. The control panel in a cockpit implements a facade design pattern, for example. The moving parts responsible for the plane's flight are not isolated in the nose of the plane, beneath the control panel. They, like the functions and code libraries in a Unity project, are distributed across the system. A facade, then, is the hub through which subcomponents connect, exposing their functionality to the user through a discrete interface.

To prompt the cascade of events that culminate in an object responding to a user's touch, we will begin with our old friend, the Unity Axis 1D Action component. In your Scene Hierarchy, create an empty game object and name it RightTriggerAxis. In the Inspector, click Add Component to add a Unity Axis 1D Action component (Figure 8-18).

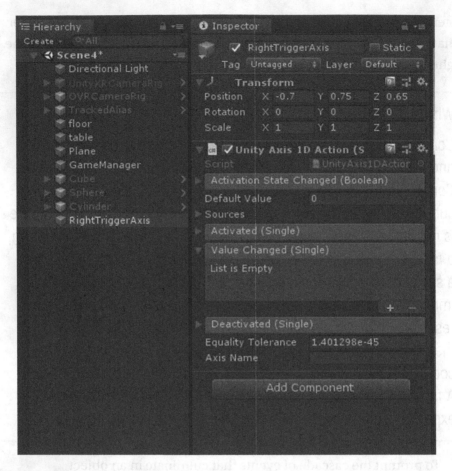

Figure 8-18. *Add an Axis 1D Action component to an empty game object called RightTriggerAxis*

Navigate to the Unity Input Manager through Menu Bar ➤ Edit ➤ Project Settings. Locate the Input Axis named VRTK_Axis_12_RightGrip (Figure 8-19).

Figure 8-19. *Locate the Right Grip Axis information in the Input Manager*

Copy the value of the Name property: VRTK_Axis12_RightGrip. Paste the name of the axis in the Axis Name field of the 1D Axis Action component connected to the RightTriggerAxis game object (Figure 8-20).

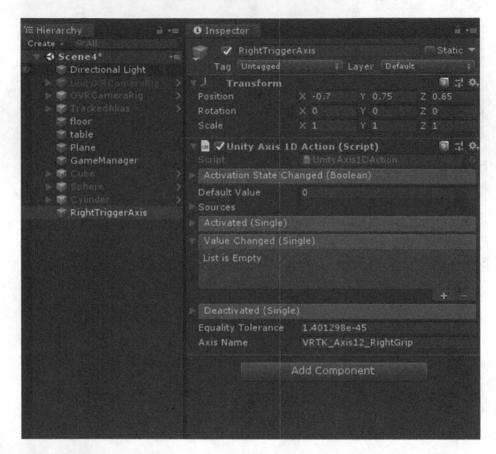

Figure 8-20. *Pasting the name of the Right Grip Axis input as the Axis Name in a 1D Action component connects trigger input to a Unity event handler*

Now, we have an event handler listening to our touch controller's right grip trigger as mapped through the VRTK TrackedAlias prefab. The specific event to which we'd like to listen is the Value Changed (Single) event. In Chapter 7 we listened for this same event on our main trigger button to control the intensity of a point light. Listening to this input from the user will yield a float value correlated to the degree to which they've pressed their trigger.

Unlike dimming a light, however, grabbing and holding an object does not require a range of values. To grab an object, users only have to press their grip trigger button past a certain point to determine whether they've grabbed the object or not. Therefore, a continuous range of float values is not helpful toward our goal of allowing users to grab, hold, and move an object with their hand. We need a mechanism that converts the information communicated by the 1D Axis Action Value Changed event handler from a float value to a boolean value. The boolean value will allow us to determine, simply, whether the user has grabbed an interactable object or whether not.

Step 8: Convert the Float Value to a Boolean Value

VRTK offers a convenient component to help us accomplish this task. It is called, appropriately, Float to Boolean. To map the float value captured by the Unity Axis 1D Action component to a bool we must chain the 1D Action component to a Float to Boolean component. To do this we first create another empty game object in our Hierarchy called RightTriggerPressed. With the new game object highlighted in the Hierarchy, click Add Component in the Inspector and search for Float to Boolean.

After adding a Float to Boolean component to the RightTriggerPressed game object, you will see the component contains two fields: (1) the Transformed (Boolean) event handler list, and (2) the Positive Bounds parameter. Set the Positive Bounds parameter to 0.75, as shown in Figure 8-21.

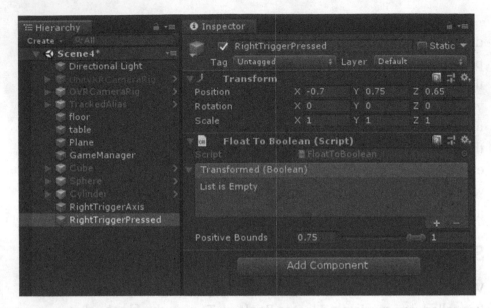

Figure 8-21. *The Positive Bounds parameter of a VRTK Float to Boolean component sets the threshold at which a trigger event sparks an action. VRTK normalizes the boundary of a trigger input's range: 0 is no pressure, and 1 is fully pressed*

The Positive Bounds field on the Float to Boolean component sets the threshold at which the Transformed event will fire. Pressing the right grip trigger only halfway, for example, will not trigger the event. The user must press the grip trigger at least 75% of the way down to trigger the function that converts the Unity Axis 1D Action float value to a transformed boolean. This serves our purpose well because we'd only like the users to be able to grab and hold an object if they intentionally clench their fist on the controller in the presence of an Interactable object.

Once our Float to Boolean action transforms our `float` value to a `boolean` value we need to capture the `boolean` value somewhere to connect it to the Grab Action on our Interactor prefab in our TrackedAlias game object. To accomplish this, we will use the Boolean Action component we introduced in the Interest Calculator exercise of Chapter 6. Recall that

in that exercise we connected the CalculateInterest script to a button
on our controller by attaching it to our cake object and wiring it through
the Activated (Boolean) event. For this exercise, attach a Boolean Action
component to the RightTriggerPressed game object, the same game object
to which we've added the Float to Boolean component (Figure 8-22).

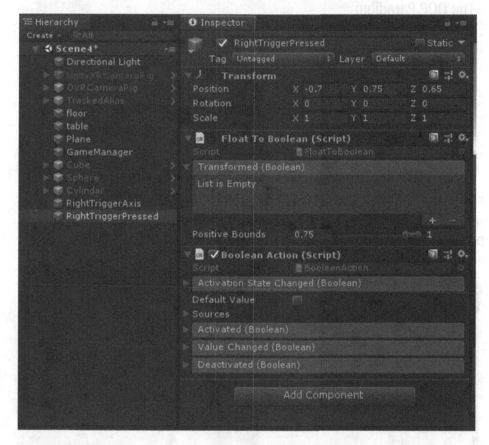

Figure 8-22. *Add a VRTK Boolean Action component to the same
game object as a VRTK Float to Boolean component to receive the
boolean value created by the Transformed event*

A Boolean Action is a VRTK-specific data type, which means it is a unique class VRTK has constructed from the elements of a base class. The creation of classes that build on the functionality of other, broader classes is called inheritance, and it is one of the main principles of the OOP paradigm.

The OOP Paradigm

Most developers agree that the four main principles of OOP are encapsulation, abstraction, inheritance, and polymorphism. We've addressed all four in this text, broadly, but I'll leave it to the more ambitious among you to delve deeper into the numerous resources for OOP available online.

The VRTK Boolean Action class builds on the broader VRTK Action class, which contains as part of its definition the methods we can see inside the Unity Editor's Inspector: Activated, ValueChanged, and Deactivated (Figure 8-23).

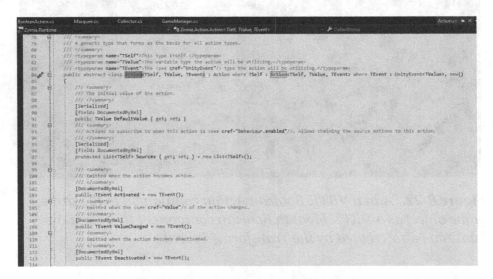

Figure 8-23. *A view of the abstract* Action *class in the VRTK code base, from which* Boolean Action *inherits*

The Action class definition also contains methods we do not see in the Unity Editor directly. One of these methods, seen in Figure 8-24, is called Receive.

```
/// <summary>
/// Acts on the value.
/// </summary>
/// <param name="value">The value to act on.</param>
[RequiresBehaviourState]
public virtual void Receive(TValue value)
{
    if (IsValueEqual(value))
    {
        return;
    }

    ProcessValue(value);
}
```

Figure 8-24. *The method signature for the Receive function in the VRTK Action class*

Because the BooleanAction class inherits from the more general Action class, it too has the Receive function as part of its definition. It is the Receive method from the BooleanAction class (and its component in our editor) that we would like to call to save the boolean value converted from our Axis 1D Action float value.

> **Trigger ➤ Axis 1D Action ➤ Float to Bool ➤**
> **Boolean Action ➤ Grab Action**

This is the chain of actions we are attempting to devise to avoid creating any original code to drive our users' ability to grab, hold, and move objects in our scene. To connect our Boolean Action component to our Float to Bool component on our RightTriggerPressed game object, we need to call the Boolean Action Receive() method from the Float to Boolean component's Transformed() event handler.

With the RightTriggerPressed game object highlighted in the Scene Hierarchy, click + beneath the Float to Boolean Transformed (Boolean) event handler in the Inspector. Drag and drop the RightTriggerPressed game object from the Hierarchy into the empty game object field on the Transformed event handler in the Float to Boolean component. From the function pull-down menu in the Transformed (Boolean) event handler, select BooleanAction ➤ (Dynamic Bool) Receive as shown in Figure 8-25.

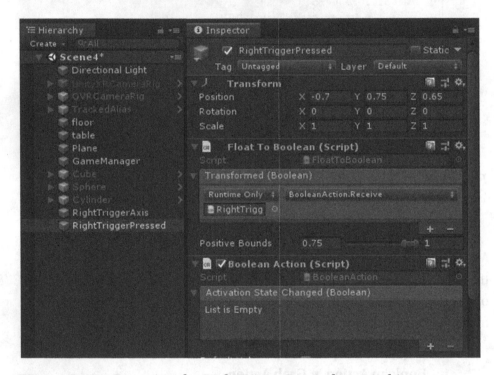

Figure 8-25. *Dragging the RightTriggerPressed game object on to its Float to Boolean component chains the Boolean Action Receive method to the Transformed event handler*

By this point, we've created a mechanism to measure the input from the user's right grab trigger through the RightTriggerAxis game object's Unity Axis 1D Action Component; we've created a mechanism to convert the float value from the Axis 1D Action component into a boolean value; and we've sent that boolean value to a Boolean Action component on the RightTriggerPressed game object. There are two steps remaining to complete the chain of events.

Step 9: Connect the RightTriggerPressed Object to the RightTriggerAxis Object

The first step is a step we glossed over to create our RightTriggerPressed game object. We haven't yet defined how our float value captured by our RightTriggerAxis Axis 1D Action component will reach the Float to Boolean action component on the RightTriggerPressed game object. To do so, let's add a listener to our Value Changed event handler on our RightTriggerAxis Unity Axis 1D Action component.

With the RightTriggerAxis game object selected in the Hierarchy, click the + sign on the Unity Axis 1D Action component's Value Changed (Single) event handler. Drag and drop the RightTriggerPressed game object on to the empty game object field, and in the event handler's function pull-down menu select FloatToBoolean ➤ (Dynamic Float) DoTransform (Figure 8-26).

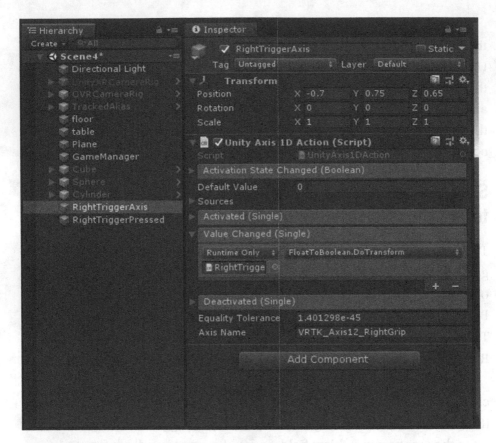

Figure 8-26. *Dragging the RightTriggerPressed game object on to the RightTriggerAxis's 1D Action component creates a listener on the Trigger Axis's Value Changed event*

Step 10: Connect the Controller to the Interactor Facade

The final step we take to complete the creation of our right grip trigger grab action is to connect our Boolean Action event on our RightTriggerPressed game object to the Grab Action property on our right controller interactor (Figure 8-27).

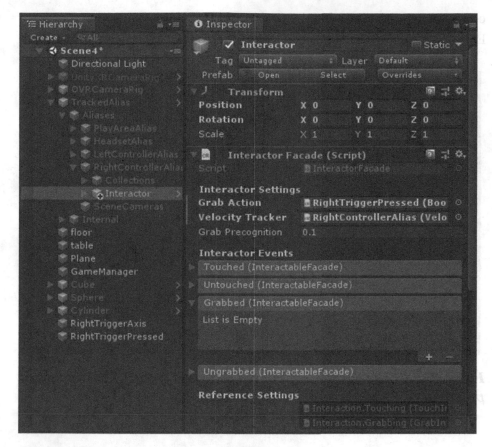

Figure 8-27. *The Grab Action property on the Interactor object's Facade component connects the value emitted by the RightTriggerPressed object's Boolean Action Receive event*

The Interactor prefab created by VRTK, which we added as a child object to our TrackedAlias game object in the Hierarchy early in this exercise, contains a VRTK component called Interactor Facade (Figure 8-28). Because we can attach the Interactor Facade to a game object, we know it inherits from the UnityEngine class MonoBehaviour. Therefore, it is a C# script. After opening the InteractorFacade script in an IDE by double-clicking the script's name in the Interactor Facade component, we can see that the Grab Action property exposed in the Unity Editor's Inspector window is of data type BooleanAction (Figure 8-29).

Figure 8-28. *The Facade component attached to the VRTK Interactor prefab is a C# script we can view in an IDE*

```
/// <summary>
/// The public interface into the Interactor Prefab.
/// </summary>
public class InteractorFacade : MonoBehaviour
{
    /// <summary>
    /// Defines the event with the <see cref="InteractableFacade"/>.
    /// </summary>
    [Serializable]
    public class UnityEvent : UnityEvent<InteractableFacade> { }

    #region Interactor Settings
    /// <summary>
    /// The <see cref="BooleanAction"/> that will initiate the Interactor grab mechanism.
    /// </summary>
    [Serialized, Cleared]
    [field: Header("Interactor Settings"), DocumentedByXml]
    public BooleanAction GrabAction { get; set; }
    /// <summary>
    /// The <see cref="VelocityTrackerProcessor"/> to measure the interactors current velocity.
    /// </summary>
```

Figure 8-29. *The Interactor Facade component is a C# class inheriting from Unity's MonoBehaviour class. The data type of its GrabAction property is a BooleanAction, which means it can hold the result returned by a Boolean Action method like Receive( )*

We also know that the last link in our chain of events we touched was the BooleanAction component on our RightTriggerPressed game object. Therefore, we know the value published by our Receive( ) method on our BooleanAction component on our RightTriggerPressed game object will be of type BooleanAction. To complete our chain of events, we simply need to connect the message sent from our BooleanAction.Receive( ) method to our Interactor object's InteractorFacade.GrabAction property.

The BooleanAction.Receive( ) method receives the boolean value from the Float to Bool component on the RightTriggerPressed game object. The Receive( ) method then passes that value as a parameter to a function called ProcessValue( ) also in the VRTK Action class (Figure 8-30). The ProcessValue( ) class in turn sends a delegate that updates the Interactor Facade's Grab Action property with the most recent boolean value—true if the user has pressed the right grip trigger button down further than 75%, and false if they have not.

```
/// <summary>
/// Processes the given value and emits the appropriate events.
/// </summary>
/// <param name="value">The new value.</param>
protected virtual void ProcessValue(TValue value)
{
    Value = value;

    bool shouldActivate = ShouldActivate(value);
    if (IsActivated != shouldActivate)
    {
        IsActivated = shouldActivate;
        EmitActivationState();
    }
    else
    {
        ValueChanged?.Invoke(Value);
    }
}
```

Figure 8-30. *The Boolean Action* `Receive()` *method calls the* `ProcessValue()` *method, which invokes a delegate whose responsibility it is to update the Interactable object's* `GrabAction` *property with a true or false* `BooleanAction` *value. This complex chain of event messaging is what VRTK conveniently, and invisibly, handles for us*

We connect the `BooleanAction.Receive()` method with the `InteractorFacade.GrabAction` property by simply dragging and dropping the RightTriggerPressed game object, the game object to which we've attached the `Boolean Action Receive()` method, into the GrabAction field on the RightControllerAlias's Interactor child's Interactor Facade component (Figure 8-31).

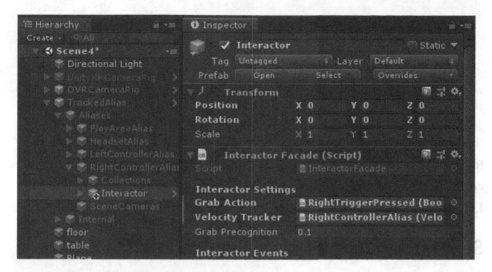

Figure 8-31. *Dragging and dropping the RightTriggerPressed game object into the Interactor Facade's Grab Action field wires up all the communication scripting that VRTK handles behind the scenes. Such is the convenience provided by a facade design pattern*

With the Grab Action property on our Interactor connected with the Axis 1D Action component, we have successfully wired up our chain of events from user input to object interactable. To review, the chain of events transpires as follows:

1. User pulls trigger.

2. Unity Axis 1D Action Value Changed event fires.

3. At 75% pressure Float to Boolean Transformed event fires.

4. Float value converted to bool.

5. Bool value received by Boolean Action Receive event.

6. Sends the bool value to the Grab Action property on the Interactor prefab.

7. The Interactor prefab attaches to the users' virtual hand to simulate grabbing and moving an object.

Save the scene and press Play to test the application. When you are through, if everything has worked according to plan, and you are able to pick up the interactable shapes by gripping the correct trigger on the controller, then repeat the steps we covered to create a Grab Action for the Left Trigger Grip button.

Step 11: Add User Interface Canvas Object to Scene

One fundamental element of VR design we have not addressed yet is UI design. The UI of an application is the client-facing portion that often handles visual input and output. Text, for example, is a common, simple component of UI design.

Unity offers a graphical text library through its package manager called TextMeshPro. Navigate to the Unity Package Manager through the Window tab of the menu and download the Text Mesh Pro library (Figure 8-32).

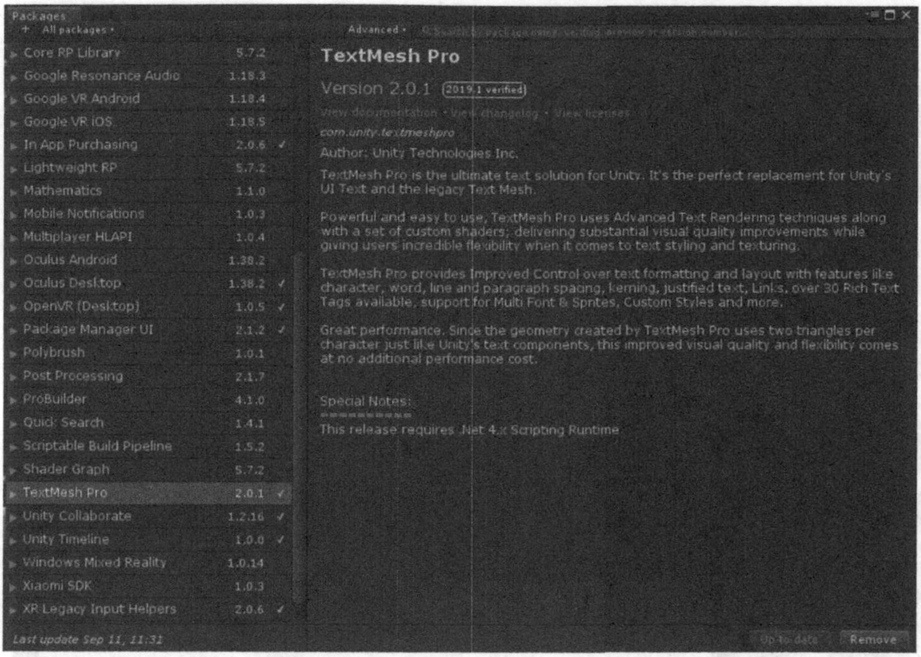

Figure 8-32. *The TextMesh Pro library, available through the Unity Package Manager, provides features for creating custom UI assets*

Once the library has been added to Unity, right-click in the Scene Hierarchy and select UI ➤ Text - TextMeshPro (Figure 8-33).

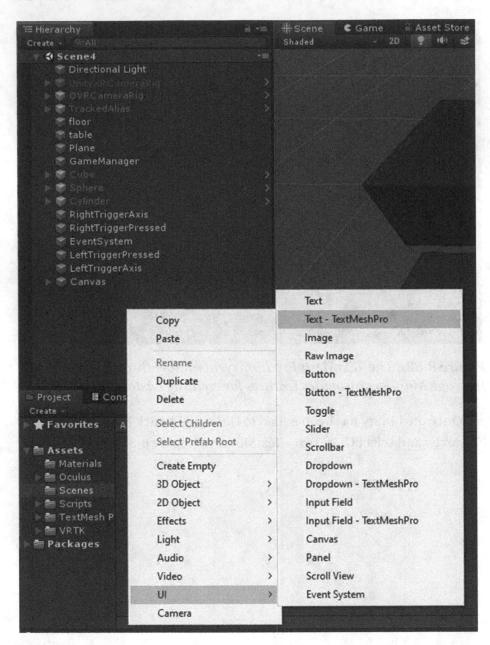

Figure 8-33. *Right-click in the Scene Hierarchy to add a TextMeshPro object to the scene*

A Canvas with a Text child and an EventSystem object will appear. With the Canvas object selected, turn your attention to the Inspector. A Canvas object in Unity comes with four components. The second component, Canvas, has a property called Render Mode, which has three options in its drop-down menu: Screen Space - Overlay, Screen Space - World, and World Space. Select World Space, leaving the Event Camera field empty as shown in Figure 8-34.

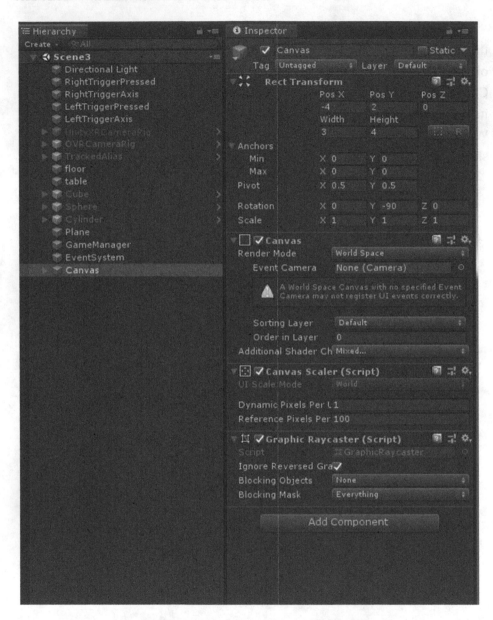

Figure 8-34. *The Render Mode parameter of the Canvas component determines where the Canvas will render its UI objects*

Set the Rect Transform properties of the Canvas object to the values shown in Figure 8-34.

Step 12: Add a Second TextMeshPro Object as a Child to the Canvas Object

With the Canvas object selected in the Hierarchy, right-click and add a second Text - TextMeshPro object. Name the first text object Text_go and the second object Text_response.

Set the Rect Transform properties of each text object to the values shown in Figures 8-35 and 8-36.

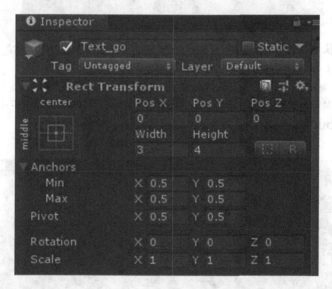

Figure 8-35. *Rect Transform settings are shown for the Text_go game object*

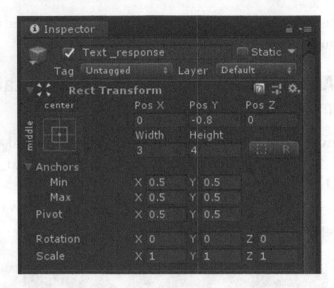

Figure 8-36. *Rect Transform settings are shown for the Text_response game object*

Once you have set the Canvas and TextMesh objects' properties in the Inspector, your scene should resemble Figure 8-37.

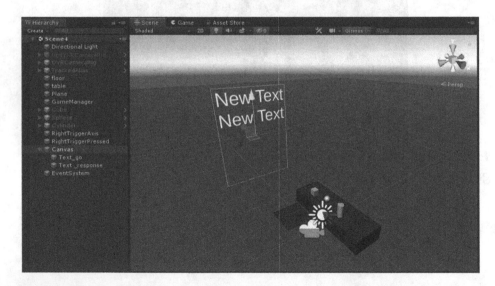

Figure 8-37. *This is a view of the Canvas object rendered in World Space*

If you play-test the scene you should see the text fields appear slightly above your head to the left through your HMD. You can set the parameters of the Canvas and text object transforms to your liking.

The larger takeaway from adding the Canvas object and its TextMeshPro children is the role of the Render Mode property on the Canvas's Canvas component. Placing a Canvas in a scene in World Space allows us to manipulate the size and appearance of the Canvas relative to the size and appearance of other objects in our scene. As it is a game object unto itself, the Canvas and its children reside in our scene just like every other game object, and like every other game object we can transform the value of its properties through scripting, even its text.

Part 2: The Code

By now you've learned all there is to know about connecting Interactors and Interactables in a Unity scene using VRTK. Without touching any C# code, you leveraged the Unity Event System to create event handlers, assign publishers, assign listeners, send delegates, and fire events.

What's All This Talk of Delegates?

Delegates are usually discussed in advanced sections of C# instruction. For the scope of this book, it is sufficient to understand a delegate as a variable for a function. Much like variables, which can store the values of objects, delegates can store the value of a function. The principles of OOP frown on exposing the innards of classes to other classes. As a result, accessing the methods of classes from outside their scope can be difficult. The benefit is loosely coupled code; the cost is the overhead of extra planning. By storing the values of functions, delegates serve as a messenger service that can call functions between classes. VRTK Actions and Unity Events are a relative of delegates in this regard.

What follows is a quick and dirty prototype of a program that executes the logic of Dr. Pallavi's test. Whereas she, as the physician, can control the flow and pace of the exercise in person, in a virtual application we need software to serve the role of adjudicator. The detail of the code I have written is beyond the scope of our lessons together, but it is available on the course GitHub page with commentary. I have taken pains to keep the code limited to concepts we have already discussed in this book. Although the code is not production-ready, I do feel it adequately stays within the scope of our lessons. I include images of the complete code in this text, but I only sparingly draw attention to its details for the sake of both clarity and brevity.

Step 1: Set Up the GameManager Script

To begin, create a folder called Scripts in your Assets folder in the Project window and create a new C# script. Name the script GameManager and open it in your IDE. Beneath the class title define eight public properties: three GameObjects called "shape" 1, 2, 3, respectively, and three Vector3 objects called "origin" 0, 1, 2, respectively. Create two public arrays, one of type GameObject and one of type Vector3.

Finally, create a Marquee property called marquee, a Collector property called collector, and an integer property called round and initialize it to 0. The content of the script should appear as shown in Figure 8-38.

```
public class GameManager : MonoBehaviour
{
    public GameObject[] shapes_array;
    public GameObject shape1;
    public GameObject shape2;
    public GameObject shape3;

    public Vector3[] origins_array = new Vector3[3];
    public Vector3 Origin0;
    public Vector3 Origin1;
    public Vector3 Origin2;

    Marquee marquee;
    Collector collector;

    public int round = 0;
```

Figure 8-38. *Define the public properties of the GameManager class in Visual Studio 2017*

The Start() function of the GameManager class does the following:

1. Creates an array of three indexes called shapes_ array, which holds three shape objects of type GameObject.

2. Creates an array of three indexes called origins_ array, which holds three Vector3 objects that save the starting location of the three interactable shape objects in our scene.

3. Stores references to the Plane, Collector, and Marquee objects in our scene.

What's an Array?

An array is a primitive data structure that holds objects in indexes. The first index of an array is conventionally identified as index 0. Arrays commonly hold collections of values that together comprise a set. Notably, arrays in C# require an exact number of indexes specified on creation. Capping the size of an array at compile time allows the computer to allot the exact amount of memory required to store the collection.

You might also notice that in the Start() function of the GameManager class we added two original components to the Plane object in our scene (Figure 8-39). These original components are original classes I created called Marquee and Collector. If you're following along with your own IDE, the Collector and Marquee data types probably appear with a red line beneath them indicating an error. To correct this, let's create our original classes.

```
// Start is called before the first frame update
void Start()
{
    // setup the game array
    shapes_array = new GameObject[3];
    shapes_array[0] = shape1;
    shapes_array[1] = shape2;
    shapes_array[2] = shape3;

    // create a known origins array for each shape
    Origin0 = shapes_array[0].GetComponent<Transform>().position;
    Origin1 = shapes_array[1].GetComponent<Transform>().position;
    Origin2 = shapes_array[2].GetComponent<Transform>().position;
    origins_array[0] = Origin0;
    origins_array[1] = Origin1;
    origins_array[2] = Origin2;

    // Locate the "Trigger Plane" game object
    GameObject plane = GameObject.Find("Plane");

    // Attach the Collector component to the trigger plane
    plane.AddComponent<Collector>();

    // connect the GameManager script to the collector component on the trigger plane
    collector = plane.GetComponent<Collector>();

    // attach a marquee to the trigger plane to receive broadcast
    plane.AddComponent<Marquee>();

    //connect the GameManager script to the marquee component on the trigger plane
    marquee = plane.GetComponent<Marquee>();
```

Figure 8-39. *The GameManager's* Start() *method adds two original components to the Plane object in our scene*

Step 2: Create the Marquee and Collector Classes

Back in Unity, create two new scripts in your Scripts folder: Marquee.cs and Collector.cs. In the Marquee class, create the properties as seen in Figure 8-40.

```
public class Marquee : MonoBehaviour
{
    public string object_name;
    public bool isCorrect;

    GameManager gameManager;
    Collector collector;

    TextMeshProUGUI textMesh_go;
    TextMeshProUGUI textMesh_response;
```

Figure 8-40. *The properties of the* Marquee *class are shown here*

In the Collector class, create the properties shown in Figure 8-41.

```
public class Collector : MonoBehaviour
{
    public string objectName;
    public string collected_ObjectName;
    public GameObject collectedObject;
```

Figure 8-41. *Create the properties of the* Collector *class shown here*

In the Marquee class, create a function called void Awake() and copy its code block from Figure 8-42.

```
private void Awake()
{
    TextMeshProUGUI[] textMeshes = FindObjectsOfType<TextMeshProUGUI>();
    foreach(TextMeshProUGUI textMesh in textMeshes)
    {
        if(textMesh.name == "Text_go")
        {
            textMesh_go = textMesh;
        }
        else
        {
            textMesh_response = textMesh;
            textMesh_response.text = null;
        }
    }

    gameManager = FindObjectOfType<GameManager>();
    collector = FindObjectOfType<Collector>();
}
```

Figure 8-42. *The* Awake() *method is part of the UnityEngine library,
like* Start() *and* Update()*.* Awake() *is like* Start() *except Unity
calls the Awake method before the* Start() *method, which it calls
immediately before the first Update.*

The Awake() function in the Marquee script executes before Unity
calls the Start function in the GameManager class, even though the
GameManager's Start() function initializes the Marquee object. It is a good
rule of thumb to use the Awake() method on a MonoBehaviour to initialize
any components that need to be present before the game loop executes.

In the Marquee class, the Awake function essentially stores references to
the TextMeshPro objects we placed as children of the Canvas object in the
Scene Hierarchy. In this regard, the Marquee script controls the appearance
of the billboard, or marquee, represented by the Canvas in the scene. Using
the FindObjectOfType() method, which is also part of the UnityEngine
code library, the Marquee class stores references to the other classes in our
project.

Beware: Tightly Coupled Classes

Storing references to other classes in a class is a great way to stumble into bad coding behavior. The result is what is called tightly coupled code. Tightly coupled code leads to spaghetti code, the horrible condition of interdependent logic with the potential to break at every point of connection. As the master of software architecture, Grady Booch, noted, designing classes and their interactions is a fine art derived through iteration. It is near impossible to write loosely coupled code on a first pass. As this application is an exercise in prototyping, I won't stress ideal software design composition. It is valuable to understand that although loosely coupled code is the goal, perfection cannot be the enemy of good when prototyping rapidly through iteration. However, as always, practice makes perfect.

If the GameManager is the brains of our application, setting everything up and coordinating the flow of control, and the Marquee class is the logic of our Canvas billboard, what then is the Collector class?

Step 3: Create a Trigger Collider

Returning to the Unity Scene Hierarchy in the Unity Editor, we can find the Plane game object we created in Step 3 of Part 1 in this exercise. Selecting the Plane object and opening its properties in the Inspector, notice the component called Mesh Collider. There are two check boxes at the top of the Mesh Collider components: Convex and Is Trigger. Select both check boxes as shown in Figure 8-43.

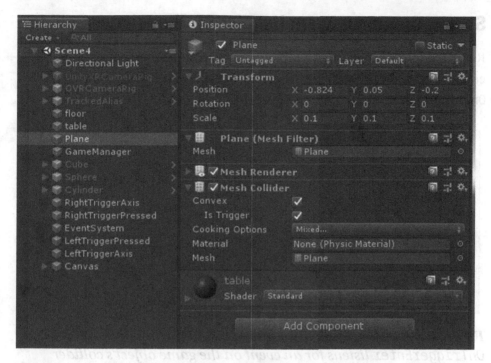

Figure 8-43. *Check the Convex and Is Trigger check boxes on the Plane object's Mesh Collider component*

Selecting both Convex and Is Trigger creates an actionable area around the Plane object. Any object with a RigidBody component attached can trigger an event on entering the Plane's mesh collider. Because the Interactable prefabs we dragged and dropped from the VRTK prefab folder have RigidBody components attached to them by default, they have the potential to trigger an action on entering the Plane's mesh collider. We will use this trigger event handling feature of the Plane's mesh collider to prompt a change in our Marquee object.

Step 4: Create an Event Handler for the Trigger Collider

Return to the Collector.cs script in your IDE and create a function called void OnTriggerEnter. Copy the signature and body of the OnTriggerEnter method from Figure 8-44.

```
private void OnTriggerEnter(Collider other)
{
    Debug.Log(other.gameObject.GetComponentInChildren<MeshFilter>().name);

    this.collected_ObjectName = other.gameObject.GetComponentInChildren<MeshFilter>().name;
    this.collectedObject = other.gameObject;
    if (this.objectName == this.collected_ObjectName)
    {
        BroadcastMessage("SetCorrect", true);
    }
    else
    {
        BroadcastMessage("SetCorrect", false);
    }
}
```

Figure 8-44. *Unity implicitly understands a method named OnTriggerEnter listens for an event on the game object's collider*

When the Is Trigger and Convex check boxes are selected on a mesh collider, Unity knows to listen for an OnTriggerEnter event handler. We are then free to wire up the event handler to the action we'd like to drive as a result. The code I have written in the body of the OnTriggerEnter() method stores the name of the shape entering the Plane's mesh collider and compares it to the name of the shape the Marquee is expecting for a correct answer (CUPCAKE!). If the shape the user drops into the collider matches the shape the billboard asked the user to select, then my script sends a message to the other components on its game object (Figure 8-45).

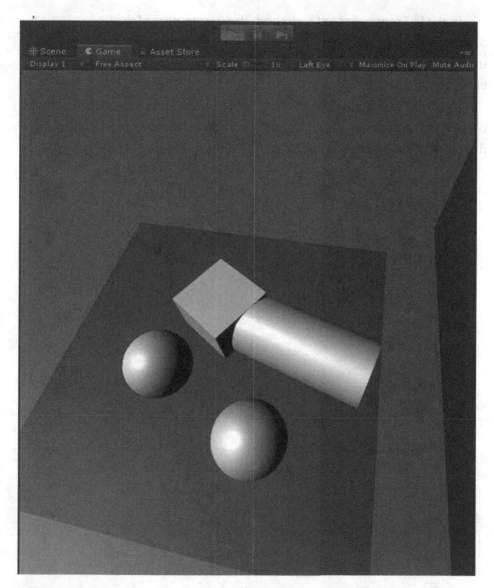

Figure 8-45. *Interactable objects dropped on the Plane object fire the plane collider's* OnTriggerEnter() *method, which exists in the* Collector *class attached to the Plane as a component*

In the OnTriggerEnter() method, the parameters of the BroadcastMessage() function, which comes from the Component class of the UnityEngine code library, are the name of the function to call and the value to send to it.

If you are wondering how the Collector class knows the name of the object the Marquee class is expecting for a correct answer, then look at the final line of the GameManager's Start() method (Figure 8-46).

```
// Start is called before the first frame update
void Start()
{
    // setup the game array
    shapes_array = new GameObject[3];
    shapes_array[0] = shape1;
    shapes_array[1] = shape2;
    shapes_array[2] = shape3;

    // create a known origins array for each shape
    Origin0 = shapes_array[0].GetComponent<Transform>().position;
    Origin1 = shapes_array[1].GetComponent<Transform>().position;
    Origin2 = shapes_array[2].GetComponent<Transform>().position;
    origins_array[0] = Origin0;
    origins_array[1] = Origin1;
    origins_array[2] = Origin2;

    // locate the "Trigger Plane" game object
    GameObject plane = GameObject.Find("Plane");

    // Attach the Collector component to the trigger plane
    plane.AddComponent<Collector>();

    // connect the GameManager script to the collector component on the trigger plane
    collector = plane.GetComponent<Collector>();

    // attach a marquee to the trigger plane to receive broadcast
    plane.AddComponent<Marquee>();

    // connect the GameManager script to the marquee component on the trigger plane
    marquee = plane.GetComponent<Marquee>();

    // load the first shape into the marquee
    this.SetMarqueeObjectName(round);

}
```

Figure 8-46. *The GameManager, in its Start() method, calls a function on itself that sets the application in motion. The this keyword that precedes the function call refers to the fact that the method exists on the object that is calling it. In this context, this refers to the GameManager object created by Unity on the application's start*

Step 5: Create a Method to Tell User Which Shape to Select

The final line of the GameManager class's Start() method calls a method on the GameManager class called SetMarqueeObjectName(). I define the signature and body of the method below the Start() method in the GameManager class (Figure 8-47).

```
public void SetMarqueeObjectName(int round)
{
    if (round < this.shapes_array.Length)
    {
        marquee.object_name = shapes_array[round].name;

        marquee.WriteToObject(marquee.object_name);
        this.SetCollectorObjectName(marquee);
    }

    else
    {
        this.GameOver();
    }

}
```

Figure 8-47. *Because the GameManager class's Start() method stored a reference to the Marquee class, a method defined in the GameManager class can call a public method defined in the Marquee class. Events and delegates are more mature mechanisms for handling interclass communication than publicly defined methods*

The SetMarqueeObjectName() method takes an integer as a parameter. The integer represents the "round" of the test the user is in. Each round corresponds to one shape object in the GameManager's shapes_array collection, which is comprised of the interactable objects we placed in our scene—cube, sphere, and cylinder. As long as the round number is lower than the number of shapes in our array (considering we initialized our "round" variable to begin at zero), the Marquee object will broadcast what shape the user is to select to the billboard in our scene. The GameManager asks the Marquee to set the name of the object it would like the user to select by calling the Marquee's WriteToObject() method and passing as a parameter the name of the shape pulled from the array.

Step 6: Create a Method to Tell Collector Which Shape Is Correct

The SetMarqueeObjectName() method in the GameManager class also calls another function on the GameManager object through the code, this.Set CollectorObjectName(marquee). Beneath the SetMarqueeObjectName() method on the GameManager class, I have created another method called— you guessed it—SetCollectorObjectName(), as shown in Figure 8-48.

```
public void SetCollectorObjectName(Marquee marquee)
{
    collector.objectName = marquee.object_name;
}
```

Figure 8-48. *Chaining methods to access public properties in different classes is the type of bad coding practice events and delegates exist to replace. However, understanding how to connect classes through events in a rudimentary fashion leads to deeper appreciation of the structural complexity the VRTK interface and the Unity Event system abstract away*

Called by the SetMarqueeObjectName() method,
SetCollectorObjectName() sets the objectName property on the
Collector class equal to the name of the shape the Marquee has broadcast
to the user to select.

When you've completed the scripts, the Marquee object will instruct
the Canvas object to display the name of the first shape in the GameManager
shapes_array in the TextMeshPro Text_go text object (Figure 8-49). By
storing a reference to this shape's name in its own member variable, the
Collector object, attached to the Plane trigger collider game object,
knows what shape entering the Plane's mesh collider triggers a correct
response.

Figure 8-49. *The name of the first interactable in our scene arrives on the Canvas object through an event passing pipeline provided by the Marquee class*

The Collector's `OnTriggerEnter` method grabs the name of the RigidBody entering the Plane's mesh collider trigger sensor and stores it in its member variable `collected_objectName`, as shown in Figure 8-50. Because the `GameManager` has already set the value of the Collector object's `objectName` property in its `SetCollectorObjectName()` method, the Collector knows what shape the Marquee object has instructed the user to select through the Canvas's text field.

```
public class Collector : MonoBehaviour
{
    public string objectName;
    public string collected_ObjectName;
    public GameObject collectedObject;

    private void OnTriggerEnter(Collider other)
    {
        Debug.Log(other.gameObject.GetComponentInChildren<MeshFilter>().name);

        this.collected_ObjectName = other.gameObject.GetComponentInChildren<MeshFilter>().name;
        this.collectedObject = other.gameObject;
        if (this.objectName == this.collected_ObjectName)
        {
            BroadcastMessage("SetCorrect", true);
        }
        else
        {
            BroadcastMessage("SetCorrect", false);
        }
    }
}
```

Figure 8-50. *The* `Collector` *class contains the logic that will evaluate whether the shape dropped by the user into the Plane collider matches the name of the shape published to the Marquee*

If the value of the `objectName` variable matches the value of the `collected_objectName` value, then the Collector broadcasts a message to the other components attached to its game object, calling the `SetCorrect` method and passing as a parameter the value `true`.

In its `Start()` method, the `GameManager` class also set the Collector and Marquee objects, which both derive from the `MonoBehaviour` class, as

components of the Plane game object that holds the mesh collider trigger
(Figure 8-51). Because the Collector and Marquee objects both exist as
components on the same game object, Plane, they can communicate via
the BroadcastMessage() function, which exists on every Unity
Component class.

```
// Start is called before the first frame update
void Start()
{
    // setup the game array
    shapes_array = new GameObject[3];
    shapes_array[0] = shape1;
    shapes_array[1] = shape2;
    shapes_array[2] = shape3;

    // create a known origins array for each shape
    Origin0 = shapes_array[0].GetComponent<Transform>().position;
    Origin1 = shapes_array[1].GetComponent<Transform>().position;
    Origin2 = shapes_array[2].GetComponent<Transform>().position;
    origins_array[0] = Origin0;
    origins_array[1] = Origin1;
    origins_array[2] = Origin2;

    // Locate the "Trigger Plane" game object
    GameObject plane = GameObject.Find("Plane");

    // Attach the Collector component to the trigger plane
    plane.AddComponent<Collector>();

    // connect the GameManager script to the collector component on the trigger plane
    collector = plane.GetComponent<Collector>();

    // attach a marquee to the trigger plane to receive broadcast
    plane.AddComponent<Marquee>();

    //connect the GameManager script to the marquee component on the trigger plane
    marquee = plane.GetComponent<Marquee>();

    // load the first shape into the marquee
    this.SetMarqueeObjectName(round);

}
```

Figure 8-51. The GameManager's Start() function attaches
Marquee and Collector components on to the Plane object to establish
communication between the Canvas and the trigger collider

Step 7: Define a Listener Function for the OnTriggerEnter Event Handler

Speaking of which, the BroadcastMessage() method called from the Collector's OnTriggerEnter() event handler requests a message from all attached components within earshot (on the same game object) to call a method called SetCorrect and set as its argument either true or false, depending on whether the user has provided the same shape expected by the Marquee.

SetCorrect is a method I created in the Marquee class to control the value of its isCorrect member variable (Figure 8-52). The logic of the function isn't germane to the larger lesson we're addressing so I won't go too deep into it. It is sufficient to explain that if the user's answer is correct, then the Marquee writes "Correct" to the Canvas object (Figure 8-53), moves the application into the next "round," and writes "Game Over" to the Canvas when no more shapes exist in the GameManager's shapes_array.

```
public void SetCorrect(bool value)
{
    isCorrect = value;

    if (isCorrect == true)
    {
        Debug.Log(true);
        textMesh_response.SetText("Correct!");
        gameManager.round++;
        if (gameManager.round < gameManager.shapes_array.Length)
        {
            this.object_name = gameManager.shapes_array[gameManager.round].name;
            collector.collected_ObjectName = null;
            gameManager.SetMarqueeObjectName(gameManager.round);
        }
        else
        {
            gameManager.GameOver();
        }
    }

    else if (isCorrect == false)
    {
        Debug.Log(false);
        textMesh_response.text = "Wrong!";

        for (int i = 0; i < gameManager.shapes_array.Length; i++)
        {
            if(collector.collected_ObjectName == gameManager.shapes_array[i].name)
            {
                Instantiate(gameManager.shapes_array[i], gameManager.origins_array[i], Quaternion.identity);
            }
        }

        gameManager.SetMarqueeObjectName(gameManager.round);
    }
}
```

Figure 8-52. *The* SetCorrect() *method on the* Marquee *class responds to the* BroadcastMessage() *function called from the* Collector *class's* OnTriggerEnter() *method*

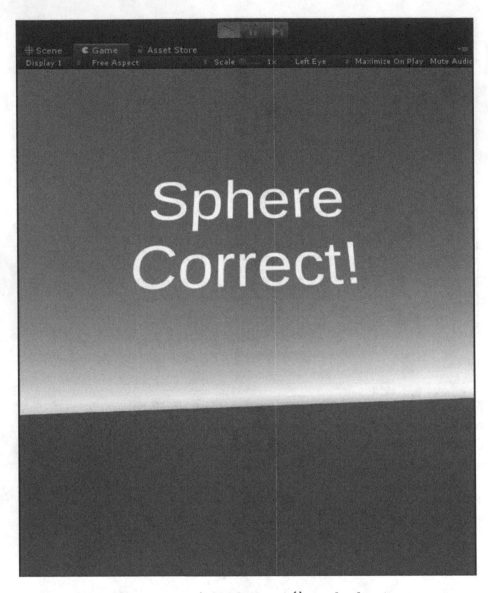

Figure 8-53. *The Marquee's* `SetCorrect()` *method writes the result of the* `Collector` *class's evaluation method to the* `TextMesh_reference` *object on the Canvas. A correct response prompts the text shown*

If the user's answer is incorrect, the function writes "Wrong" to the Canvas (Figure 8-54), replaces the shape selected by the user back to its origin, and moves the game to the next round.

Figure 8-54. *The Marquee's* SetCorrect() *method writes the result of the* Collector *class's evaluation method to the* TextMesh_reference *object on the Canvas. An incorrect response prompts the text shown*

Step 8: Create a `GameOver()` Method in the `GameManager` Class

Whether the user's answer is correct or incorrect, the `Marquee` class's `SetCorrect()` method moves the test into the next round by calling the `GameManager`'s `SetMarqueeObjectName()` method, the definition of which can be seen in Figure 8-55. Of course, as we've already seen, if the "round" is greater than the number of shapes in the scene, the program jumps to the `GameManager`'s `GameOver()` method.

```
public void GameOver()
{
    marquee.WriteToObject("");
    marquee.WriteToResponse("Game Over");
}
```

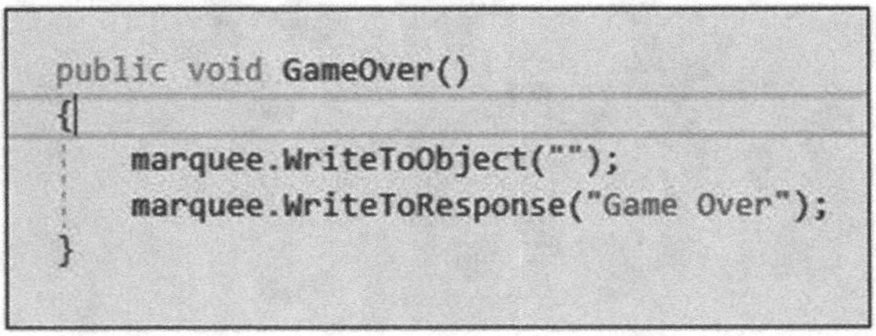

Figure 8-55. *The signature of the `GameOver()` method is defined in the `GameManager` class*

Step 9: Define Methods in the Marquee Class to Write to the Canvas Object's Text Fields

The `GameManager`'s `GameOver()` method makes a call to a function the `GameManager` has called once before in its `SetMarqueeObjectName()` method: `marquee.WriteToObject()`.

The `Marquee` class's `WriteToObject()` and `WriteToResponse()` methods set the words to appear in the TextMeshPro fields on the scene's Canvas object (Figure 8-56). The `Marquee` class saved references to the TextMeshPro game objects in its `Awake()` method.

```
public void WriteToObject(string word)
{
    textMesh_go.SetText(word);
}


public void WriteToResponse(string word)
{
    textMesh_response.SetText(word);
}
```

Figure 8-56. *The Marquee methods defined in the figure control the text that appears on the canvas*

Step 10: Connect the GameManager Script to an Empty Game Object

Finally, to connect our game logic to our Unity Scene, create an empty game object in the Scene Hierarchy in the Unity Editor and name it GameManager. If you have coded along with the exercise, attach the GameManager.cs script as a component to the GameManager game object.

Step 11: Drag and Drop the Interactable Shape Objects into the GameManager

In the Inspector, you will see the public properties exposed in the GameManager's class definition. Drag and drop the Interactable shape objects from the Scene Hierarchy into the fields of the GameManager's Shapes_array property (Figure 8-57). The values of the Origins_array property you can leave as is because they will be defined by Unity at runtime.

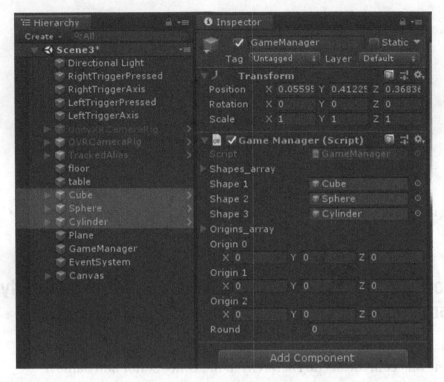

Figure 8-57. *Drag and drop the interactable shapes from the Scene Hierarchy into the GameManager object's Game Manager script to create references to the objects in code*

Step 12: Play-test

After making sure there are no errors in any of your scripts and that all files have been saved and compiled, press Play to test your scene. The scene should begin with the name of the shape to select broadcast to the Canvas in your HMD or monitor. If your touch controllers are activated, then holding the grip action triggers while hovering within the container of any interactable shape object should activate that shape's Grab Action. Dropping the incorrect shape onto the Plane trigger should reset the shape to its original position and write the incorrect selection text to the Canvas marquee. Correct responses should trigger a correct message.

After cycling through the shapes, the game loop should call Game Over in the Canvas's text (Figure 8-58).

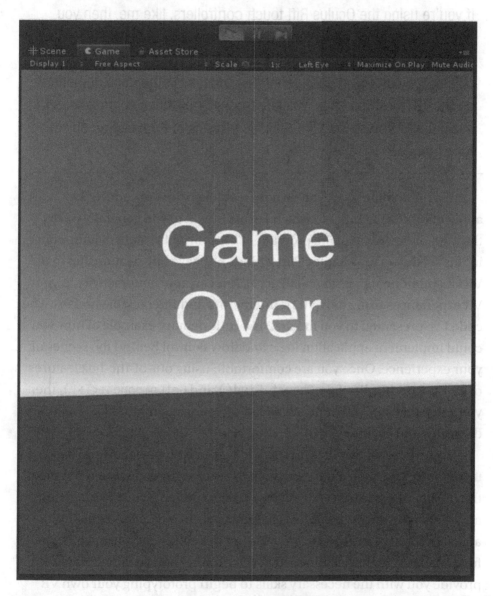

Figure 8-58. *The Game Manager's* GameOver() *method sends a string to the* Marquee *class to print to the canvas*

What's Up with My Velocity Tracking?

If you're using the Oculus Rift touch controllers, like me, then you have to go through a few more steps to correctly calibrate the velocity trackers on your controllers with the VRTK TrackedAlias object. You can find details about this process in the documentation on the VRTK GitHub page. Velocity tracking for touch controllers is essential for re-creating the realistic physics of throwing an object, for example.

In a roundabout way, you've now seen every line of code in the application. The manner in which I presented it to you generally traces the path of execution of the program. It's important to note that the code in this section of the chapter, Part 2, does not have any relationship to the VRTK components we set up in Part 1. You can apply interactivity to your VR experiences using only VRTK Interactors and Interactable prefabs. The code I've presented to you in Part 2 is a rudimentary example of how you could implement application logic and flow control behind the scenes of your experience. Once you are comfortable using out-of-the-box features of Unity scripting, like `GameObject.Find()` and `GetComponent<T>()`, then you can begin study of more advanced scripting techniques like custom delegates and events.

However, until then it is no small feat to prototype behavioral logic using Unity and C#, even if the design of your or my code would not meet the muster of a startup's code review. Design patterns such as Singletons and Mediators are tremendously helpful tools to create functionality and should serve as goals for your further development. Meanwhile, the fundamentals we have addressed in this chapter and so far in this book provide you with the necessary skills to begin prototyping your own VR experiences immediately. After all, updating game objects, such as text, in response to a user's input is but one example of many simple events achievable through beginning-level code that can facilitate convincing immersion in a VR scene.

Summary

Running Dr. Pallavi's test with the VRTK components wired up and the GameManager script applied provides a reasonable prototype for the doctor. She approves of the work we've done for her and looks forward to iterating the project with more bells and whistles.

In this chapter you added Interactable prefabs from the VRTK library into a scene. You facilitated user interaction with those prefabs by connecting the user's VR controllers with VRTK's Interactor prefabs. Using the VRTK Float to Boolean component, you converted a user's pressure on a trigger button into a yes/no event. Through C# code you created trigger events connected to game objects' Collider components. You used built-in Unity functions to broadcast messages to game objects to create complex logic, and you configured code to write dynamic text to a canvas in VR world space.

In the next and final chapter, we address the last looming concept in VR design left for us to explore: getting around a scene in a way that collapses geography into geometry. In other words, how do we create movement without moving? Until VR-synced omnidirectional treadmills become commonplace, it is our responsibility as immersive experience designers to devise ways for users to travel through a scene while taking into account the limitations of their bodies, systems, and environments. Fortunately, VRTK has tools for that. They're called Pointers and Locomotion, and we dive into them next.

CHAPTER 9

Movement in VR

We've made it. Here begins the final chapter in our journey together. We've gone from an introduction of the vertex to the creation of interactive VR scenes with dynamic UI text. What's taken me four years to understand, you hopefully have grasped within the confines of these pages. There's still one more feature of VR design that we have not addressed.

In this chapter you will do the following:

- Learn the principles of movement in VR.

- Explore how to design VR for user comfort.

- Create your own VR building and environment.

- Add the ability to move around a virtual scene while wearing a headset.

- Write a simple sorting algorithm to locate the nearest game object.

The Elusive Nature of Movement

Movement in VR is an odd concept. Throughout the exercises we have already completed, we have dealt with vectors, which define the length and direction of a line in space. The physics engine within Unity uses vectors to calculate physics properties like force. Unity even has functions that handle the creation of simulated gravity. All of these parameters affect

© Rakesh Baruah 2020
R. Baruah, *Virtual Reality with VRTK4*, https://doi.org/10.1007/978-1-4842-5488-2_9

what we, in our real lives, understand to be movement. Yet, movement in VR can be a very tricky thing.

The reasons for movement's complicated relationship with VR are things we explore shortly. First, though, it'll be helpful to come to a clear understanding of the types of movement in VR.

Movement vs. Motion

Movement, as I use it in the context of this chapter, is distinct from motion. Motion, for the sake of our conversation, is the act of objects traveling between two points over time. In Chapter 8, the action performed by our interactors on interactables included motion. With our controllers, we moved interactable shapes from a table to a bin. The shapes underwent the process of motion, which itself was the product of force, mass, and gravity. Movement, however, I define as something more psychological. Movement, in my definition for the basis of the exercises to follow, is the impact motion of the virtual camera in our environment has on the user. Movement, therefore, is subjective. It requires consciousness. It is the name of the valley between expectation and reality.

Perhaps the most obvious example of movement as a mental model is the distinction between 3DoF and 6DoF VR headsets. DoF is an acronym that stands for degrees of freedom. A VR headset that offers three degrees of freedom, like the Oculus Go or the Google Daydream View, tracks a user's head movement through the three axes related to rotation. In a 3DoF headset, users can rotate their head in any direction. They cannot, however, move their position, or translate their position. If users were to try to translate their position while wearing a 3DoF headset, by walking, for example, then they would immediately become dizzy. Although their brain tells the user they are moving forward, for example, the headset cannot update its image to match the user's translation of position. The 3DoF headset can only track users' rotational head movement, not the movement of their body through space. On the other hand, 6DoF VR headsets, like the Oculus Rift, the Oculus Quest, and the HTC Vive, track not only a user's three degrees of rotation, but also their three degrees of movement through space—forward, backward, and sideways.

Although some VR experts might argue that headsets with more DoF allow for a deeper sense of immersion in a VR scene, I'd argue that it is how we, as VR developers, embrace the strengths and limitations of different headsets that influence the immersive power of a VR scene.

VRTK Tools for Movement

Whether you are designing for a 3DoF or 6DoF headset, VRTK offers specific tools in its Pointers and Locomotion libraries to help streamline the creation of movement actions for users. Pointers in VRTK refer to the design elements that allow a user to visualize direction and distance through the use of a touch controller. Straight VRTK pointers operate like laser pointers, whereas curved VRTK pointers function like parabolas. Locomotion in VRTK refers to the movement, or translation, of a user's position in virtual space. Two popular examples of locomotion in VRTK are dash locomotion and teleportation.

Before we get into the shortcuts VRTK offers developers for creating user movement in a VR scene, let's first build up the foundation of this chapter's exercise.

Exercise: Virtual Tour Guide

Placido Farmiga is a world-renowned contemporary artist. He's bringing his most recent collection, which wowed at the Pompidou Center in Paris, to the Milwaukee Contemporary Art Museum in Milwaukee, Wisconsin. As tickets for the event sold out in minutes, the museum has asked Penny Powers, an associate in the member services department, to help design a VR experience that museum members who were unable to purchase tickets can use to experience Placido's work remotely.

As Penny in this exercise, you will do the following:

- Create a building environment using only primitive Unity objects.

- Create a C# script that moves a virtual camera through a scene.

- Create a button action that controls UI events.

Creating the Environment

As always, before we begin the exercise, create a new Unity 3D project. This time, however, we won't immediately mark our project for VR support. We won't install XR Legacy Input Mappings or the VRTK files, just yet. First, we'll set up a standard 3D scene to begin our understanding of movement in VR.

Step 1: Create the Foundations of a Building

In previous examples we've imported 3D models created by different artists to serve as environments and props in our scenes. Convincing 3D models of large spaces, however, are difficult to find and even harder to create. The few that do exist for our use cost money. As I cannot in good conscience ask you to spend any more money than you've already spent purchasing this book, I will instead show you how you can prototype your own 3D environment inside Unity.

The process is tedious to describe and not unlike the creation of game objects we've gone through in previous chapters. Table 9-1 displays the transform settings I have used for primitive cubes to create the walls for my model of the fictional Milwaukee Contemporary Art Museum.

Table 9-1. Transform Values for Primitive Cube Objects as the Walls for My Museum

Transform Values	Wall	Wall_2	Wall_3	Wall_4	Wall_5	Wall_6	Wall_7	Wall_8	Wall_9
Position x	-10.98	-20.24	2.17	6.19	24.59	-10.98	-10.98	-16.12	11.41
Position y	0.122	0.122	0.122	0.122	0.122	0.122	0.122	0.122	0.122
Position z	-12.60	-12.17	2.62	-13.28	-11.99	-24.48	-0.18	-25.91	-25.63
Rotation x	0	0	0	0	0	0	0	0	0
Rotation y	0	0	0	0	0	0	0	0	90
Rotation z	0	0	0	0	0	0	0	0	0
Scale x	1.02	1	1.09	1	1	1.02	1.02	1.02	1.01
Scale y	4	4	4	4	4	4	4	4	4
Scale z	9.71	28.50	45.83	12.97	28.15	3.87	6.40	9.26	27.36

Use Table 9-1 and the image in Figure 9-1 as a reference for the design of your own contemporary art museum. After you have created the Floor object of the museum and one Wall object, pause to add Materials and Textures to the assets.

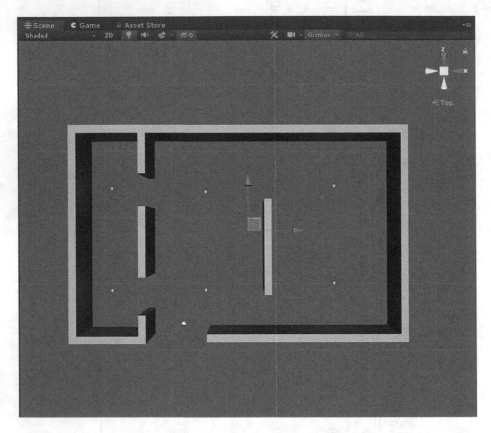

Figure 9-1. *This is an overhead view of the building layout*

Step 2: Add Materials and Textures to the Environment

To add Materials to the Floor and Wall objects, first create a new folder called Materials in your Assets folder. Create a new Material object, name it Floor, and change its Albedo color to something you prefer in the Inspector.

Do the same for a Material you name Wall. After creating both materials, add each to its respective game object in the Scene Hierarchy.

In the Scene Hierarchy, select the Wall object to which you've added the material component. In the Inspector, expand the Material component. With the Material components attached to the Floor and Wall objects in our scene, we can manipulate the textures of the objects to give our scene a bit more believability.

First, download the assets for this exercise from the course GitHub page at http://www.apress.com/source-code.

Second, import the assets into the Assets folder of your Unity project. Locate the asset called rough-plaster-normal-ogl.png in the Project window. Select the Normal Map property radio button in the Main Maps section of the Material component (Figure 9-2). Navigate to the rough-plaster-normal-ogl.png file to select it as the Normal Map for the Wall material.

Figure 9-2. *Set textures in the Material component*

Select the radio button next to the Metallic property beneath Main Maps on the Material component, too. Navigate to the project asset called rough-plaster-metallic.psd. Select it and close the menu. Use the Smoothness slider beneath the Metallic property to set the value for your desired smoothness.

Finally, beneath the heading Secondary Maps on the Wall's Material component, select the radio button next to the Normal Map property. Set the secondary normal map to the asset called rough-plaster-ao.png.

To apply textures to the Floor object in your scene, expand the object in the Hierarchy and its Material component in the Inspector. If you'd like to add the carpet texture I've provided in the chapter assets, then set the Main Albedo Map to worn-braided-carpet-albedo.png; apply the worn-braided-carpet-Normal-ogl.png asset to the Main Normal Map property; and set the worn-braided-carpet-Height.png as the Height Map (Figure 9-3). You can also use the Albedo color picker to change the color of the texture asset you've added as an Albedo. I downloaded all the texture assets for the objects from a web site called FreePBR.com, where PBR stands for physically based rendering. If you'd like to select other texture assets for your scene, you can find more at that site.

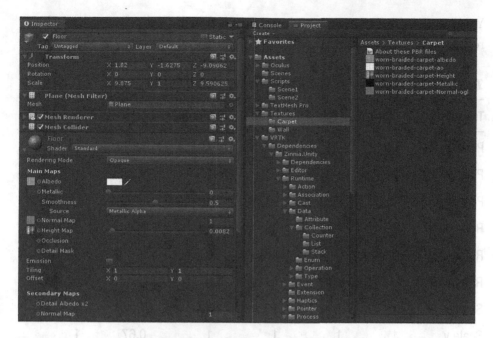

Figure 9-3. *You can select Texture settings for the floor's material*

After you've set the material and texture parameters for the building in your scene, copy the objects in the Scene Hierarchy to which you've added the Material and Texture components by selecting them individually and pressing Ctrl+D. Creating all additional wall objects from the original wall object that holds material and texture information will streamline the prototyping process. You will only have to set the material and texture properties once. The properties will cascade to all clones of the object.

Step 3: Add Lights to the Environment

Because materials and textures respond to light, add point light objects to the Hierarchy and place them around the scene. Deactivate the ceiling game object in the Inspector Window if it blocks your view of the building's interior while you are fine-tuning the details of the environment.

You can use the Transform settings I applied to the lights in my scene by referring to Table 9-2 and the image in Figure 9-4.

Table 9-2. *Transform Values for the Lights in the Scene*

Transform	Light	Light 1	Light 2	Light 3	Light 4	Light 5
Position x	-2.48	-12.28	-15.28	-2.48	15.22	15.22
Position y	1.37	1.37	1.37	1.37	1.37	1.37
Position z	-5.70	-19.29	-5.29	-19.19	-4.89	-18.30
Rotation x	90	90	90	90	90	90
Rotation y	0	0	0	0	0	0
Rotation z	0	0	0	0	0	0
Scale x	1	1	1	1	1	1
Scale y	1	1	1	1	0.67	1
Scale z	1	1	1	1	1	1

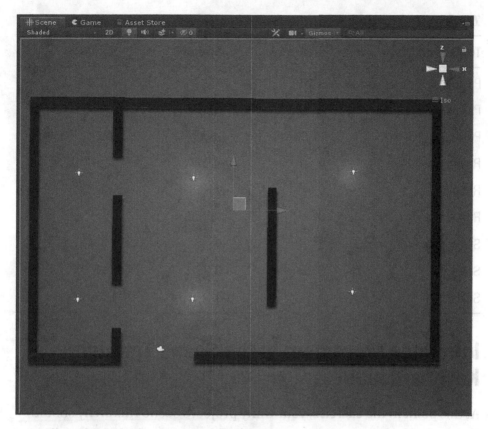

Figure 9-4. This is an overhead view of the light objects in the scene

Step 4: Add Sculptures to the Environment

Because our user story defines the setting of our scene as a museum, let's add primitive game objects that can serve as templates for art work in our scene. You can refer to Table 9-3 to use the Transform settings for three game objects I created called Statue_1, Statue_2, and Statue_3. Like the walls, I've formed the statues from primitive cube objects.

Table 9-3. *Transform Values for Statue Objects in the Scene*

Transform Values	Statue 1	Statue 2	Statue 3
Position x	-3.49	-1.11	-11.91
Position y	-0.44	-0.44	-0.44
Position z	11.03	-6.57	-5.14
Rotation x	0	27.17	0
Rotation y	0	113.85	-76.15
Rotation z	0	-17.88	0
Scale x	1	1	1
Scale y	3.25	3.25	3.25
Scale z	1	1	1

Introduce Movement to the Scene Through Keyboard Input

At this point in the exercise, your Unity project's Scene Hierarchy should include, at the least, a main camera; a building game object with walls, floor, ceiling, and point light child objects; and a statue object.

To introduce movement to the scene we will add two components: a CharacterController and a script. Because we want our users to feel as if they are moving through our museum, we will add the components to the Main Camera game object.

Step 1: Add a `CharacterController` Component to the Main Camera

Select the Main Camera game object in the Scene Hierarchy of your scene. In the Inspector, click Add Component, and search for

CharacterController. Add the `CharacterController` component to the
Main Camera game object as shown in Figure 9-5.

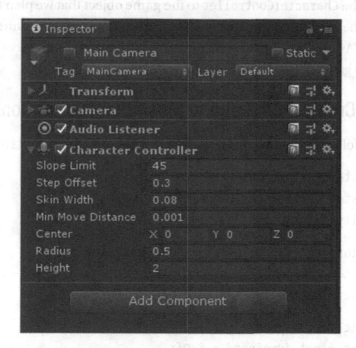

Figure 9-5. *The* CharacterController *on the Main Camera object*

What's a `CharacterController`?

The `CharacterController` is a class that inherits from the
`Collider` class in the Physics Module of the UnityEngine library.
Unity provides the `CharacterController` component as a
contained, easy-to-use `MonoBehaviour` that we can attach to an
object we'd like the user to control. As the `CharacterController`
does not contain a RigidBody component, it is not affected by
forces in the scene. Movement of the object to which it is attached,
therefore, will be under total control of the user.

The default settings of the CharacterController that appear in the Inspector are fine as is for this exercise. However, even though we have attached the CharacterController to the game object that we plan to move in our scene, we have not connected it to the input we aim to capture from our users. As we have done several times in this book, to create a connection between a game object and user input, we will create a C# script.

Step 2: Create a C# Script to Move the Camera Controller

Copy the following code into a new C# script named CameraController.

```
using System.Collections;
using System.Collections.Generic;
using UnityEngine;

public class CameraController : MonoBehaviour
{
    CharacterController characterController;

    public float speed = 6.0f;
    public float jumpSpeed = 8.0f;
    public float gravity = 20.0f;

    private Vector3 moveDirection = Vector3.zero;

    void Start()
    {
        characterController = GetComponent<CharacterController>();
    }

    void Update()
    {
        if (characterController.isGrounded)
        {
            // We are grounded, so recalculate
```

```
// move direction directly from axes

moveDirection = new Vector3(Input.
GetAxis("Horizontal"), 0.0f, Input.
GetAxis("Vertical"));
moveDirection *= speed;

if (Input.GetButton("Jump"))
{
    moveDirection.y = jumpSpeed;
}
}

// Apply gravity. Gravity is multiplied by deltaTime
twice (once here, and once below
// when the moveDirection is multiplied by deltaTime).
This is because gravity should be applied
// as an acceleration (ms^-2)

moveDirection.y -= gravity * Time.deltaTime;

// Move the controller
characterController.Move(moveDirection * Time.deltaTime);
}
}
```

The heart of the CameraController script, which I've repurposed
from the Unity documentation on the CharacterController class, lies
in its Vector3 variable moveDirection. The moveDirection variable
stores a Vector3 value created every frame update by the Input.
GetAxis() function, which takes as its argument the string names of the
horizontal and vertical axes. As we know from the Unity Input Manager,
the horizontal axis corresponds to the a, d, left, and right arrow buttons.
The vertical axis corresponds to the s, w, down, and up arrow buttons.
The Update() function of the CameraController script multiplies the

moveDirection variable by the speed parameter set in the Editor and subtracts from its y position the value of gravity, also set in the Editor. Finally, the CameraController script calls a Move() function on the CharacterController component of the game object to which it is attached.

The Move() function is a method created by Unity, available in its UnityEngine namespace, which Unity describes as, "a more complex move function taking absolute movement deltas" in a comment above its signature in the CharacterController class. If Unity describes a method as "more complex," then I feel confident concluding its details are beyond the scope of this exercise. Suffice it to say that the Move() function on the CharacterController component accepts the moveDirection variable as a parameter to create user-influenced character movement in our scene.

Step 3: Attach the CameraController Script to the Camera Game Object

After saving the CameraController script in your IDE, return to the Unity project. Attach the CameraController script as a component to the Main Camera object as shown in Figure 9-6. You will see the public properties we set to default values in the script appear in the Inspector window. The moveDirection property does not appear because we set its scope to private in our script, which means it is not accessible from outside the CameraController script.

Figure 9-6. *The Camera Controller script is added to the Main Camera object*

Step 4: Play-Test the Scene

While playing the scene you should be able to move the virtual camera by pressing the horizontal and vertical keyboard inputs as defined in the Input Manager. The Main Camera game object moves through the scene according to the parameters we've set for the CharacterController and CameraController components. Because our project does not have VR supported, yet, we can only experience the movement of our camera through the screens of our monitors or laptops.

I don't know about you, but for me, the impact of the
`CameraController` script and the mechanics of the `CharacterController`
component are pretty good. The motion of the camera through space
reminds me of video games from the early 2000s like Golden Eye and Halo.
Let's see how things translate into VR.

Continuous Movement of a Camera in VR

Now that we've connected user input to the movement of a camera in our
scene, let's apply what we've learned in the previous section to VR.

Step 1: Set Up the Unity Project for VR and VRTK

Duplicate the scene you created in the previous steps by highlighting its
name in the Project window and clicking Ctrl+D. Rename the duplicated
scene Scene2. Double-click Scene2 in the Project window to open it in the
Scene view and the Scene Hierarchy.

If you created the Unity project for this exercise without the trappings
of VR support, then take the time now to activate the necessary ingredients
with which we've become so familiar:

- Edit ➤ Project Settings ➤ VR Supported

- Window ➤ Package Manager ➤ XR Legacy Input
  Mapping

- Clone VRTK through GitHub

- UnityXRCameraRig into the Scene Hierarchy

Step 2: Adapt the `CameraController` Script for the HMD

Duplicate the `CameraController` script you created in the earlier steps. Rename the cloned script `VR_Camera_Controller`. Open the script in your IDE and change the name of the class from `CameraController` to `VR_Camera_Controller`. Remember, the name of the script has to match the name of its class for Unity to read it as a `MonoBehaviour` component. Save the script and return to Unity.

Add a `CharacterController` component and the `VR_Camera_Controller` script to the UnityXRCameraRig in the Inspector. The default settings on the components will be fine to begin with, and you can tweak them during play-testing.

Step 3: Play-Test the Scene

Press the Play button on the Unity toolbar to test the impact of the Character and Camera controllers on the UnityXRCameraRig. Because we didn't change the body of the `CameraController` class after renaming it, all the keyboard functionality related to movement remains. Press the keyboard inputs associated with the horizontal and vertical axes to experience continuous movement in VR.

Movement and VR: It's Complicated

If you play-tested the scene while wearing an HMD, then you might have noticed the challenges that arise when we try to connect VR headsets with continuous movement in the forward, backward, and sideways directions. Although some have a higher tolerance than others, most users will experience some level of discomfort when moving through a virtual scene continuously. The reasons may vary and can be mitigated by different settings for variables such as speed and gravity. In my experience, after

311

about 10 minutes in a VR experience with poorly designed continuous movement, I develop a headache. I believe my brain's inability to reconcile the movement I see with the motion I feel causes the discomfort.

I have had positive experiences with continuous movement in VR experiences that forgo gravity. Games that take place in space or through flight, for example, have been fine for me. However, these games also are professionally designed, so the reduced impact of continuous movement on my senses could result from higher quality 3D assets, higher frame rates, more efficient processing, or any other combination of factors. The larger takeaway is that especially for prototyped projects created by small teams, users do not gain more than they lose with continuous movement in immersive experiences.

VRTK to the Rescue!

One solution VR developers use to enable a user's movement through a VR scene is teleportation. Yes, it is appropriate that a futuristic medium like VR would include as part of its design a futuristic mode of transportation like teleporting. However, unlike the teleportation many of us might have become familiar with through *Star Trek,* teleportation in VR has its own limitations.

First, teleportation, as we will use it in this exercise, can only move the viewer to a location of a scene within a prescribed radius. Sure, we can create scripts that move our users across wide swaths of space instantaneously, but I would not call that teleportation. I'd call that cutting to a new scene. Teleportation, however, translates a user's position in the same scene.

Second, teleportation, again, as we will use it in this exercise, remains under the control of the user. There's no Scottie who will beam our user up. In one way, we, the developer, are the user's Scottie. However, because we cannot be in the scene with the users as they experience our design, we must create mechanisms in our program that empower the users to determine the parameters of their own teleportation.

To demonstrate how users can define the destination for a translation of their position in a scene let's first place a VRTK object called a Pointer in our scene.

Adding a VRTK Pointer to the Scene

If You're Only Seeing Black...

Because we are adding touch controller interaction to our scene, it might be helpful for you to replace the UnityXRCameraRig game object with the SDK-specific CameraRig game object for your system in the Scene Hierarchy. Although I have been able to execute this exercise in its entirety using a UnityXRCameraRig game object and the VRTK Oculus touch controller prefabs, I have encountered some hiccups in the execution. The exercise runs well when I use the Oculus VR Camera Rig prefab from the Oculus Integration package, which I downloaded from the Unity Asset Store. Please feel free to follow along using whatever virtual camera rig best suits your workflow. If you run into problems with the scene in your headset then you can troubleshoot the bug by using a different virtual camera object.

Step 1: Select the VRTK Curved Pointer Prefab from the Project Window

In the Project window of Unity, navigate to Assets ➤ VRTK ➤ Prefabs ➤ Pointers as shown in Figure 9-7. Drag and drop the ObjectPointer.Curved prefab into the Scene Hierarchy.

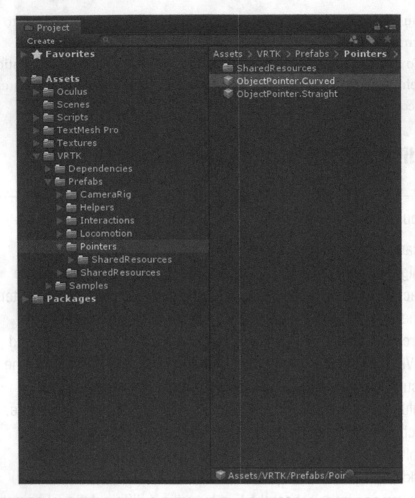

Figure 9-7. *Drag and drop the VRTK Curved Pointer prefab into your Scene Hierarchy*

Step 2: Connect the Curved Pointer to a Controller

Select the Curved Pointer prefab in the Scene Hierarchy. In the Inspector window, locate the Follow Source field on the Pointer Facade component attached to the Curved Pointer prefab game object. Expand the TrackedAlias game object in the Hierarchy, and drag and drop the

LeftControllerAlias prefab into the Curved Pointer's Follow Source field (Figure 9-8).

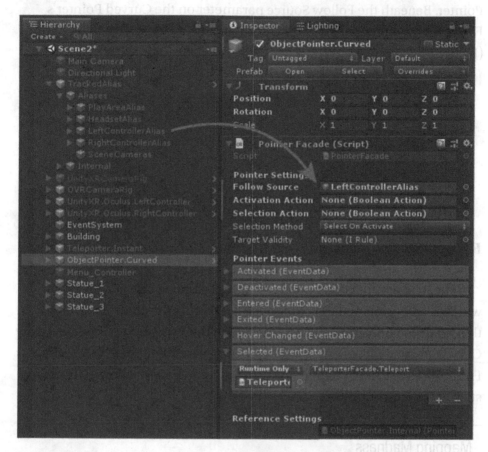

Figure 9-8. *Connect the LeftControllerAlias to the Curved Pointer object*

If you added an SDK-specific Camera Rig game object, like the OVRCameraRig for the Oculus Rift, for example, to your Scene then be sure to add a Linked Alias Collection component to the camera and connect it to the TrackedAlias Camera Rigs Elements list as we did in a previous exercise.

With a Curved Pointer connected to a controller alias in our scene, we now have to tell Unity which button on our controller activates the Curved Pointer. Beneath the Follow Source parameter on the Curved Pointer's Facade component, there is an empty object field called Activation Action (Figure 9-9).

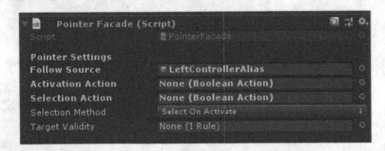

Figure 9-9. *The Activation Action field is shown on the Pointer object*

The Activation Action parameter accepts a game object attached to which is a Boolean Action component. Triggering the controller button that holds the Boolean Action connected to the Activation parameter of the Curved Pointer will, of course, activate the Curved Pointer in our scene. For this exercise, let's connect the Curved Pointer's activation to the thumb stick of the left controller.

Mapping Madness

Again, be mindful that I am using an Oculus Rift connected to a desktop with two wireless touch controllers. The mapping I use to connect my controller buttons to actions might not apply to the controllers with your system. As always, you can find the input mapping for your device's controllers in the XR section of the Unity online documentation at https://docs.unity3d.com/Manual/ xr_input.html.

To hook into Boolean Actions on our controllers we must first include references to our VR controllers in our scene. As we've done in previous exercises, we can use VRTK's Controller prefabs to point to our touch controllers. To accomplish this, navigate to the Input Mappings folder in your Project window: Assets ➤ VRTK ➤ CameraRig ➤ UnityXRCameraRig ➤ Input Mappings. VRTK comes with four Controller prefabs: two for the Oculus runtime and two for the OpenVR runtime. From the Input Mappings folder, drag and drop the Controller prefabs appropriate for your system into the Scene Hierarchy (Figure 9-10).

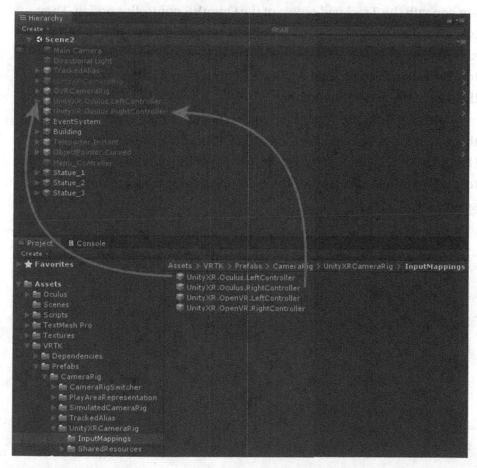

Figure 9-10. *Drag and drop the UnityXR controller prefabs into the Hierarchy*

317

In the Hierarchy, expand the UnityXR.LeftController prefab you just dragged from the Project window. Its child objects are prefabs representing the button actions available on the controller. Because I want to connect the Activation Action of my Curved Pointer to the left thumbstick of my Oculus touch controller, I will expand the Thumbstick child object. For child objects, the Thumbstick prefab has two Unity Button Actions attached to two otherwise empty game objects. For the Oculus controller, the child objects are called Touch[16] and Press[8]. If you are using the UnityXR.OpenVR controller prefab, then the corresponding child objects are beneath the Trackpad object of the OpenVR controller prefab. They, too, are called Touch[16] and Press[8]. As always, if you'd like to know more about the default input mappings between Unity and your VR system's touch controllers, refer to the Unity XR Input resources in the XR section of the online Unity documentation.

Drag and drop the Touch[16] game object from the Hierarchy onto the Activation Action field of the Curved Pointer's Facade component (Figure 9-11). The Activation Action will draw the curved pointer from the touch controller's virtual coordinates to a point on the Floor object in our scene.

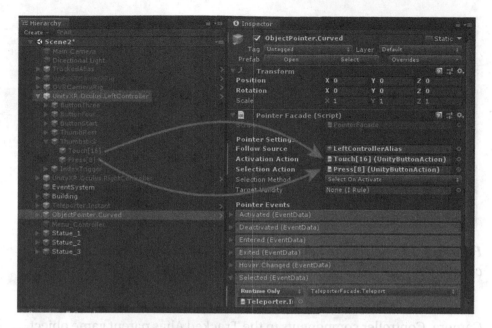

Figure 9-11. *Drag and drop Button Action objects onto the Pointer object*

To create a selection event to trigger the user's teleportation, we can use another Unity Button Action. This time we'll use the Unity Button Action attached to the Press[8] child object on the UnityXR controller prefab in the Hierarchy. Drag and drop the Press[8] child game object from the Hierarchy onto the object field of the Selection Action parameter in the Curved Pointer Facade component (Figure 9-11).

Move the Camera Controller components onto the TrackedAlias object. Whether or not you replaced the UnityXRCameraRig game object with an SDK-specific virtual camera, move the CharacterController component and the VR_Camera_Controller script onto the TrackedAlias parent game object as components. If you attached these components to the UnityXRCameraRig object earlier in this exercise, you can delete them from the UnityXRCameraRig by clicking on the gear icon next to the name of the component in the Inspector and selecting Remove Component as shown in Figure 9-12.

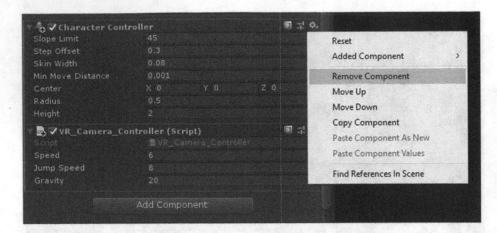

Figure 9-12. *Select the Remove Component command to delete a component*

Confirm that you have added the CharacterController and VR_ Camera_Controller components to the Tracked Alias parent game object. Further, make sure only one virtual camera object is activated in your scene. Finally, confirm that the one camera active in your scene is also included as an Element on the Tracked Alias game object, as shown in Figure 9-13.

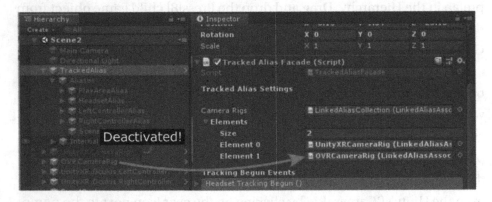

Figure 9-13. *This shows a deactivated UnityXRCameraRig in the Hierarchy*

Step 3: Play-Test

While play-testing your scene, you should see a green parabola appear at the end of your left touch controller and fall somewhere on the Floor object when your thumb touches the thumb pad as displayed in Figure 9-14.

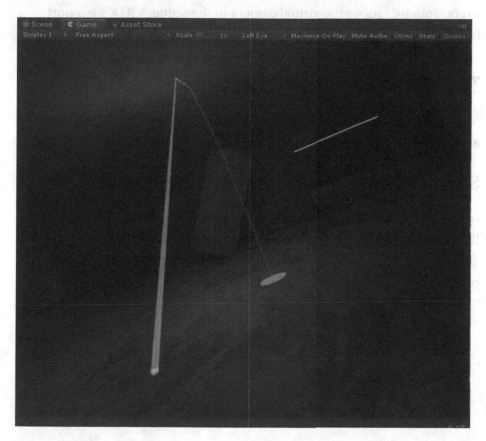

Figure 9-14. *The VRTK Curved Pointer appears as a green parabola during playback*

Because we have connected our VR_Camera_Controller and CharacterController components to our Tracked Alias, you can also move continuously in the scene by pressing the left thumb pad in the horizontal and vertical directions. If the continuous motion of the virtual camera makes you feel uncomfortable, then you can change the VR_Camera_ Controller settings in the Unity Inspector. Reducing the value of the Speed property and increasing the value of the Gravity property might improve the experience. Of course, you might find you don't even want the option to continuously move the virtual camera in the scene. VRTK's teleport function could be all that you need.

The VRTK Teleporter Object

Now that we've added a VRTK Curved Pointer object to our scene, we can add a VRTK Teleporter to make full use of the Curved Pointer's potential.

Step 1: Add a Teleporter Prefab to the Scene

In the Project window, navigate to the Teleporters folder in the VRTK library: Project Window ➤ Assets ➤ VRTK ➤ Prefabs ➤ Locomotion ➤ Teleporters. Inside the Teleporters folder, select the Teleporter.Instant prefab object as shown in Figure 9-15.

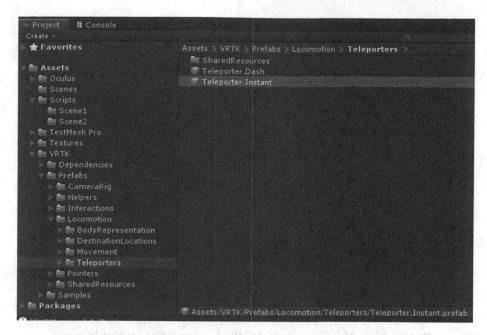

Figure 9-15. *Select the VRTK Instant Teleporter prefab*

Drag and drop the Teleporter.Instant prefab into the Scene Hierarchy.

Step 2: Configure the Teleporter Prefab in the Scene

Highlighting the Teleporter.Instant prefab in the Hierarchy opens its properties in the Inspector. Notice the first two parameters beneath the Teleporter Settings on the object's Facade component (Figure 9-16).

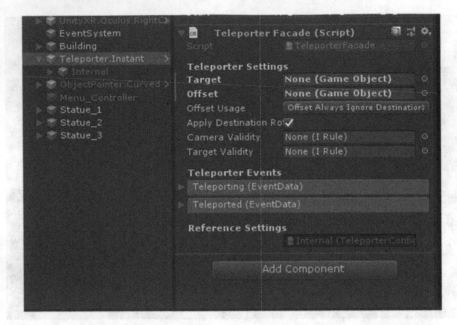

Figure 9-16. *Note the Target and Offset properties of the Instant Teleporter prefab*

The Target property on the Teleporter object instructs the Teleporter what game object to teleport, or move. Because we want our virtual camera to teleport, we *could* connect the Teleporter's Target property to the active camera object in our scene. However, this will tie the Teleporter to a single camera object. Because part of the appeal of designing with VRTK is that we can target many VR SDKs, it's best practice to connect the Teleporter to our TrackedAlias game object. Using this method, if we decide to activate our UnityXRCameraRig, or even SimulatedCameraRig for that matter, we do not have to change the Target setting on our Teleporter object.

With the Teleporter.Instant prefab highlighted in the Scene Hierarchy, expand the TrackedAlias parent prefab. Beneath the Aliases child object, locate the PlayAreaAlias grandchild object. The PlayAreaAlias points to an Observable class in VRTK that contains the game objects to which the Alias can connect. Drag and drop the PlayAreaAlias parent prefab into the Target property of the Teleporter.Instance Facade component (Figure 9-17).

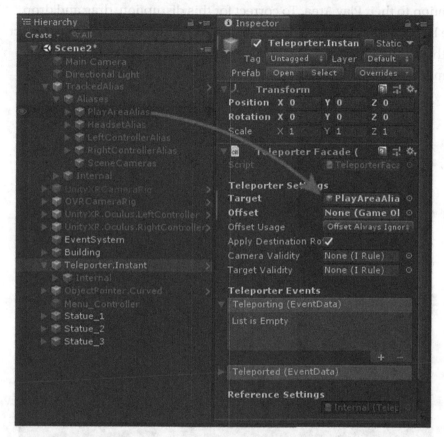

Figure 9-17. *Connect the PlayAreaAlias as the Target object of the Teleporter*

The Offset property on the Teleporter prefab refers to the difference between the user's expected location and actual location at the Teleporter's destination. For example, if the user is standing 2 feet to the left of the center of the Play Area, then he or she will still be standing 2 feet to the left of the center of the Play Area after the teleportation takes place. This creates a disruption in the immersion of the experience because most users expect the teleportation event to place them exactly on the point they

selected with their curved pointer. The Offset property of the Teleporter
prefab calculates the difference between the user's headset position in
relation to their Play Area. To correct for this disruption, drag and drop
the HeadsetAlias object, which is a grandchild of the TrackedAlias object
in the Scene Hierarchy, onto the Offset field on the Teleporter's Facade
component (Figure 9-18).

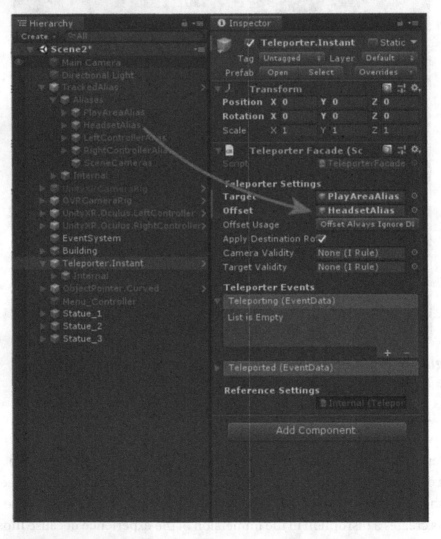

Figure 9-18. *Drag the HeadsetAlias to the Teleporter's Offset property*

Step 3: Set the Blink Parameter of the Teleporter

Both the Instant and Dash Teleporters in VRTK offer an option to provide a "blink" before translating the user's Play Area in the scene. A blink is akin to a quick camera fade-in, which can reduce the discomfort a user feels when moving through virtual space. To set the blink action on the Teleporter object, drag and drop into its Camera Validity field the SceneCameras grandchild object, which can be found beneath the Aliases object on the TrackedAlias prefab in the Hierarchy (Figure 9-19).

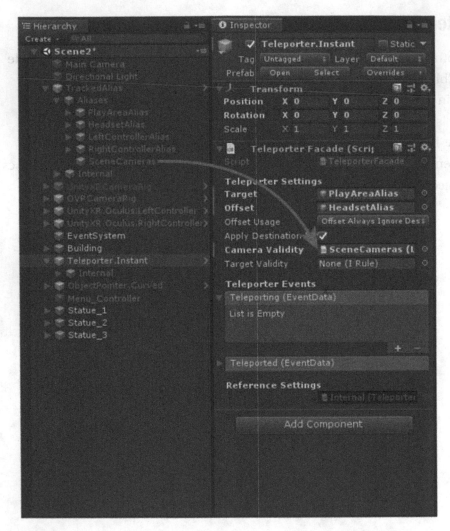

Figure 9-19. *The Camera Validity property controls the fade-in following a teleport*

Step 4: Connect the Teleporter Object to the Curved Pointer's Selection Action

Now that we have our Teleporter object set up in our scene, we need to connect it to the Curved Pointer object we set up earlier. You might recall in Step 2 of the earlier section "Adding a VRTK Pointer to the Scene" that we set up not only an Activation Action for the Curved Pointer, but also a Selection Action. The Activation Action, mapped to the touch sensor on the left controller thumb pad, makes the Curved Pointer's parabola appear. The Selection Action, mapped to the press of the left controller thumb stick, triggers the Teleporter event. Because we have already connected the Button Action of the Curved Pointer's Selection Action, we now only have to instruct the Curved Pointer which function to fire when the user trips the Select Action event.

Select the ObjectPointer.Curved prefab in the Scene Hierarchy. In the Inspector, locate its Pointer Events. The final drop-down list in the Pointer Events list is the Selected (EventData) event. Click the + in the Selected (EventData) box. Into the empty game object field, drag and drop the Teleporter.Instant prefab from the Hierarchy. From the Selected Pointer Events function drop-down menu, select the function TeleporterFacade. Teleport (Figure 9-20).

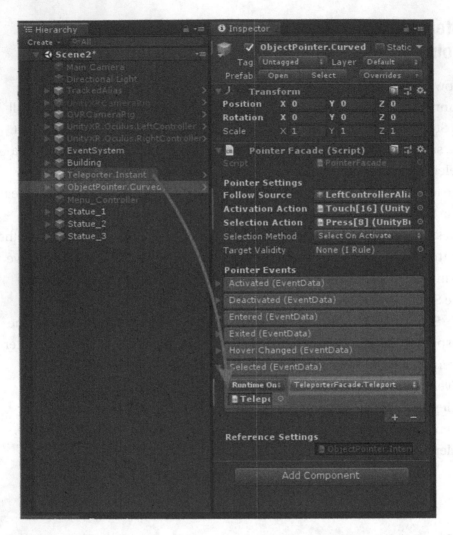

Figure 9-20. *Connect the Teleporter function to the Curved Pointer's event handler*

Step 5: Play-Test

Just prior to play-testing the scene, I recommend navigating to the VR_Camera_Controller component on the TrackedAlias prefab, if you choose to attach it. There, change the value of the Speed setting of the

VR_Camera_Controller to 1 and its Gravity value to 30. This will reduce the motion sickness that can occur for a user experiencing continuous movement in a headset.

After the settings for all your components are set to your preferences, save the scene. Make sure the requisite applications are running on your machine if your VR system requires a third-party program like Oculus or SteamVR. Then, press Play and test your scene.

If all goes according to plan, while play-testing your scene, you are able to teleport through the scene by pressing the left controller thumb pad button. If you kept the VR_Camera_Controller on your TrackedAlias object active, then you can fine-tune your position in virtual space using continuous movement, as well.

Create a Button Action to Display Statue Information

For the final section of our exercise, we will create a Button Action mapped to the right touch controller that toggles a text display of each statue on or off. We'll make things a bit more complicated than anything we've done so far in this book. Consider this, then, your grand finale.

The desired goal for this action is to provide the user with the ability to toggle on and off a Canvas object that displays information for each statue. What makes this goal challenging is the logic we will use in the script to determine which statue is nearest when the user presses the Canvas toggle button. For example, if the user's virtual camera is closest to Statue_2 then we do not want to toggle the Canvas for Statue_3. How, though, can we determine to which statue the user is nearest?

Fun with Vector Math

Finding the distance between two points in 3D space is similar to finding the distance in 2D space. Both rely on an application of the Pythagorean theorem. Our FindNearestStatue() function, then, will calculate the distance between the user and each statue in our scene using the Pythagorean theorem with the distance between the user and the statue serving as the hypotenuse of a triangle in 3D space. Of course, the Pythagorean theorem requires us to take the square root of a value to define the length of the hypotenuse. However, because the square root function can be costly to calculate in an immersive application, we will instead square the distance using Unity's sqrMagnitude() method. Because we are squaring all the distances, their relationship to each other will remain proportional. To see the code in print will be most helpful.

```
using UnityEngine;
using System.Collections.Generic;
using TMPro;
public class Menu_Controller : MonoBehaviour
{
    // Create an array to hold the Transform components of each
    statue
    Transform[] statues = new Transform [3];

    // Define 3 public GameObject fields into which we can drag
        our statues
    public GameObject statue_1;
    public GameObject statue_2;
    public GameObject statue_3;

    void Start()
    {
        // Load the statue array with our scene's statues
```

```
    statues[0] = statue_1.transform;
    statues[1] = statue_2.transform;
    statues[2] = statue_3.transform;
}

// The function fired by the Button Action click event
public void FindNearestStatue()
{
    // Define an empty variable to hold the nearest statue
    Transform bestTarget = null;

    // Define a variable to hold a ridiculously large number
    float closestDistanceSqr = Mathf.Infinity;

    // Store the user's position in a variable
    Vector3 currentPosition = transform.position;

    // Iterate over the collection of statues in the scene
    foreach (Transform potentialTarget in statues)
    {
        // Store the distance between a statue and the user
        // in a Vector3 variable
        Vector3 directionToTarget = potentialTarget.
        position - currentPosition;

        // Store the distance between a statue and the user
        // squared
        float dSqrToTarget = directionToTarget.
        sqrMagnitude;

        // Compare the distance between the statue and user
        // to the previously stored smallest distance
        if(dSqrToTarget < closestDistanceSqr)
        {
```

```
            // If the distance between the statue and the
            user is smaller than a previously calculated
            distance...
            // Store the current distance as the smallest
            distance
            closestDistanceSqr = dSqrToTarget;

            // Save the transform with the shortest
            distance as the value of the bestTarget
            variable
            bestTarget = potentialTarget;
        }
    }

    // Log the name of the closest statue for testing
    Debug.Log(bestTarget.name);

    // Store the canvas object of the nearest statue in a
    variable
    Canvas canvas = bestTarget.GetComponentInChildren<Canv
    as>();

    // Store the text object of the nearest object's canvas
    in a variable
    TextMeshPro text = canvas.GetComponentInChildren<TextMe
    shPro>();

    // Toggle the state of the nearest statue's canvas
    if (!canvas.enabled)
        canvas.enabled = true;
    else
        canvas.enabled = false;
    }
}
```

The preceding code is based on a solution to a question posed on the Unity message boards in 2014. The original poster's Unity handle is EdwardRowe, and you can follow the entire thread at `https://forum.unity.com/threads/clean-est-way-to-find-nearest-object-of-many-c.44315/`.

In the preceding code for the `Menu_Controller`, I have presented the comments in italics. The comments in the code, preceded by `//`, describe the action performed by each line. Although I've done my best to use code you've already seen in this text, there might be some functions you don't recognize. You can find more information regarding them in the online Unity documentation.

Copy the code from the `Menu_Controller` script and save it in a script of your own with the same name in Unity.

You will notice in the code an expression that sets a `Vector3` variable called `currentPosition` to the position of the game object to which the script is attached. Because the positions of the statue objects are stored in the `statues` array in the code, the position represented by `currentPosition` is the user's position in 3D space. If you recall from the step in this exercise in which we connected the PlayAreaAlias child object of the VRTK TrackedAlias prefab as the Target of our Teleporter function, then you'll remember that the PlayArea is, effectively, what identifies the user's position in the scene. Knowing this, we can attach our `Menu_Controller` script to our PlayAreaAlias object, too, as its position will always follow that of the user in the scene.

After saving the `Menu_Controller` script in your IDE, return to your Unity project. Add the `Menu_Controller` script as a component on the PlayAreaAlias object in the Hierarchy.

In Figure 9-21, notice that the public properties identified in the `Menu_Controller` appear in the Inspector when the PlayAreaAlias object is highlighted in the Hierarchy. Dragging the statue game objects from our scene into these parameters will notify Unity of the positions of the statues in our scene.

Figure 9-21. *The Menu_Controller's public statue properties are shown here*

However, before we connect our statues to the Menu_Controller script, let's first be sure that our statues contain both the Canvas and TextMeshPro objects to which the Menu_Controller script refers. If you set the statue objects in your scene according to the same Transform settings I used, then copying the Transform settings for my Canvas objects will track nicely to your project. If you set your own statue objects in the scene, you can easily attach Canvas objects and set their position to your liking.

Statue_1 Canvas Rect Transform

- Position (x,y,z): -2, 0.1, -0.6

- Width x Height: 2 x 3

- Pivot (x,y): 0.5, 0.5

- Rotation (x,y,z): 0, -48, 0

- Scale (x,y,z): 1, 0.3, 1

Statue_2 Canvas Rect Transform

- Position (x,y,z): -2, -0.2, -0.6

- Width x Height: 2 x 3

- Pivot (x,y): 0.5, 0.5

- Rotation: 0, 0, 0

- Scale (x,y,z): 1, 0.3, 1

Statue_3 Canvas Rect Transform

- Position (x,y,z): -2, 0.10, -0.6

- Width x Height: 2 x 3

- Pivot: 0.5, 0.5

- Rotation (x,y,z): 0, -48, 0

- Scale (x,y,z): 1, 0.3, 1

Further, add a TextMeshPro Text object to each canvas. Set the content of the Text field to any dummy text you'd like. Because I have tilted Statue_2 in my scene, its TextMeshPro transform requires a bit of tweaking.

Statue_2 TextMeshPro Object Rect Transform

- Position (x,y,z): -0.05, -0.50, -0.90

- Rotation (x,y,z): 5, -80, 30

With the Canvas and TextMeshPro objects set on each Statue object in the Scene Hierarchy (Figure 9-22), we can drag and drop them into the public Statue fields on the Menu_Controller script component attached to the PlayAreaAlias game object, as shown in Figure 9-23.

Figure 9-22. *The Canvas and Text objects are connected to the statues in the scene*

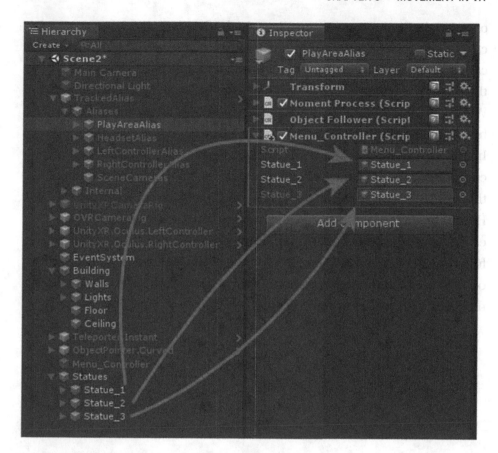

Figure 9-23. *Drag and drop the Statue objects onto the Menu_Collector script*

Once our Statues are connected to our `Menu_Controller` script on the PlayerAliasObject, all that's left for us to do is connect the `FindNearestStatue()` function to a Button Action. As we did with the Curved Pointer earlier in this exercise, we will attach the object holding our desired method to the Button Action of a VRTK Controller prefab.

We already have a UnityXR Left Controller prefab in our scene; we attached our Curved Pointer functions to it. If you haven't already done so, drag and drop a UnityXR Right Controller into the Scene Hierarchy, too. I'm going to map the `FindNearestStatue()` function to the A button on my right Oculus touch controller, which VRTK's UnityXR.Oculus controller prefab defines as ButtonOne. ButtonOne includes a press event called Press[0]. Selecting the Press[0] prefab in the Hierarchy opens it in the Inspector, where I see the familiar Unity Button Action component. Whether you are using the Oculus or OpenVR VRTK controller prefab, highlighting the button object will open a Button Action script in the Inspector. Expand the Activated (Boolean) event in the Button Action component and click the + to add an event. In the empty game object field that appears, drag and drop the PlayerAreaAlias game object from the Hierarchy. In the Function pull-down menu on the Activated (Boolean) event, select the Menu_Controller script and the FindNearestStatue() function, as depicted in Figure 9-24. Once you've set these two properties on the Unity Button Action component, you have completed connecting the Menu_Controller to your scene.

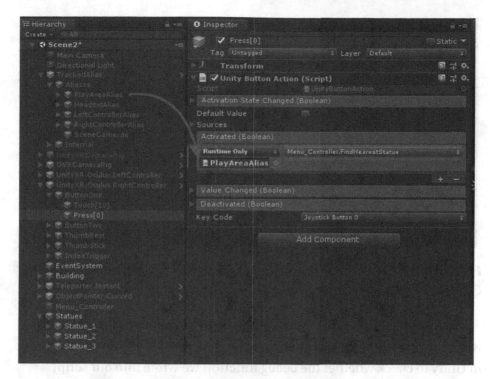

Figure 9-24. *Connect the* `FindNearestStatue()` *method to the Button Action event handler*

Play-Test

When play-testing the scene, not only should you be able to use the Curved Pointer Teleportation functionality we connected to the left touch controller, but you should also be able to toggle the Canvas object of the statue nearest you by pressing the main button (A on the Oculus touch controller) on the right touch controller. Toggling a Canvas on should display the text you entered into the TextMeshPro object of the canvases attached to each statue (Figure 9-25).

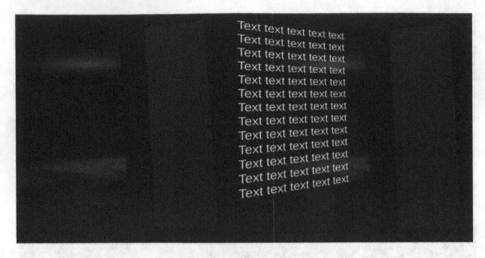

Figure 9-25. *The image on the left is the result of a statue object with Canvas toggled off. On the right, the Canvas is toggled on*

If, for some reason, the Canvas objects do not appear in your scene when you press the main button, you can look at the Console window in Unity to check whether the Debug function we wrote into our script printed to the console. If your console shows the name of the Statue object to which you were nearest when you pressed the activation button on the right touch controller, as in Figure 9-26, then you know the FindNearestStatue() function is connected to your event handler.

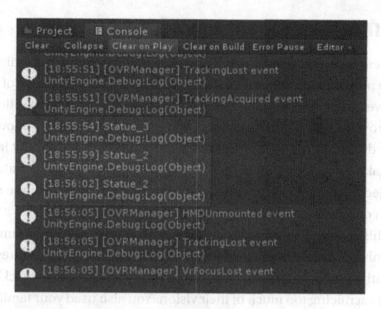

Figure 9-26. *Check the Console to see if the Debug function executed*

Complete! Congratulations! As Penny Powers, you completed the prototype for the Milwaukee Contemporary Art Museum's Placido Farmiga exhibit. Your supervisor in the Members' Benefits Department has forwarded the application on to the Art Department, where designers will swap out the primitive assets you created with higher end work digitized from Placido's sculptures. The Museum was so impressed with your work, in fact, that they have commissioned a special photography team to capture a 3D scan of the museum's interior to include in your project as an asset. Sit back and enjoy the countdown to the raise in salary you will inevitably receive for an excellent job.

Summary

Movement is a tricky beast in VR. Camera motion for some users might pose no problem; for others it could cause illness. The best course of action we, as developers, can follow is to provide our users with options. Tools provided by VRTK, like Pointers and Locomotion prefabs, allow us to provide different experiences for users. Fundamentally, movement in VR is not a make-or-break component of a piece. Like lights, textures, materials, and objects, movement is but one more instrument in our case, one more color on our palette as designers of VR.

In this chapter you learned how to prototype your own environment using only primitive objects in Unity. Applying materials and textures to primitive game objects can help developers prototype ideas quickly without sacrificing too much of their vision. You also used your familiarity with Unity Button Actions and the TrackedAlias game object to place a VRTK pointer and locomotion component in your scene. Finally, using original scripting you created two different custom actions: one to move the user through space, and another to create a smart function that not only determines the nearest statue to a user, but also toggles the state of its informational menu.

Conclusion

So ends our time together in this book. I hope you had as positive of an experience learning how to use VRTK with Unity as I did passing on my lessons to you. VR continues to expand as a medium, and every day its promises grow. As the new media of VR, AR, and MR converge, the skills and knowledge you have picked up in these pages will serve you well. I am sure of it. Earlier in the book I offered you a guarantee that you would reach the final page confident that you could prototype any original VR experience you could imagine. I hope you are not disappointed. Although you might feel like you have only seen the tip of the iceberg, I assure you that there are very few additional skills or secrets that you do not know. The only difference between you, now, and a professional VR developer is time and practice. Fortunately, the one thing that for certain makes a strong VR developer you already have—your own unique imagination.

If you close this book curious about what you can make in VR on your own, then I will have considered my job a success. If, however, you feel more confused than you did during Chapter 1, I encourage you to give it time. A year and a half ago, when I started to learn how to program C#, an instructor at a bootcamp told me that learning to code is really learning how to think about problems in a new way. The further I explore the systems and patterns of designing applications, the better I understand what he meant. Coding is not the language. It's not even the rules of the interface of an application like Unity. Coding is thinking about a problem, breaking it into smaller problems, and solving each smaller problem step-by-step.

If you read all the chapters in this book, if you completed each exercise, then you already know the tools at your disposal to solve the problems you might face. The true, unbridled creativity of programming, especially in a medium like VR, in my opinion, lies in the innumerable ways you can decide to solve a problem. Some solutions might be easy, whereas some might require months of patient research. No matter the answers we find, however, every step of the way is a step into a new idea, a new version of ourselves. The fantasy of VR has been with us ever since man touched paint to stone. The only difference between then and now is that today creating VR is possible. Who knows what tomorrow will bring?

Index

A

Awake() function, 269

B

Boolean Action component, 219
BooleanAction.Receive()
    method, 253, 254
Bunny multiplier
    counter, 93
    data type, 90
    VRTK, 91
Button action creation
    Canvas objects, 336
    code, 332–334
    currentPosition, 335
    FindNearestStatue()
        function, 340, 341
    goal, 331
    Menu_Controller, 335, 336
    PlayAreaAlias game object,
        337, 339
    playing the scene, 341–343
    Pythagorean theorem, 332
    TextMeshPro Text object, 337, 338
    UnityXR Controller, 339
    vector math (see Vector math)

C

CalculateInterest() function,
    141, 142, 144, 147, 148,
    151, 152, 156
CalculatorManager's Boolean
    Action component, 161
CenterEyeAnchor, 135
CharacterController, 305
Components, attributes, 58
Creative Commons licensing
    agreement, 171
Cubemap
    Api compatibility level, 41
    console window, 42
    globehopper app, 40, 51
    lighting settings, 46, 47
    mapping property, 45
    rocky_dawn_4k.hdr file, 43
    rotation property, 48
    skybox shader, 42, 49–50
    texture shape, 43, 44
    360-degree HDRI, 39, 52–54

D

Debug class, 198
Debug.Log() function, 215

W, X, Y, Z